SAFER CARE

Human Factors

for

Healthcare

TRAINER'S MANUAL

Edited by Patrick Mitchell

Prepared on behalf of the North East Strategic
Health Authority Patient Action Team

Safer Care—*Human Factors in Healthcare: Trainer's Manual*
Edited by Patrick Mitchell

First published 2013
ISBN: 978-1-909675-00-1
Copyright © 2013 Swan & Horn
All rights reserved.

Notice
Clinical practice is constantly evolving in terms of standard safety precautions, responsibility of practitioners, and treatment options. While every effort has been made to ensure the accuracy of information contained in this publication, no guarantee can be given that all errors and omissions have been excluded. Neither the publisher nor the authors assume any liability for any injury and/or damage to persons or property arising from this publication.

The Publisher
For information and orders, contact Swan & Horn:
Swan & Horn • Woodside Tower •
Cove • Argyll and Bute G84 0NT
Tel: (44)1436 842748 • Fax: 07092 373804
Email: info@swanandhorn.co.uk
www.swanandhorn.co.uk

Cover artwork by Virginia Brailsford
Editorial and production by Shoreline BioMedical
Printed in England by Ferguson Print, Keswick

Contents

With special thanks to:
Professor Graham Towl, Professor David Crighton
and Durham University Department of Psychology

Preface

Safer Care is a training course on human factors for healthcare professionals. It was developed by the Safer Care Action Team, NHS North East of England. It consists of eight modules dealing with cognitive processing, decision-making, situation awareness, personality types, teamwork, leadership, communication skills, and stress management; these can be delivered in separate sessions or as a single intensive course. This *Manual* gives detailed and referenced accounts of each subject, and other components of the course are provided in an e-learning package (www.safercare.eu/human/) and a *Handbook* for participants.

Human factors training is widely used in safety-critical industries, but healthcare is a relative late-comer to the field. There are two main differences from other industries that must be addressed. The first, and more obvious one, relates to those issues that are specific to healthcare as opposed to those of primary relevance in other industries.

The second is less obvious, but more important. It relates to the fact that healthcare professionals tend to be more sceptical than workers in many other industries – they are disinclined to accept statements of benefit without seeing the evidence. This course has been specially designed with this important difference in mind.

Contributors

CLIVE BLOXHAM

Clive Bloxham is a consultant pathologist at County Durham and Darlington Hospitals with an interest in cognitive factors in medical practice and how errors occur.

GUY HIRST

Guy Hirst was a pilot with British Airways from 1972 until 2006 and was one of the pioneers of Human Factors Training in the airline culture. Since 2001 he has been writing and presenting courses in healthcare and is involved in research on healthcare safety.

PHIL LAWS

Phil Laws is a consultant in intensive care medicine and anaesthesia in Newcastle, and medical lead for the Advanced Critical Care Practitioner Programme and Outreach, with an interest in communication, crisis communication for junior doctors and mandatory training for critical care staff.

PATRICK MITCHELL

Patrick Mitchell is a consultant neurosurgeon in Newcastle upon Tyne with a research interest in surgical safety and decision-making.

EMMA NUNEZ

Emma Nunez is a registered midwife who now works in patient safety. She is the Safer Care North East Programme manager and chaired the Human Factors Faculty responsible for developing this course.

NANCY REDFERN

Nancy Redfern is a consultant anaesthetist in Newcastle upon Tyne specialising in obstetric and neuro-anaesthesia, with an interest in medical education, appraisal and mentorship.

GAVIN THOMS

Gavin Thom is a consultant anaesthetist with interests in perioperative and operative safety, and related human and cultural factors. He is currently joint lead on Project OASIS on surgical safety in South East Asia and recently led the international Global Oximetry Project aimed at improving anaesthetic safety.

Introduction

Being human, by its very nature, makes us all fallible. The additional titles we bear – doctor, nurse, midwife, pharmacist, dentist, chief executive, non-executive director (the list is endless) as a result of our education, training and technical ability – will never change the fundamental imperfections found among humans.

Our day-to-day lives provide numerous opportunities to make mistakes that generally have limited adverse consequences. You might forget to put the bin out on collection day because of some distraction, or you might walk down the stairs with the intention of emptying the washing machine, only to forget what you came down for when you reach the kitchen. These lapses are only minor, no more than an irritation, meaning that you have to make alternative plans for refuse disposal or you have to stop in your tracks and retrace your steps to work out what it was you had meant to do. These kind of mistakes do not harm anyone.

However, some lapses carry greater risks. A midwife, for example, driving home in the early hours after finishing her nightshift, pulled to a stop at a red traffic light. As she sat and waited for the lights to change, the CD she was playing came to the end and the player automatically changed to the next disc in the library. At this point she drove off again, right through the red light. She had confused the change in what she heard with the change she was waiting to see in the traffic signals. She laughed about it at the time, but she was well aware of how easily she could have killed or seriously injured herself or someone else.

Let us not make the error of thinking that the processes we experience that lead to mistakes in our personal and social lives are any different from the processes we experience that lead to mistakes in our professional life. Why do we tend to think that the title of our professional group removes our fallibility? Why is it that we forget such risks when it comes to delivering some of the most technologically advanced and effective healthcare in the world? What has led us to think this way?

When we talk about improving safety and reliability in healthcare, we make regular references to the aviation industry. The aviation industry has considerable knowledge and learning that can be shared with and applied to healthcare, but the industry embarked on a difficult journey when it first introduced human factors training. The following quote is from Jeremy Butler, the General Manager of Flight Training in British Airways at that time. We thank him for allowing us to use his comments here, which reveal a rational, balanced view based on both his own experience and expertise in aviation, and latterly in healthcare.

> "Flight Ops in British Airways (BA) had for a few years been considering, rather idly, the issues of what we might now call non-technical skills on the flight deck. I had become interested in Human Factors, both at the managerial and front-line levels, and became informed through attending seminars and conferences in the USA. I participated in the United Airlines CRM programme (called something else but I can't remember the exact name). I was asked by

Operating Standards Group (OSG) in BA whether this had any relevance to us. I enjoyed the experience but it was a very psychological course at that time, and I concluded that British pilots were not ready for 'psychobabble'. Also I believed that the Standard Operating Procedures of BA were greatly superior to those of the manufacturer, which are usually adopted by airline operators. It seemed to me that the principles of the 'monitored approach' with workload distribution and shared responsibilities were conducive to achieving safe flight and that Crew Resource Management (CRM) was not necessary in BA.

"I believe the Kegworth accident changed the thinking in BA (there was probably active consideration prior to Kegworth, and this confirmed the thinking, but I can't remember the exact sequence). The Board Air Safety Committee (not sure of the exact name now), decided that we would develop and introduce a CRM programme. The responsibility for this fell to me. This was devolved to various managers and interested flight crew, and we recruited a number of CRM instructors. It is noteworthy that CRM was introduced in BA well before the Civil Aviation Authority (CAA) had made it a requirement (even though it was hugely expensive). I have always believed that leading world operators have a responsibility to be generative and not simply respond to the Regulatory Authority. This is an example of BA leading in the UK and influencing the Authority as well as other airlines worldwide.

"At some point (1992, I think) I became Chair of International Air Transport Association (IATA) Human Factors Group and worked with Dan Maurino in International Civil Aviation Organisation (ICAO) and we took Human Factors/CRM to the world's airlines!"

Jeremy has also worked in several different roles within the NHS, which have allowed him to reflect on the years he spent in aviation.

"During my time working in the NHS, I have also pondered why the messages so obvious to us were not being universally received. I am now working with a NHS Research and Ethics Committee and a member of the National Research Ethics Advisors' Panel. This new insight has demonstrated something of which I was certainly aware, but not in so dominant a fashion, and that is that the medical profession will not do anything without evidence. In healthcare this evidence is accrued over many years of research studies, perhaps in some cases (a very few) resulting in new treatments or new medications. This evidence base is the safety mechanism of healthcare, and I support it. In aviation, I fear that we have not gathered in sufficient detail or depth the evidence for human factors/ CRM interventions as a necessary component in improving safety. I introduced CRM to BA on an instinctive feel, after attending conferences and seminars in the USA, but with very little research or analysis and no idea of how to measure outcomes of safety improvement. Of course we struggle with these measures as the data is very limited. Do you remember 'Cockpit 2000', a highly controversial component of our CRM programme? I thought it seemed a good idea at the time, and to this day I have no idea of its worth, although I am aware of the aggro.

"All this preamble is to say that we, involved in aviation human factors, have been remiss in not acquiring and documenting the evidence that HF and CRM have improved aviation safety. We should have been measuring the effects of our interventions, doing genuine research and writing learned articles in Aerospace for years, but we haven't. Is it too late to start? I don't know, as I am not closely involved anymore, but I am sure that the medical profession will continue to ask 'What is the evidence?' "

These intimate reflections on both the aviation and healthcare industries reinforce the question *why are we not doing this already*? Professionals from other high-risk industries are often stunned to learn that this is not already a part of our mandatory professional education and progression; they assume that "clinical" human factors must be an intrinsic part of how we train.

This is not the place for a debate on the definition of "clinical human factors' – there are many other places where such a debate is on-going. However, the fact that that we are even talking about the subject in the context of delivering healthcare is a positive step forward. The aim of this book and course, therefore, is to support the individuals and teams involved in delivery of healthcare, to understand the connection between the "psychobabble" surrounding the analysis of the human mind, and what it means to you in practice. It explains how cognition (the process of how we "think"), decision making, situation awareness (our view of what is happening around us), our personalities and their differences, team working, leadership, communication skills, and stress and fatigue apply to us when we are providing care and treatment to patients. Perhaps more importantly, it enhances understanding of these factors and therefore assists us in delivering care and treatment safely.

Many have argued that we cannot apply all the information gained from the aviation industry to healthcare, saying *I don't deal with planes. I deal with patients!* Is this not an even stronger argument for the need to understand human factors within healthcare? We cannot programme patients, or their disease, injury or illness, but we can avoid deluding ourselves that our years of technical training and experience remove our vulnerability as humans. We are, after all, "only human".

Emma Nunez

List of Figures

Thinking About Thinking: Cognitive Processing

1

Key points for reflection

❶ We all have biases in our cognitive processing which will influence decision-making. For example, evidence in support of a decision may be more readily attended to than evidence that contradicts it.

❷ It is important to distinguish between automatic or unconscious thinking and actions, and analytic and conscious thinking and action.

❸ It is possible to recognise biases in our cognitive processes and adjust for these accordingly, where it is appropriate to do so.

Human reasoning, or *cognition*, is the set of mental processes that deals with the acquisition and use of knowledge. It is studied by developing general models of observed behaviour, then comparing these models with reality. Applied cognitive modelling gained an early following in economics and this led to the award of two Nobel prizes [1,2].

It is now an important area of research in subjects such as the law, the aviation industry, economics and politics, but it is only recently that academic interest has developed in medical thinking [3]. So far, cognitive models remain largely outside mainstream medical education and clinical practice, mainly because it is not obvious that applying such models leads to any practical benefits [4], but it has been estimated that 70% of medical errors are due to faulty reasoning [5], with the remainder being due to system failures or being 'no-fault' incidents, due to apparently random events. This observation motivates the study of reasoning in medical settings. The study of cognition involves cognition about cognition so is sometimes called *metacognition* [6].

In the setting of clinical judgement and decision-making, results suggests that habits of thought are skills that are every bit as important as the more traditional diagnostic and procedural dimensions of medical education [7]. As with more conventional skills, they are open in principle to refinement and improvement through appropriate training.

Dual-process model

Over the last few decades, the study of cognition has become dominated by a Dual Process Model which is simple and accessible [8–12]. This is illustrated by the two scenarios described in **Vignette 1.1** and **Vignette 1.2**.

Vignette 1.1   Making a fire

One warm, sunny afternoon a man is sitting outside by a heap of dried grass and various types of stone artefacts with which he is trying to make a fire. He is not having much success and experiments with different approaches: scraping, hitting, small stone on large, flint on granite, and so on, when he hears what is probably the noise of a wild animal. Without hesitation he drops the stones and climbs up a tree.

Vignette 1.2   Performing a cholecystectomy

Some 50,000 years later, a surgeon is performing a routine cholecystectomy operation. The atmosphere is relaxed, music is playing, and the conversation around the table includes some non-clinical dialogue. Suddenly large pools of blood appear in the peritoneal cavity. All non-essential noise in the theatre ceases and the surgeon and assistants discuss and actively explore the possible sources of this haemorrhage to regain control over the situation.

Despite the difference between these scenarios in time and space, they reveal a fundamental aspect of human cognition that appears to be highly conserved over the course of human evolution, namely the existence of two broad categories of mental activity – 'automatic' and 'analytic' – and the transition from one to the other under appropriate circumstances.

The consequences of failing to make this transition are serious in both cases: on the one hand death will follow, and on the other a personal, professional and medicolegal disaster will occur.

Were early humans conscious?

There is some doubt about whether early modern humans were 'conscious' in the sense of being self-aware [11]. One proposal is that they had a limited form of consciousness, with swift memory loss and minimal awareness of time [12]. Another is that they had no consciousness at all but acted in an automatic – but nevertheless competent – mode [13].

The two categories correspond to the common descriptors of thought: automatic (or intuitive) and analytic (or rational) respectively. Their principle characteristics are summarised in **Table 1.1**. More recently the terms 'system 1' and 'system 2' have been used to describe them [9], but we will use the terms *automatic* and *analytic* as they are easier to remember.

Table 1.1 *The Dual Process Model*

Property	Automatic (System 1)	Analytic (System 2)
Reasoning style	Intuitive, heuristic, associative, concrete	Conscious, normative, deductive, abstract
Working memory	Not involved	Involved
Awareness	Low	High
Action	Reflexive, skilled	Deliberate, rule-based
Automaticity	High	Low
Speed	Fast	Slow
Effort	Minimal	Considerable
Cost	Low	High
Vulnerability to bias	Yes	Less so
Reliability	Low, variable	High, consistent
Errors	Common	Few
Predictive power	Low	High
Hard-wired	May be	No
Scientific rigour	Low	High
Context importance	High	Low

The advantages of the Dual Process Model are multiple. As the model is intrinsically simple, we can generally recognise our own reasoning when we look back on it after the event. Furthermore, third parties who are familiar with the model are also able to recognise it in real time and hopefully respond accordingly. A clinician may appreciate that a colleague is following an unproductive or dangerous automatic line of thought and should change to analytic.

More complex models involving multiple cognitive biases or *heuristics*, often with subtle conceptual definitions, are not so useful in practice. The whole range of human factors influencing judgement can be incorporated into the Dual Process Model, and analysed according to their facilitation or inhibition of either system. This includes *situational awareness* and *personality factors* [10].

This classification into two processes makes no inherent claim that one system is 'better' that the other. The automatic system occasionally gets a bad press as a 'primitive' evolutionary vestige that has unfortunately not yet been completely superseded by the more advanced analytic system. This argument is countered by the conservation and persistence of the automatic system in human history, and the better view is that they both have equally valuable roles in reasoning. Indeed, medical practice itself, with its limited information availability and time, could not proceed without the engagement of both systems. According to Croskerry [14] and Kovacs and Croskerry [15], without automatic thinking:

" ... emergency departments would inexorably

grind to a halt."

Fodor [16] has stated in a related context:

"Nature has contrived to have it both ways,
to get the best out of fast dumb systems and slow contemplative ones,
by simply refusing to choose between them."

This view is supported by considering both systems working in tandem, as a 'rational' process – if rationality is defined as a mental mechanism for achieving one's goals [17].

Automatic cognition

Heuristics are rules that automatic cognitive processes follow. They are not rules of the explicit kind such as 'look both ways before crossing the road', but take the form of deep *tacit knowledge* [18], which is not easily formulated, shared or transmitted to others. They are learned from repeated personal experience. They are information-processing short-cuts, sometimes described as cognitive *rules of thumb*. They are generally used where exhaustive searching and processing would be too slow or demanding. Internet search engines are an example of the effective use of heuristics. Here the sheer quantity of available information makes exhaustive searching impractical and undesirable. Effective heuristics will generally provide enough relevant items and do so quickly.

We are generally not aware of using heuristics, only of their outcomes. More than fifty different types of heuristic have so far been described [7], a selection of which are given in **Table 1.2**. These heuristics are selected by conscious or unconscious pattern recognition; then they determine further action. A common theme in the heuristics listed in **Table 1.2** is that they are largely concerned with improving the speed of response.

Table 1.2 *A selection of heuristics and their characteristics*

Heuristic	Characteristic
Availability	The tendency to judge an event as more likely if it readily comes to mind (e.g. recent exposure to a disease)
Anchoring	The disposition to persist with an initial judgement regardless of new information to the contrary
Confirmation	The tendency to actively seek evidence to support a given position, rather than evidence that might refute it
Representative	Decisions based on recognising a prototype, or 'typical' example of a class of diseases without considering base rates or atypical variants
Premature closing	The premature closing of the decision-making process before it has been fully verified
Sutton's slip	The diagnostic approach of going for the obvious without considering alternative possibilities. The name derives from the story of the Brooklyn bank-robber Willie Sutton who when asked by the judge why he robbed banks answered '*Because that's where the money is!*'

Heuristics are also referred to as *cognitive biases* because they determine our preference for drawing one conclusion over another due to psychological factors, rather than objective evidence [19]. The word 'bias' has a negative implication in common parlance, but actually this refers to a normal and (in most circumstances) valuable mental asset.

Heuristic cognition is fast. There is no appreciable delay between pattern recognition and guide to further action. It also requires little mental effort. For these two reasons it is the *default* mental process. Unlike analytic cognition, automatic heuristic cognition appears to operate in multiple parallel pathways. It is not clear whether these are really parallel or whether the speed of heuristic cognition allows effective multitasking through a single channel but the effect is, for the practical purposes quite similar [20].

Automatic cognition is promoted by distracting influences that make it difficult for us to give a problem the attention necessary to switch to analytic thought. These include emotional states, tiredness, fatigue and multiple interruptions.

Emotional states

This is especially true of negative emotions, such as frustration and anger, which make it particularly difficult to switch into analytical mode. It also appears that successful switching to analytical thought has the effect of lessening the intensity of such emotions. This is an important part of conflict resolution, where a valuable strategy involves leading an agitated person towards analytical thinking.

Tiredness and fatigue

Tiredness is a short-term state aggravated by sustained concentration, sleep deprivation and stressful situations. Switching to analytical thinking is more difficult when we are tired. The solution to tiredness is simply a good night's rest. Fatigue has a similar meaning to tiredness, but is often used to describe a longer-term state aggravated by long periods of high-intensity cognitive effort over weeks, cumulative sleep deprivation, and other life stresses. As with tiredness, fatigue reduces our ability to switch to analytic thinking. The solution is a holiday rather than the good night's rest (see *Module 8*). Other problems requiring analytic attention such as financial concerns, family matters, and so on, do not impair our ability to switch into analytic thinking mode but do occupy the single and slow analytic channel.

Multiple interruptions

Multiple interruptions have little impact on *automatic* thinking for two reasons. Firstly, it is faster than analytic thinking. Secondly, it is largely unconscious. Multiple interruptions have a profound effect on analytical thinking because the processing speed is slow and therefore more prone to interruption; and it is more complex, so after interruption more backtracking has to be done to get back to the same point.

How do errors arise?

Errors can arise if we remain in automatic mode when we should switch to analytic. This switch usually happens appropriately, but the risk of failing to switch, or to consciously guide automatic processes, rises with the above factors. We cannot get stuck in automatic mode, like we can in analytic mode, but we can drift *by default* in an automatic mode of working until we consciously direct such thinking in response to events.

Vignette 1.3   Accidental anaesthesia

A caesarean section requires antibiotic cover with co-amoxiclav, which is drawn up in a syringe in advance. Thus it is ready for intravenous administration to the mother just after the umbilical cord is cut.

In this scenario, a woman had a caesarean section under spinal anaesthesia and was cuddling her new baby with her partner present. The anaesthetist had previously asked the operating department practitioner (ODP) to draw up the drug, then checked it with her. (Since this approach involves two checkers, it is arguably sounder than the alternative, in which the anaesthetist prescribes, selects from the cupboard, draws up, dispenses, checks, administers and then records a drug, all without any other person involved.)

The anaesthetist checked with patient and staff for allergy to antibiotics, then gave the drug over three to four minutes. The patient rapidly became unconscious and required emergency intubation and ventilation, thus running various risks, however she remained well oxygenated and was otherwise stable.

Later it emerged that the drug given was the anaesthetic induction agent, thiopentone, which is also drawn up ahead, also in a 20 mL syringe, and is also a pale-straw coloured liquid.

Analytic cognition

Analytic cognition is a slow, fully conscious, cognitive process. It consumes more mental effort than automatic thinking and is much more tiring. It is associated with physiological changes, such as raising blood pressure and heart rate.

Its great *advantage* over automatic thinking is its flexibility. Automatic thinking depends on pattern recognition. It does not work well when no pattern is recognised and is prone to the error of recognising the wrong pattern. Analytical thinking is capable of assessing and avoiding both of these errors. Its *disadvantage* is that – unlike automatic thinking – it must be positively engaged. We default to automatic rather than analytic mode.

When a new situation presents itself, it is tempting to think that we can 'choose' to engage in heuristics or conscious analysis from the outset, according to the importance of the outcome. However, the evidence suggests that even when making critical judgements, as in medical practice, or when large incentives are offered under laboratory conditions, people rely on heuristics, with its rapid, efficient, but error-prone mechanisms. Although most errors occur because reasoning has been held up in heuristics, it can also be detrimental to be stranded in conscious analysis thinking. For example, obsessive–compulsive type behaviours might exemplify such a situation, or 'paralysis by analysis' in managerial parlance. It is not a good use of time to spend an hour deciding which can of baked beans to buy in a supermarket. The problem is the cause of Craster's well-known poem *Centipede's Dilemma*.

The centipede was happy—quite!
Until the toad in fun
Said 'Pray, which leg comes after which?'
Which brought his mind to such a pitch
He lay distracted in a ditch
Considering how to run.

Because it is a slow single-channel process, our ability to respond to situations with analytical thought can be impaired if the channel is preoccupied by other matters. Our consciousness is dominated by analytical thinking when we are engaged in it, and the conscious threshold for external stimuli rises. In extreme cases, this situation is known as *fixation*. In fixation, analytical thought is so dominated by one issue that the conscious threshold for sensory inputs is greatly raised, so high in fact that things such as warning sounds or lights or other people speaking are not registered at all. We *drift* into automatic thinking, but in this way we can get *stuck* in analytical thinking.

For some problems there may be no viable solution from analytic thinking. Gerd Gigerenzer gives the simple example of catching a baseball. Here the analytic approach suggests calculating all the variables involved, the speed of the ball, the angle and speed of the bat, the wind resistance and so on. In reality, any such effort is quickly overwhelmed by the number and interaction of variables and fails in the face of limited capacity to process these in time. A simple heuristic of observing the ball and adjusting position to meet it works more quickly and more accurately [21].

Switching between automatic and analytic thinking

Heuristics are reliable as long as we have recognised the correct pattern or process, and they are usually appropriate. In our daily non-clinical environment, the sole operation of heuristics can lead to outcomes that are perfectly adequate, but not truly optimal. This effect has been named 'satisficing' by Herbert Simon [22], reflecting the 'bounded rationality' of human evaluative mechanisms, which are often limited by incomplete knowledge of data and their associated likelihoods. In professional healthcare decision-making, the bar is set higher; there is a greater need for optimal decisions, and thus a greater need for analytical input.

Whether automatic and analytic cognition are mutually exclusive at any one time remains controversial, but it is clear that under appropriate circumstances a transition between them will occur, and the two states may 'oscillate' [23] according to task demands. **Vignette 1.4** describes a common clinical situation. A patient has an initial wrong diagnosis induced by the similarity of their case to a more common or recently seen condition (an availability heuristic), and which also appears to be a typical example of its class (a representative heuristic).

Vignette 1.4 An acute abdomen

A 42-year-old woman presented to accident and emergency with an acute abdomen and was seen by a casually officer who considered appendicitis the most likely diagnosis. They called the surgical SHO who came to review the patient and found signs of peritonism with guarding and rebound tenderness, and history consistent with acute appendicitis. The more general signs of a bacterial infection such as a coated tongue and foetor were lacking but this does not exclude the diagnosis. The patient appeared reasonably stable. She was given antibiotics, painkillers and an intravenous drip, kept nil by mouth and scheduled for surgery the following day.

Over the course of the next six hours her condition worsened significantly. When the surgical registrar did his night-time round before going home, he found the most obvious thing about her was not abdominal pain but that she was pale and sweaty. A pregnancy test was positive.

An immediate laparotomy was arranged and bleeding from her ectopic pregnancy was successfully controlled. She made a full recovery

This initial diagnosis is then reinforced by several other well-established heuristics (anchoring bias, confirmation bias and premature closure) which can all be contained within the scope of automatic cognition. Treatment failure should then force a switch to conscious cognition, which is more analytical in nature and may include the formal consideration of the combined probabilities of the various individual signs, symptoms and investigations pertaining to the case. In the clinical example in **Vignette 1.3**, if executed in a sufficiently timely manner, the sequence of events was rational, with the appropriate outcome, even though the initial engagement of heuristics had been misleading. Without the switch to analytic cognition, the mechanism would have failed. However, in other situations heuristics may have provided the correct answer faster and more efficiently, and with less use of cognitive resources.

Attention should therefore be focused on those triggers or stimuli that might promote or inhibit these two systems, and – because the final system to be engaged is the most crucial in determining outcomes – in particular those factors that modulate the transition between them. This concept is summarised in **Figure 1.1**, which displays stimuli for this transition that may originate externally from the environment or from primarily internal sources. Clearly there is an interaction between these two main initial engagement groups and more than one is likely to be in operation at any one time, but they offer a useful approach to formulating a strategy that will promote analytic thinking when required.

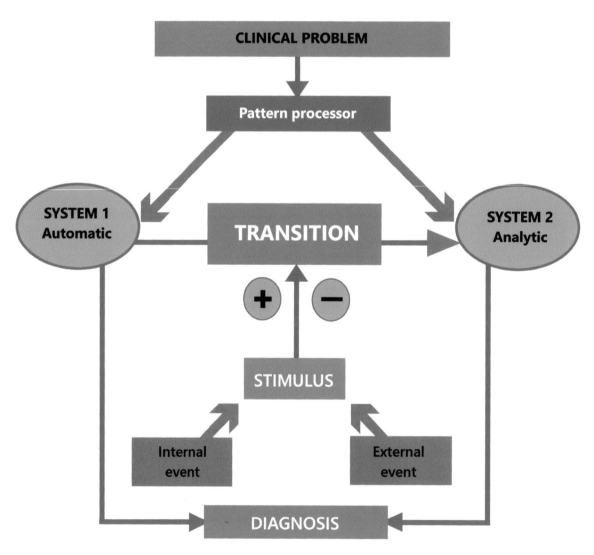

Figure 1.1 *The transition between thinking systems.*

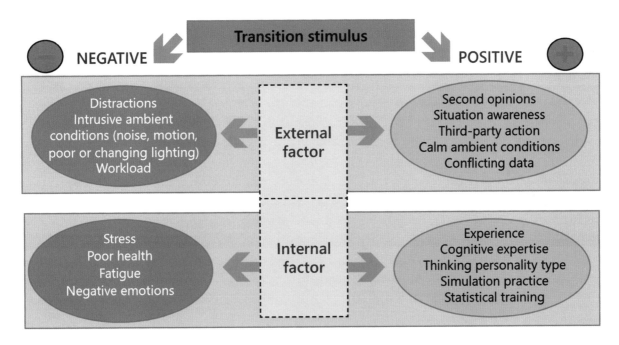

Figure 1.2 *Factors influencing the transition between the two thinking systems.*

A selection of the most significant determinants is given in **Figure 1.2.** Here they are classified according to their source and whether they have a positive or negative influence on the transition process. Even without the influence of environmental factors and experiences, individuals will vary in their disposition towards adopting heuristics or conscious analysis to make judgements and decisions. This would inevitably depend upon their personality, but their ability to adopt conscious analysis – either de novo or in overriding heuristics – is also a function of other characteristics, including their working memory capacity and performance on standardised intelligence tests [24].

Even clever people are quite capable of making gross errors of judgement through the automatic engagement of heuristics, as illustrated in a 2007 study by Gigerenzer involving 160 experienced gynaecologists. All were given relevant information in the form of conditional probabilities given as percentages, as shown below.

Women in a particular region are being screed for breast cancer with mammography. In this region the following observations apply:

- The probability that a woman has breast cancer is 1% (prevalence).
- If a woman has breast cancer, the probability is 80% that she will have a positive mammogram (sensitivity).
- If a woman does not have breast cancer the probability is 9% that she will have a positive mammogram (false-positive rate)

A woman who has tested positive asks what the probability is that she actually has breast cancer. What is the best answer to give her?

(a) 'It is not certain that you have breast cancer, yet the probability is about 81%.'
(b) 'Out of ten women who test positive, as you did, about nine have breast cancer.'
(c) 'Out of ten women who test positive, as you did, only about one has breast cancer.'
(d) 'The chance that you have breast cancer is about 1%.'

The percentage of gynaecologists giving each answer were:

(a) 14%
(b) 47%
(c) 20%
(d) 19%

The best answer was in fact (c), that about one in every ten women testing positive has breast cancer. However, only 20% of gynaecologists gave this answer.

Elements other than intelligence, experience and expertise are clearly operating here and need to be considered. Contextual and environmental circumstances matter greatly, and heuristic-based errors are more likely when there are distractions or time pressures that reduce the attention and effort required for the functioning of conscious analysis [25,26]. The manner in which information is presented and received also seems critical.

A major determining factor comprises the nature of the judgement itself. Matters such as deciding on what car to buy, with numerous complex factors to consider, engage analytic thinking. Deciding which way to go on a familiar route to work engages automatic thinking.

For the same issue, whether it is dealt with automatically or analytically is dependent on the way in which information is presented. A junior doctor asking his or her consultant about treatment may present a clear and typical history with appropriate treatment suggested and ask 'Do you agree?'. The consultant is likely to say 'Yes' automatically. If there are ambiguities or inconsistencies between the clinical picture and the proposed treatment, the consultant is likely to deal with the case analytically. Each approach is appropriate to its situation. Analytic thought is not necessarily the best.

Unconscious processing

In this section we look at work in the field of human learning and information processing that occurs *outside* of conscious awareness. Ideas about the subconscious mind are polarised between psychoanalytic and behavioural psychology. Psychoanalysis and behavioural psychology use different methods of evidence gathering.

Psychoanalysis adopted detailed case studies, whereas behavioural psychology or *psychometry*, emerged from laboratory-based physiological experiments such as those of Pavlov. This division became even more pronounced in the UK and later North America by the development and growth of the psychometric and behavioural genetics approach of Galton (which strongly influenced British, and especially English, psychology until the 1960s and 70s). Galton's approach stressed the study of population characteristics compared to the case-based analysis of psychoanalytic schools.

The other major influence on psychology was radical behaviourism, often based on case studies but completely rejecting any study of unconscious processes. An example of this is the controversial study of an acquired phobia in *Little Albert* conducted by Watson and Raynor in 1920 [27]. These combined influences resulted in British and North American psychology being (with a few exceptions) a rather curious and philosophically incoherent hybrid during much of the twentieth century.

Freud's psychodynamic theory

Freud's theory of mind was an early and pivotal attempt to explain human behaviour in terms of basic physical and chemical mechanisms without recourse to any dualist or supernatural effects. The great significance of Freud's theory was its position in removing the last barrier to viewing humans as physical 'machines'. This dealt what Freud called his 'third blow' to the medieval theistic view of man. (The first was the cosmological blow of Copernicus who ended the geocentric view of the universe; the second blow was Darwin's theory of evolution.)

Freud considered the mind as an 'energy system'. In this system, mental content does not simply reside in storage, waiting to be accessed, but exerts pressure on behaviour. Psychodynamic theory concerns the source of such energy, how it flows, gets side-tracked, becomes dammed up and is expressed. The essential features of Freud's theory are that:

- mental energy is strictly limited and energy use for one purpose is not available for another;

- mental energy is conserved so that if it is blocked from expression in one channel it becomes diverted inevitably into another (rather than disappearing);

- the mind operates to relieve tension created by bodily needs (e.g. a shortage of food leads to a tension called hunger which is eliminated by the mind by seeking environmental factors that mitigate hunger, namely food, and thereby achieving quiescence);

- all behaviour is directed towards achieving pleasure, either from the reduction of tension or the release of energy;

- these processes are largely unconscious.

Freud proposed three different levels of awareness of mental processes:

- **Level 1:** At the *conscious* level are thoughts we are aware of at the time we are having them. This is still the definition used for the content of consciousness.

- **Level 2:** The *preconscious* content of the mind includes thoughts and memories that we are not conscious of at the moment, but could easily become aware of if we attended to them. It includes things such as your birthdate or home address, or the outline and progress of projects you're involved with.

- **Level 3:** The *unconscious* content of mind includes things that we cannot become aware of except under specific circumstances. Freud's idea was that these are inaccessible because of the positive action of mental processes. They are suppressed because of the level of stress they create. The circumstances under which they become manifest (according to Freud) are: slips of the tongue, neuroses, works of art, psychosis and dreams. These unconscious processes nevertheless have a profound and continuing effect on conscious thought and behaviour.

Freud's conscious and preconscious levels of awareness clearly do exist. He based his unconscious level on evidence from hypnosis. Freud used the technique extensively but abandoned it because not everyone could be hypnotised. Under hypnosis, he found that patients can access verifiable memories they were previously not aware of [28]. Freud noted that such recollections were often associated with strong and painful emotional reactions. More conclusive is that if a person is asked to remember something while hypnotised, when they are woken up they cannot remember it or they do not even know that they have forgotten it, yet if hypnotised again they often remember it, showing it must have been stored unconsciously.

Id, ego and superego

Freud added to his three-tiered theory of consciousness in 1923 with the three concepts of the *id*, *ego* and *superego* [29]:

- **Concept 1—The id:** He proposed the id as the source of all mental energy. Its purpose is simply to reduce tension arising from biological drivers to return to a peaceful mental state. It does this by following the pleasure principle of seeking pleasure and avoiding pain. The id is entirely unconscious, and entirely uncomplicated. It does not plan or temporise, but merely seeks immediate pleasure or release of tension. It has a tenuous link to the physical world and can be satisfied by imagination as well as action.

- **Concept 2 —The superego:** Freud's superego represents the learnt moral aspects of social behaviour, including standards of ethics and conduct. It is an internal model of the societal rules of the external world. The superego exists largely in the unconscious and has limited ability to interact with the external world.

- **Concept 3 —The ego:** The ego is the principle constituent of the conscious mind and stands between the id and the superego. The ego directly controls conscious thought and actions and is guided by the 'reality principle'. It moderates the demands of the id and superego according to what is reasonable and achievable in practice. Unlike the other two, the ego has the ability to plan, weigh options and temporise.

Freud's theory is one of an unconscious pressure-cooker of highly motivational tensions and mental energy. These can be controlled and redirected but they must be manifested, sometimes in ways apparently unrelated to their origin such as irrational beliefs or psychosomatic illness.

Experimental evidence of unconscious processes

As early as 1884, researchers investigated their own ability to distinguish between differing amounts of pressure applied by weights. They then plotted their conscious confidence in the difference between pressures against the accuracy of their judgements. They found that even when they had no conscious confidence at all that the weights were significantly different, the pure 'guesses' were still correct 60% of the time, with high statistical significance [30].

Psychological research into the unconscious largely fell from favour from the nineteenth century to the first half of the twentieth century. Interest in the unconscious remained common among European psychologists, with Jean Piaget being perhaps the best known. Frederick Bartlett, at Cambridge from the 1930s onwards, was an exception in British psychology because he was interested in cognition and unconscious processes . Before the 1960s, his work was largely excluded by the dominance of the behaviourist psychometric hegemony.

In the 1960s and 1970s, experimental research on what we now call *subliminal perception* gained significant ground and increasing academic acceptance in both British and North American psychology. It was confirmed that the threshold for unconscious registration of presented information is lower than the threshold for conscious registration for all sensory modalities. This threshold can be in terms of the duration the information is presented for, or the level of intensity at which it is presented. Note that this threshold varies with the factors listed above which promote automatic thinking.

A key instrument for research into the unconscious that exploits this threshold difference is the *tachistoscope*. This instrument allows images or text to be shown to subjects for brief periods of time. The time period can be adjusted so that is above the threshold for subliminal perception, but below the threshold for conscious perception. In this way, experimenters can expose subjects to purely unconscious stimuli and observe the effect they have on their behaviour. Numerous experiments have been done using the tachistoscope that leave no doubt that there is an unconscious mind. More controversial is whether (and in what way) the properties of the unconscious mind differ from those of the conscious mind. It is of note that while Freud's psychodynamic theory is based on case studies, there is some experimental evidence to support certain aspects of it.

Perceptual defence

In perceptual defence, the unconscious mind withholds information from the conscious mind, as if it is in some way threatening. Freud based this theory on observations on hypnotised patients recalling painful 'suppressed' memories. In an early experiment [31] subjects were shown words that were either neutral such as *apple* or emotionally charged such as *whore*. The duration of exposure of these words was slowly lengthened so that it passed from *below* to *above* the conscious registration threshold. Subjects were asked at what point they became aware of the word, and were also monitored using skin conductivity (a measure of physiological stress). It was found that emotionally charged words were recognised later than the neutral words and that skin conductivity changes came before reported recognition.

Subliminal psychodynamic activation

The theory of subliminal psychodynamic activation is that messages presented subliminally that contain elements of tension or stress (as opposed to reassurance or calm) can affect behaviour or cognitive performance after the message has been presented without the subject being aware of it. This effect has been demonstrated in a number of experiments. In one series of experiments, Silverman and colleagues [32] tested Freud's theory that guilt about love for one's father is a source of stress that leads to conflicting sexual ideas in some females. Female undergraduates were shown the message *Loving daddy is wrong* or the message *Loving daddy is okay* via a tachistoscope. They were all unaware of having been shown these messages, and after exposure they all underwent memory psychometric testing. Subjects performed poorly *only* if they had seen the message *Loving daddy is wrong* [32].

In another example Patton [33], and later Gerard and colleagues [34], investigated the effect of the term *Mamma is leaving me* on the behaviour of people with eating disorders. This was based on Freud's theory that eating disorders were a response to feelings of loss and abandonment by a person's mother. Subjects were shown this phrase and similar (but not emotionally loaded) phrases such as *Mamma is loaning it* via a tachistoscope. Afterwards they were given the opportunity to eat wheat crackers. They were all unaware of being shown the phrases, but those with eating disorders who saw the phrase *Mamma is leaving me* ate significantly more crackers.

Most experimental evidence that has been collected refers to laboratory tasks and games, rather than Freudian theory. Typical experiments ask subjects a question and show them the answer subliminally, then assess responses and how they vary with time or other factors.

Current views of the unconscious

There is broad agreement in psychology that the unconscious exists and that it is responsible for many – if not most – of our beliefs and actions. More controversial is the highly motivated, irrational and basic biology-driven subconscious proposed by Freud. Research into the mind has three means of investigation. These are surveys, laboratory experiments, and case studies.

By case studies, we mean detailed psychological examinations of people, largely those who are undergoing psychotherapy. They involve numerous sessions spread over months or years, as well as great trust between the therapist and patient and intimate enquiry. The strength of the method is that it can achieve a level of complexity and depth of understanding about the minds of individual people the other methods cannot. The weakness is that they contain a substantial subjective component in the interpretation of results, which are therefore poorly repeatable by other investigators. This weakness has made the method fall out of favour as the fashion in both medicine and science has moved towards repeatability of findings. Freud exclusively used case studies as his evidence and based his theory on powerful, but deeply hidden, biological forces connected with alimentation, voiding, aggression and sex. In the field of psychoanalysis where case studies still form the principle evidence base, Freud's theories have proved durable, but this is not the case in psychology.

There are two main reasons for this. First, they are difficult issues to access via psychometric or laboratory experiments and, second, with psychoanalytic and psychodynamic approaches out of fashion there is little interest among psychologists in testing its predictions. Research that has been done focuses more on reactions to everyday social goals and often mundane laboratory tasks.

The current, dominant view of psychology of the *cognitive unconscious* differs in a number of respects from that of Freud. In this view, the unconscious does not have motivations that are hidden or independent of those of the conscious mind and there is no specific significance associated with the biological motivations described by Freud. Mental processes are unconscious because they do not receive the prominence necessary for them to cross the threshold into consciousness, or because they have become automatic by regular practice (as shown by activities like playing the piano, typing on a keyboard or tying shoelaces). According to this theory, unconscious content is not primarily motivational but may provide *implicit motives* that we are not aware of – as opposed to *explicit motives* that we are aware of [35].

Implicit knowledge

Implicit learning and *implicit memory* refer the knowledge acquired by people and their ability to recall it without being consciously aware of it or to verbalise it. Implicit learning is the *non-intentional* and *incidental* acquisition of knowledge, and implicit memory is the *non-intentional* recourse to this knowledge. *Unconscious knowledge* is the information itself. Examples are the grammatical rules used when someone speaks in their mother tongue. This is particularly striking in children aged between four and six, before they have any notions of grammar. When asked how it is that they speak correctly they are unable to say anything other than it *seems* right.

There do appear to be differences between conscious and unconscious knowledge. There are two areas where conscious and unconscious processing takes place in anatomically distinct locations.

- **Vision:** The first and most studied of these areas is *vision*, and there is extensive data on the difference between the conscious ventral visual stream to the visual cortex and the unconscious dorsal visual stream to the posterior parietal cortex. This is not expanded on here because its relevance to human factors is limited.

- **Memory:** The second area is *memory*. Korsakoff's syndrome, head injury and strokes affect the anatomical structures in the brain known as fornices, mamillary bodies and medial temporal lobes. These conditions impair *explicit* memory, but experiments on affected people find that implicit memory is substantially intact [36].

A particularly dramatic example of this was an 'experiment' carried out by Claparède [37] (original publication 1911) who took a profoundly amnesic patient and shook hands with her. In his own hand he had concealed a pin with which he pricked her. Following this, the patient could not remember having their hand pricked, but refused to shake hands with Claparède again, claiming it was well known that people often hid pins in their hands.

There are some specific features of implicit memory. It is:

- **Durable**: Experimental evidence in normal people suggests that knowledge that is acquired and stored unconsciously is retained more reliably in unconscious memory than knowledge that is gained explicitly is retained in explicit memory.

- **Holistic:** Although it is possible to communicate with the unconscious mind using text and language, unconscious knowledge tends not to be linguistic in nature. Rather it is procedural. It also tends to be holistic, such that the compositional structures (such as the sequence of letters 'P–Q') are not decomposed into constituents (such as 'P' and 'Q') but are remembered with no internal structure [38].

- **Inflexible:** Subconscious knowledge requires stereotypical pattern recognition for its exercise. Unlike conscious knowledge, It cannot be applied via analysis to unfamiliar situations [39].

- **Independent from explicit knowledge:** Performance in implicit learning is said to be independent of the performance of explicit memory. Implicit learning is consistent in any one person, so that people who perform well on one experiment also tend to perform well on others. The correlation between a person's performance in implicit learning and their performance in explicit learning is relatively weak and there is little or no correlation with learning or memory [40].

- **Has little age or IQ dependence:** This hypothesis is less well established through the evidence, but it seems that implicit learning is independent of both age and IQ, and shows lower variance in populations than that shown by explicit learning [41].

Why should there be an unconscious kind of knowledge? One reason is that we only have one conscious channel of processing, but we can process many things without consciously doing so. We can think of disparate subjects while competently driving a car. It may be that the evolution of consciousness occurred at a relatively late stage in human development and therefore unconscious processes are older in evolutionary terms. In addition, humans appear to start learning – at the latest – immediately after birth, when mental life is thought to be for the most part unconscious [42].

So how important is unconscious cognition? Psychodynamic theory holds that it is by far the most important of our mental processes. In contrast, behavioural psychology denied or marginalised its importance, particularly during the days when radical behaviourism was in fashion, but this has again changed and is now thought to be of great importance in determining performance and decision-making, if not as devious as the psychodynamic unconscious of Freud.

Unconscious decision-making

This topic is covered in more detail in *Module 2* on decision-making. Two theories predominate in contemporary psychology addressing the question of unconscious decision-making, although both have been subject to criticism. These are the *somatic marker hypothesis* and the *unconscious thought theory*.

SOMATIC MARKER HYPOTHESIS

This suggests that unconscious cognitive processing leads to somatic changes, such as 'gut feelings', which influence decision-making. Learning starts with an association between a perceived situation and an emotion. The relevance of the physical bodily response is that experimenters can measure it. For example, you might be a cold dark room with blue light coming in through the window when something jumps out at you. This invokes fear and an adrenergic 'fight or flight' response. When you are next in a cold dark room with a blue light, the fight of flight response may be invoked again and the somatic changes that occur invoke fear. This hypothesis has been criticised on the grounds of inefficiency, with the suggestion that such an indirect route is unlikely to have evolved and that reinforcement learning based in the orbitofrontal cortex and amygdala would be sufficient to account for such learning [43].

UNCONSCIOUS THOUGHT THEORY

This theory actually concerns *conscious* decision-making with information that is consciously accessible. The theory is that with highly *complex* situations and involved decisions, the *quality* of any decision is improved if the cognitive processing is subconscious (**Figure 1.3**). This kind of decision is taken by addressing an issue consciously, then 'sleeping on it' or turning attention elsewhere for a few days or weeks before returning to the question, if the solution does not 'pop into your head' first. The reverse is true of simple analytic decisions that are better taken directly in consciousness. Recent research has

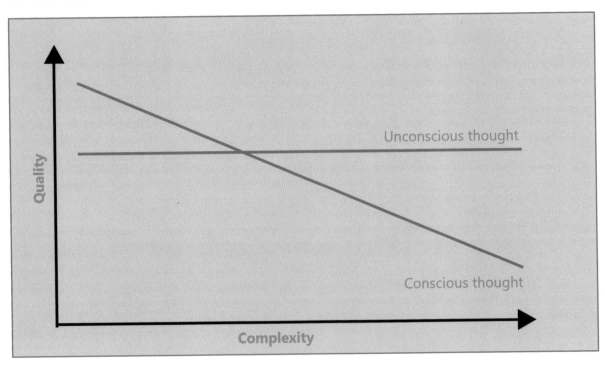

Figure 1.3 *The unconscious thought theory (adapted from* Dijksterhuis A. and Nordgren L.F. A theory of unconscious thought. *Perspectives on Psychological Science,* 2006; 1: 95–109*)*.

replicated findings that suggest that better decisions are made after distraction than deliberation, but they have questioned the general superiority of such decision making and suggested additional complexity: with decisions often being made quickly using conscious thought and being accessed more easily after distraction [44].

Emotion

The relationship between the emotions and reason has been debated since the time of the Ancient Greeks. Aristotle believed that there was a mutual relationship between judgement and emotions, and made the latter the basis of his theory of morality. During the enlightenment in the eighteenth century, the philosopher David Hume went so far as to state that reason was 'passion's slave'.

During the romantic period in the nineteenth century, this symbiotic viewpoint was rejected and replaced by the idea that the intellect and emotions were fundamentally in conflict with each other constantly struggling for control of the self and its destiny. However, fundamental research over the last twenty years or so has reunited these two domains irreversibly, and has clearly established that intelligent behaviour is a function of the harmonious interaction between emotion and reason, whereby they can rightly be described as together forming a 'rational' unit – a real-life Dr Spock would probably face many of the difficulties in functioning seen in people with autistic spectrum disorder.

The generic importance of the emotions and the specific brain regions responsible for them emerged from the study of unfortunate brain-damaged patients, such as Phineas Gage in the nineteenth century. Gage suffered a penetrating head injury in 1848. A recent study using modern techniques suggested that his brain injury must have been limited to the left frontal lobe and spared the superior sagittal sinus, as a lesion here would have posed a double threat to his life by causing a massive haemorrhage or an air embolism – or both [45] – but against expectations, he survived.

Following this injury Gage's ability to plan and structure his life deteriorated markedly, although recent reviews have suggested he experienced a greater degree of recovery of function than was initially thought. A number of modern studies have yielded similar findings [46]. Such people display defects in the late stages of reasoning, where the weighting and selection of different decisions are random and without planning, and normal social functioning is not possible. The emotions thus function to yoke the outer world to the inner self and its goals and objectives. They form the communication pathway from the unconscious to the conscious mind and are responsible for all human motivation.

However, the interaction between emotion and cognition is not always beneficial and any inappropriate or high level of emotion can interfere with attention, memory and logical reasoning [47]. The consequences may be a loss of flexibility in thinking and the consideration of alternative possibilities, together with distraction, poor concentration and a distorted world view.

Furthermore, chronic stress from any source can cause significant somatic health problems and even cell death in the hippocampus region of the brain, thus leading to memory loss [48]. The significant morbidity associated with clinical depression and anxiety states is well documented [49].

A notorious example of the catastrophic effects of stress and fear on rational decision-making is the behaviour of the commander of the American Fleet in Pearl Harbour during the attack by the Japanese forces in 1941 [50]. Despite increasing intelligence reports of an impending raid, Admiral Kimmel failed to take any measures to defend his base and his fleet was destroyed. His prevarication demonstrates the effects of the anchoring and confirmation biases in his denial of the evidence, but also reveals how anxiety in the face of a severe threat can reduce flexibility in thinking, and – in this instance – fatal inertia. What's more is that Kimmel received reassurances from his staff, possibly out of military respect, which is a gesture that illustrates the negative effect of the authority gradient in facilitating analytic thinking. Similar processes are also evident in the public health response to the 1918 pandemic of so-called 'Spanish flu'. Despite rising rates of infection and death there was widespread prevarication and denial among most public health departments, and, with few exceptions, fatal inertia that lead to large-scale mortality [51].

It is easy to imagine many clinical scenarios whereby acutely stressful situations preclude an optimal outcome. The importance of emotions in automatic thinking is well captured in the concept of the 'affect' heuristic [52], whereby emotional 'tags', positive or negative, are generated by a given representation or situation, and promote a rapid judgement or decision in the same way as the 'availability' or 'representativeness' heuristic, and with the same advantages and potential dangers associated with this class of response.

Beyond these generic effects, the individual emotions appear to display specific features that have relevance for the work environment. Anger, for example, stimulates stereotypical, heuristic-type thinking, but it also leads people to attribute blame to other individuals, rather than the situation and circumstances that surround negative outcomes [53]. On the other hand, requiring a person to explain and account for their feelings may reduce such punitive attributions, and allow more complex, conscious reasoning [53].

By contrast, positive emotions promote long-lasting, durable increases in personal resources – physical, social and intellectual – building resilience and the ability to cope with stress. People who are experiencing positive emotions appear more capable of 'stepping back' from their current problems and to 'consider them from multiple angles' [54], which is another way of describing aspects of analytic system thinking. The personal benefits [55] are therefore translated into tangible, professional and organisational rewards.

The way forward

Organisations that want to facilitate better decision-making can take measures to promote engagement of the optimum system for a given situation. Minimising unnecessarily stressful working environments and excessive workloads favours analytic thinking, as does effective communication that encourages a 'collective cognitive responsibility' of teams, which allows them to 'understand what is happening' and stay 'cognitively on top of events as they unfold' [56].

Flattening authority gradients encourages any member of a team to contribute to a decision without fear of retribution. The *authority gradient* refers to the 'steepness' of a command hierarchy. Steep authority gradients tend to be associated with an unwillingness to express concerns, to question, or even to clarify instructions. Most teams require an authority gradient to define roles and responsibilities, but effective team leaders consciously establish the shallowest hierarchy appropriate to the capabilities of the team members. Steep gradients result in automatic thinking in juniors; shallow gradients result in analytic thinking. An example of the powerful nature of such gradients is given by the civil aviation disaster that occurred in Tenerife in 1977, in which two Boeing 747 planes crashed. The events surrounding the disaster were complex but it was evident that a relatively inexperienced flight engineer was reluctant to question the decision of one of the most experienced training Captain's in the KLM fleet to proceed to take off, when they felt there may be an aircraft on the runway, even where this threatened their life.

The full spectrum of environmental factors that facilitate better decision-making – from the 'usability' of the physical design of instruments [57], to the support of harmonious human dynamics – has been described as 'environments that make us smart' [58]. The most difficult, and possibly the most important, challenge is for individuals themselves to form mental habits that adopt the optimum system, and to move towards 'cognitive de-biasing' [14]. Given the apparent hard-wired nature of heuristic decisions, there has been a persuasive pessimism about this as a realistic goal [4]. However, there are several promising strategies that offer 'cognitive pills for cognitive ills' [59] to improve thinking expertise. They start with a consciousness-raising exercise to familiarise subjects with how reasoning processes happen in the real world, namely the discipline of *metacognition* itself, and that the normative, idealised theories of 'rational' or Bayesian-type thinking are not foremost in everyday situations. Such Bayesian logic seems to present particular difficulties in terms of recall and application.

Following on from this, there are several approaches that could be taken, such as simulations [60], specific training (e.g. probability theory) and feedback to decision makers. In principle, the latter is a well-established forum for discussion of serious errors, whether due to system failures or cognitive biases. This is the serious untoward incident (SUI) reporting process. Historically the emphasis has been on biases in cognition and the unconscious and intractable nature of these. This largely derives from the early paradigms in this area of research drawing largely on the work of Kahneman [1] and Tversky [19]. Other research has suggested a more positive outlook [61]. It has been suggested [5] that:

> *"... root-cause analysis, so powerful in understanding other types of medical error, is less easily applied when the root causes are cognitive."*

This means that those tragic cases that have as their source heuristic-type reasoning and failure to engage analytic thinking, will not provide the deep learning opportunity that they deserve, thus compounding the loss and perpetuating the risk of a similar future event.

Conclusions

The last thirty years of cognitive research has produced profound insights into human reasoning, judgement and decision-making. The application of these towards improved medical outcomes necessitates understanding and engagement of all members of the health service. This is a difficult intellectual and practical challenge, and will require imagination, resources and endurance in order to achieve it.

References

1 Kahneman D. *Maps of Bounded Rationality.* Nobel Prize Lecture, 2002. Available at: http://www.nobelprize.org (last accessed January 2013).

2 Simon H. *Rational Decision-Making in Business Organizations.* Nobel Prize Lecture, 1978. Available at: http://www.nobelprize.org (last accessed January 2013).

3 Groopman J. *How Doctors Think.* Boston: Houghton Mifflin, 2008.

4 Graber M. Metacognitive training to reduce diagnostic errors: Ready for prime time? *Academic Medicine,* 2003; 78: 781.

5 Graber M. Diagnostic errors in medicine: A case of neglect. *Journal in Quality and Patient Safety,* 2005; 32: 106–13.

6 Quirk M. *Intuition and Metacognition in Medical Education: Keys to Developing Expertise.* New York: Spring Publishing Company, 2006.

7 Croskerry P. Achieving quality in clinical decision-making: Cognitive strategies and detection of bias. *Academic Emergency Medicine,* 2002; 9: 184–204.

8 Croskerry P. Clinical cognition and diagnostic error: Applications of a Dual Process Model of reasoning. *Advances in Health Sciences Education,* 2009; 14: 27–35.

9 Evans J. Dual-processing accounts of reasoning, judgement and social cognition. *Annual Review of Psychology,* 2008; 59: 255–78.

10 Pacini R, Epstein S. The relation of rational and experimental information processing styles to personality, basic beliefs and the ratio-bias phenomenon. *Journal of Personality and Social Psychology,* 1999; 76: 972–87.

11 Mithen S. *The Pre-History of the Mind.* London: Thames and Hudson, 1996.

12 Dennett D. *Consciousness Explained.* London: Penguin, 1992.

13 Jaynes J. *The Origin of Consciousness in the Breakdown of the Bicameral Mind.* Boston: Houghton Mifflin, 1976.

14 Croskerry P. The importance of cognitive errors in diagnosis and strategies to minimize them. *Academic Medicine,* 2003, 78: 775–80.

15 Kovacs G, Croskerry P. Clinical decision-making : An emergency medicine perspective. *Academic Emergency Medicine,* 1999; 6: 947–52.

16 Fodor J. *The Modularity of Mind.* Cambridge, MA: MIT Press, 1983.

17 Baron J. *Thinking and Deciding,* 4th edn. Cambridge: Cambridge University Press, 2007.

18 Polanyi M. *The Tacit Dimension*. New York: Doubleday, 1966.

19 Tversky A, Kahneman D. Judgment under uncertainty: Heuristics and biases. *Science*, 1974; 185(4157): 1124–31.

20 Reichle ED, Liversedge SP, Pollatsek A, Rayner K. Encoding multiple words simultaneously in reading is implausible. *Trends in Cognitive Science*, 2009; 13(3): 115–19.

21 Gigerenzer G. *Rationality for Mortals: How People Cope with Uncertainty*. New York: Oxford University Press, 2008.

22 Simon HA. Rational choice and the structure of the environment. *Psychology Reviews*, 1956; 63(2): 129–38 (Epub 1956/03/01).

23 Hammond K. *Human Judgement and Social Policy: Irreducible Uncertainty, Inevitable Error, Unavoidable Injustice*. New York: Oxford University Press, 2000.

24 Feldman-Barrett L, Tugade MM, Engle RW. Individual differences in working memory capacity and dual-process theories of the mind. *Psychological Bulletin*, 2004; 130: 553–73.

25 Ferreira MB, Garcia-Marques L, Sherman SJ, Sherman JW. Automatic and controlled components of judgement and decision. *Journal of Personality and Social Psychiatry*, 2006; 91: 797–813.

26 Finucane ML, Alhakami A, Slovic P, Johnson SM. The affect heuristic in judgements of risks and benefits. *Journal of Behavioural Decision-making*, 2000; 13: 1–17.

27 Watson JB, Rayner R. Conditioned emotional reactions. *American Psychologist*, 2000; 55(3): 313–17.

28 Freud S, Brill AA. *The Interpretation of Dreams: Completely* Revised Edition. London, New York: Allen & Unwin/Macmillan, 1937.

29 Freud S, Strachey J. *The Ego and the Id*. New York: Norton, 1989.

30 Peirce CS, Jastrow J. On small differences in sensation. *Memoirs of the National Academy of Sciences*, 1884; 3: 73–83.

31 McGinnies E. Emotionality and perceptual defence. *Psychological Review*, 1949; 56: 244–51.

32 Silverman LH. Psychoanalytic theory: The reports of its death are greatly exaggerated. *American Psychologist*, 1976; 31: 621–37.

33 Patton CJ. Fear of abandonment and binge eating. *Journal of Nervous and Mental Disease*, 1992; 180: 484–90.

34 Gerard HB, Kupper DA, Nguyen L. The causal link between depression and bulimia. In: Masling JM, Bornstein RF, (eds) *Psychoanalytic Perspectives in Psychopathology*. Washington, DC: American Psychological Association, 1993; pp. 225–52.

35 Bargh JA, Morsella E. The unconscious mind. *Perspectives in Psychological Science*, 2008; 3(1): 73–79.

36 Graf P, Squire LR, Mandler G. The information that amnesic patients do not forget. *Journal of Experimental Psychology: Learning, Memory, and Cognition*, 1984; 10: 164–78.

37 Claparède E. Recognition and selfhood. *Consciousness and Cognition*, 1995; 4: 371–78. (Originally published 1911; translated by Bonnel AM, Baars BJ.)

38 Roberts PL, MacLeod C. Representational consequences of two modes of learning. *Quarterly Journal of Experimental Psychology*, 1995; Section A(48): 296–319.

39 Dienes Z, Berry D. Implicit knowledge: Below the subjective threshold. *Psychonomic Bulletin and Review*, 1997; 4: 3–23.

40. Hayman CAG, Tulving E. Contingent dissociation between recognition and fragment completion: The method of triangulation. *Journal of Experimental Psychology: Learning, Memory, and Cognition*, 1989; 15:28–40.

41 Kaufman SB, De Young CG, Gray JR, Jimenez L, Brown J, Mackintosh N. Implicit learning as an ability. *Cognition*, 2010; 116(3): 321–40.

42 Augusto LM. Unconscious knowledge: A survey. *Advances in Cognitive Psychology*, 2010; 6: 116–41.

43 Rolls ET. *The Brain and Emotion*. New York: Oxford University Press, 1999.

44 Waroquier L, Marchiori D, Klein O, Cleeremans A. Is it better to think unconsciously or to trust your first impression? A reassessment of unconscious thought theory. *Social Psychological and Personality Science*, 2010; 1(2): 111–18.

45 Ratiu P, Talos IF, Haker S, Lieberman D, Everett P. The Tale of Phineas Gage, digitally remastered. *Journal of Neurotrauma*, 2004; 21(5): 637–43.

46 Damasio AR. Descartes' *Error: Emotion, Reason, and the Human Brain*. London: Penguin, 1994.

47 Evans D. *Emotion*. New York: Oxford University Press, 2001.

48 Sapolsky RM. *Why Zebras Don't Get Ulcers*. New York: Freeman, 1994.

49 Kessler RC, Birnbaum HG, Shahly V, Bromet E, Hwang I, McLaughlin KA, *et al*. Age differences in the prevalence and co-morbidity of DSM-IV major depressive episodes: Results from the who world mental health survey initiative. *Depression and Anxiety*, 2010; 27(4): 351–64.

50 Janis IL, Mann L. *Decision-making: A Psychological Analysis of Conflict, Choice, and Commitment*. New York: Free Press, 1977.

51 Barry JM. *The Great Influenza: The Epic Story of the Deadliest Plague in History*. New York: Penguin Books, 2005.

52 Slovic P, Finucane M, Peters E, MacGregor DG. The affect heuristic. In: Gilovich T, Griffin D, Kahneman D (eds) *Heuristics and Biases: The Psychology of Intuitive Judgement*. Cambridge: Cambridge University Press, 2002.

53 Lerner JS, Goldberg JH, Tetlock PE. Sober second thought: The effects of accountability, anger and authoritarianism on attributions of accountability. *Personality and Social Psychology Bulletin*, 1998; 24: 563–74.

54 Fredrickson BL, Branigan C. Positive emotions broaden the scope of attention and thought : Action repertoires. *Cognition and Emotion*,2005; 19: 313–32.

55 Seligman M. *Flourish: A Visionary New Understanding of Happiness and Well-Being*. New York: Free Press, 2011.

56 Scardamalia M. Collective cognitive responsibility for the advancement of knowledge. In: Smith B (ed.): *Liberal Education in a Knowledge Society*. Chicago: Open Court, 2002; pp. 1–14.

57 Norman D. *The Design of Everyday Things*. New York: Basic Books, 1990.

58 Todd PM, Gigerenzer G. Environments that make us smart. *Current Directions in Psychological Science*, 2007; 16: 167–71.

59 Plous S. *The Psychology of Judgment and Decision-making*. New York: McGraw-Hill, 1993.

60 Bond WF, Deitrick LM, Arnold DC, Kostenbader M, Barr GG, Kimmel SR, *et al*. Using simulation to instruct emergency medicine residents in cognitive forcing strategies. *Academic Medicine*, 2004; 79: 438–45.

61 Gigerenzer G, Edwards A. Simple tools for understanding risks: From innumeracy to insight. *British Medical Journal*, 2003; 327(7417): 741–44.

Decision Making

2

Key points for reflection

❶ It is important to understand the automatic and analytic decision-making, their applications and consequences.

❷ The progress of learning may often be from conscious incompetence to unconscious competence via conscious competence. Each of us is at different points on this pathway, depending upon the specific area of knowledge or experience focused upon.

The subject of decision-making ranges from 'gut instinct' choices made in the blink of an eye, to government and business policy judgements based on months of analytic research. Slow-moving decisions regarding policy, training, engineering choices and design are often significant for safety, but human performance and limitations are more apparent at the fast end of the spectrum, which will be our focus.

When things go wrong in healthcare, flawed decision-making is often to blame [1] as noted in the National Confidential Enquiry into Patient Outcome and Death report on team-working [2]. This has led to research into the specific issue of healthcare decision-making [1,3,4]. Decision-making can go wrong in several ways. The most obvious way is when we choose the wrong option. We might also consider the options, but fail to make a decision; or we might make the correct decision but take too long over it; or we might miss the trigger to make a decision at all and thus continue doing what we are doing with adverse results.

We make decisions in different ways to suite different situations. Several schemes have been proposed to classify these different ways. These schemes are somewhat arbitrary and are usually used to help *describe* decision-making. The emphasis here is on improving decision-making, and that is reflected in the classification system we use. We divide decisions into automatic versus analytic and conscious vs unconscious.

When choosing a new car we might (in analytic decision mode) appraise brochures, try out different models and discuss colours and the deals available, finally leading to a moment of decision. On the way to the dealership, the traffic lights go red; so we follow the rule to stop. However if we are blocking the progress of a fire-engine we might judge that there is reason enough to break the rule on this occasion. If we then find the road ahead is blocked by a fallen tree, and we know the area well, we could divert from the planned route and take back roads instead, still arriving at the dealership more or less as planned. This involves a pattern-matching automatic decision based on previous knowledge and experience.

Analytic decision-making MODULE ONE

Analytic decisions are those in which we have the time and information to consciously consider various options, to gain further information as necessary and to reach a reasoned choice. Most of the research done on decision-making has involved experiments on college undergraduates with carefully contrived analytic decision tasks. This led to a classical theory of specific steps we go through in decision-making. Several of the stages refer not to the decision itself, but to its associated *situation awareness*. This is included because good decision-making requires good situation awareness and the point of making a decision is an appropriate time to check and update one's situation awareness. These are the steps:

- Step 0—Decision trigger
- Step 1—Assessment
- Step 2—Options check
- Step 3—Project and decide
- Step 4—Review

Decision trigger (Step 0)

The decision trigger is not actually part of decision-making, which is why it is numbered as 0 in this list. It is, however, part of situation awareness and this is covered in more detail in the triggered check situation awareness model in *Module 3*.

Assessment (Step 1)

This involves not assessing the decision itself, but assessing its consequences and the time and resources that are available to make it. Assessment involves questions like:

- *How long have I got?*
- *Do I have all the facts?*
- *What is the ultimate objective?*
- *What are the risks here?*

A recurrent error in decision assessment relates to time and there is potential for improving safety by training people in this aspect. The natural tendency, particularly with inexperienced decision makers, is to hurry to the first available option. Time is rarely that pressured and for inexperienced staff it is usually better to prolong mental assessment at the expense of reduced time for action, rather than the other way round.

The quality of decision-making depends on the accuracy of information gathering in the assessment phase. As an example, consider deciding whether to do an appendectomy operation. Features relevant to this decision include a coated tongue, rebound peritonism, anorexia, and tender lymph nodes in the groin. Less relevant features are hair colour, tendon reflexes and visual acuity. In the assessment phase of this decision, the surgeon prioritises gathering the relevant information by specifically looking for it. This principle can be applied to analytic decisions in general.

The best assessments involve identifying the *most important* out of the large number of perceptual features, and specifically *looking* for them to ensure they are accurately registered [5]. The situation in

> ## Vignette 2.1 Assessment of sudden intraoperative bleeding
>
> A fit 23-year-old dancer underwent diagnostic laparoscopy. The gynaecologist and anaesthetist immediately noticed a small amount of bright pink blood spurting from the Verres needle (the first needle to go through the skin at the start of the procedure). There was cardiovascular stability but the anaesthetist was concerned because there was only one twenty-gauge cannula and no invasive monitoring or cross-matched blood.
>
> The anaesthetist had to decide whether or not to escalate access and monitoring in case of serious haemorrhage. Communications from the gynaecologist were unclear for the next ten minutes while a laparoscopic examination was carried out. Specifically there was no briefing on whether damage had been done, or the possible problems to prepare for.
>
> The anaesthetist decided to raise the alarm to obtain help from colleagues, to improve venous access and monitoring, and to order O-negative blood followed by cross-matched blood and blood products. A pressure infuser was set up, two large intravenous lines and an arterial line were inserted, and a bed arranged on the intensive care unit. Two litres of crystalloid were given proactively.
>
> A general surgeon then arrived and performed a laparotomy, during which the patient's blood pressure suddenly fell to 60/40 mmHg accompanied by pallor and reduced expired carbon dioxide tension (signifying a fall in heart output). This occurred around the time that a large retroperitoneal haematoma (major leakage of blood over the previous period, contained within a natural barrier) was announced. Continuing rapid fluid resuscitation, blood and blood products, as well as two boluses of adrenaline (epinephrine) corrected the situation while the general surgeon contained the bleeding. A vascular surgeon then attended to over-sew the damaged iliac artery.
>
> The patient made an uneventful recovery.

Vignette 2.1 involved a relatively rapid assessment stage, over perhaps five minutes or so, where information was in short supply. The anaesthetist's successful decision-making was based on an accurate assessment. He accurately identified the key feature – the pink blood – from the range of other information available to him, and saw the potential for haemorrhage. He was unable to get further information but recognised that he had time, which was currently sufficient – but not unlimited. He considered that whatever the risk was, it was enough to act on, and he took appropriate steps. Things would have been different if he had missed the bright pink blood, as he easily might have. Then communication from the gynaecologist would have been instrumental.

Options check (Step 2)

The options check is a concept that we have introduced for this course. It is a mental habit analogous to the situation awareness check of *Module 3*. It is one of the more practical take-home messages presented here.

The check begins with a deliberate, conscious identification of the *ultimate objective* of the decision and the options in hand, then it involves stepping back to see if there are further options that have not so far been considered. This is illustrated in **Figure 2.1** (overpage).

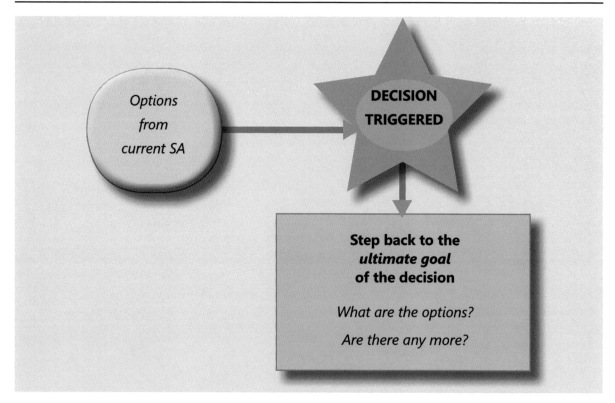

Figure 2.1 *The options check.*

Other authors have described this process under various headings including *creative* and *adaptive* decision-making [6]. We include it because we want to *encourage* it, rather than *describe* it. Decisions with particularly thorough and creative option checking make good stories and may lead to new practices or new ways of thinking.

Option checking is at its best when no existing options look attractive, as shown in **Vignette 2.2**.

Vignette 2.2   Option checking at 35,000 feet [7]

Orthopaedic surgeon, Professor A.W. Wallace, showed thorough and creative option checking when he was travelling from Hong Kong to London on an aeroplane.

He was asked to care for a passenger who had developed chest pain (who had been involved in a motorcycle accident before boarding the plane). The passenger rapidly became seriously unwell. A pneumothorax was suspected by the Professor (this happens when a damaged lung leaks air into the pleural space, between the chest wall and the lung; when the air becomes trapped, the lung collapses and threatens life).

With minimal aids to diagnosis, the Professor asked for a second opinion from a junior doctor, Dr T. Wong, who was also on the plane. Dr Wong agreed with the diagnosis. They then improvised a chest drain set using a urinary catheter, a coat-hanger as a trocar, adhesive tape, oxygen tubing and a plastic bottle of mineral water as a water trap. They used five-star brandy as a disinfectant.

The patient recovered.

Making the diagnosis was the difficulty here and both doctors conferred about it. Once they had made the diagnosis they initially had no acceptable options for treatment. They asked for advice from the ground about what equipment was on board – but none came. They considered a diversion, but time was too short. The catheter in the aircraft's medical kit would do for a drain, but it would let air into the chest as well as letting it out. Therefore they needed a one-way valve system and they devised one from whatever was at hand. Their option checking was prompted because there was no acceptable option to hand. This is often the case, as illustrated by the anonymous phrase *necessity is the mother of invention.*

Option checking is a good habit to get into, even without such prompting. **Vignette 2.3** is another example from an accident and emergency department.

Vignette 2.3   Option checking in Accident and Emergency

A patient (now affectionately known as Chuck) used an electric drill in a suicide attempt, and damaged his neck severely, including one of his carotid arteries and his trachea. Presenting at the emergency department, the drill bit was still present, passing through the skin into the trachea.

Medical staff had to deal with the severe blood loss and control the damaged, partially obstructed and bleeding airway. As the drill bit was removed, a wire was introduced into the trachea through the entry wound, enabling dilation and then intubation for airway control.

The standard options for controlling an airway are intubation via the mouth or nose, and surgical tracheostomy. In this case there were several factors complicating both options. There was a drill bit passing through the trachea, and blood and swelling were obscuring the surgical and laryngoscopic (intubation) views. The patient's anatomy was also distorted. Simply removing the drill risked closing the airway and there would be insufficient time to re-open it. The standard options were not attractive and this therefore prompted a search for alternatives. By placing a guide wire through the wound into the trachea, they were able to remove the drill bit and confidently place an endotracheal tube in the right place, quickly enough to avoid hypoxia.

Project and decide (Step 3)

The principle tool of analytic decision-making is predicting the consequences of – or *projecting* – the options. It involves looking at the predicted consequences of each option, and comparing them; the best one is chosen. Slow strategic and policy decisions (e.g. *Do we merge these hospitals?* or *Do we add bariatrics to our general surgery service?*) are analytic and involve acquiring data over a substantial time and perhaps teams of analysts to model the data. Their purpose is to provide projections for all options that are as accurate as possible. In medicine, many diagnosis, treatment and place of care decisions require careful appraisal, time and a search for information with the same intention – that is, *accurate* projection.

This occurs in fast decisions as well. To illustrate this, we can analyse the decision-making process that the doctors looking after Chuck (**Vignette 2.3**) went through.

● **Option one** was to orally intubate the patient in the conventional fashion. This was tried, but it failed.

● **Option two** was a surgical airway. This was considered, but projection indicated a high risk that the severely damaged and bleeding trachea would be difficult to approach and identify from a conventional tracheostomy incision and there could be a long delay between removing the drill bit and securing the airway, which could lead to critical hypoxia; on the basis of this projection, the option was rejected.

At this point, new options were needed so they did an options check. The possibility of intubation via the wound presented itself. This was seen as feasible using a guide-wire technique. Projection indicated a high probability of removal of the drill bit followed by rapid and accurate location of the endotracheal tube via the wound. The decision was made and the projection proved correct. The quality of this decision depended on imaginative option checking and the accuracy of the projections of the various options.

ACCURACY VS UTILITY OF PROJECTIONS

Accuracy *vs* utility refers to a well-developed mathematical model of decision-making. We have not used this model as our focus but its results are relevant to the process of projecting. Suppose we have to decide whether or not to remove a patient's appendix. The options are to do it or not to do it. If we choose to do it and the appendix turns out to be normal, then that option was incorrect. If we chose not to do it and the patient makes a rapid and full recovery then the no-surgery option was correct. At the time when the decision is made these results are unknown. Instead we define an option's *accuracy* as the probability that it will prove to be correct.

An option's *utility* refers to its consequences, whether or not it proves to be correct. Take the appendix example again. The utility of the option to operate has the positive component of curing a potentially life-threatening disease if it is correct, plus the negative component of doing an unnecessary operation with its attendant risks if it is not. Mathematically the utility of an option is calculated as the product of the probability that it is correct (accuracy) and a measure of its consequences if correct *plus* the product of the probability of its being incorrect (1 *minus* accuracy) and a measure of its consequences if incorrect. Ultimately it is the utility of an option rather than its accuracy that drives decision-making. Consider this extreme example:

> It is a nice sunny day and Emma and some friends are going sailing on a lake. Should Emma wear a life jacket? Option One is to wear one; this will be the correct option if and *only* if it helps Emma, that is if she falls in the water and cannot swim to safety. This is highly improbable, so the *accuracy* of Option One is very low. *Utility*, on the other hand, shows that the cost of Option One – if incorrect – is low. Emma just has to wear a not uncomfortable jacket. Utility – if the option is correct – is saving Emma's life! Therefore, Emma wears it.

Both *accuracy* and *utility* can be improved by identifying and gathering *relevant* information, and this improves what is called *decision quality*. For a given decision quality, there is a trade-off between accuracy and utility. The model is used to optimise this trade-off in deciding things like the best diagnostic criteria for cancer screening programs [8]. In human factors, its value is that specifically asking the questions *What is this option's accuracy?* and *What is its utility?* can improve projection quality.

In the case of Chuck in **Vignette 2.3** above, the accuracy of the option to place a guide-wire through the wound (i.e. the chance of success) was not known and perhaps not thought high, but the *utility* was high. The consequence of success was quick and safe intubation; the consequence of failure to get the wire in the right place was *no harm done*!

Review (Step 4)

The purpose of reviewing a decision is to re-visit it in the light of updated information. This information is used for two purposes:

1. *To suggest new options.* A positive options check is an important part of review.

2. *To update projections.* The most obvious projection to update is the one about the chosen option, but other projections should also be updated. In **Vignette 2.4**, the first option was oral intubation. This was rejected on review, but other options including laryngoscopy were re-examined and new projections were made.

Vignette 2.4   Intubation options

The constant stream of phone messages to Dr Brown's android phone was irritating enough, but he had a management team meeting at midday to prepare for and was very behind. One more hernia repair to go, on a patient who was obese and would need intubating and might take ages to recover.

The patient (weighing in at over a hundred and fifty kilos) had been seen and pronounced fit and well by the registrar. At induction, the light bulb in the large laryngoscope failed; then the replacement, which was a size smaller, did not give an adequate view. The patient's oxygen saturation fell rapidly and several attempts to intubate with various scopes and airway aids were equally unsuccessful. When he asked about fibreoptic equipment (a device that is threaded through the airways to enable intubation under direct vision) he learned that it was in use, but should be available in twenty minutes. Time for taking stock!

With a simple bag and facemask, a simple (Guedel) airway and two-handed ventilation, an oxygen saturation of 85% could be maintained. It was not brilliant but neither was it lethal for the patient. The surgery was non-urgent, and no drugs had been given that could not be rapidly reversed. Therefore, the patient was woken up, his drugs were reversed and he was half sat-up, to reduce the work of breathing. After a stormy few minutes, he was back in recovery (complaining bitterly that his surgery had not been done).

This frustrating situation illustrates a continuous cycle of option checking, choosing and reviewing by Dr Brown. He was under time pressure but decided to go ahead with the operation anyway. He initially decided on conventional intubation. He chose the large laryngoscope, but the bulb failed. An option to check led to the use of the second largest laryngoscope, but this too failed.

Review showed falling saturation and an urgent need to gain airway control. Various airways were tried without success. The fibre-optic option was identified and projected well; then it failed too because it was not available. Dr Brown reviewed the situation again.

With limited options, he realised he could keep oxygenation at a tolerable – but not ideal – level for enough time for the induction drugs to be reversed. He therefore cancelled the surgery and woke the patient up. The situation involved an unfortunate conspiracy of circumstances but Dr Brown managed it successfully.

Vignette 2.5   Too much insulin

The patient was a 32-year-old woman with longstanding kidney failure who had been transplanted. She was admitted four weeks after the transplant, very ill with obvious internal bleeding that needed an operation to fix. She was also noted to have a dangerously high serum potassium of 8.5. The Accident and Emergency consultant prescribed insulin to lower the potassium. Insulin also lowers glucose so he gave her an intravenous glucose drip as well.

In the theatre suite upstairs, the consultant anaesthetist had been running an aortic aneurism. The patient had just reached the stage of being stable enough to leave with a junior doctor. A call from Accident and Emergency persuaded the consultant to agree to meet the patient in the anaesthetic room of in another theatre, where she was briefed by juniors. She noted that this patient had a good pulse and blood pressure and the surgeons were impatient to commence, so she agreed to proceed.

Five minutes into the operation, the consultant requested blood for transfusion. In the briefing, cross-matched blood was said to be under way, so she was taken aback when the transfusion service claimed no blood had yet been cross-matched. Rapidly organising sampling and cross-matching, she gave colloids for volume replacement, together with two units of O-negative blood, in the meantime. She was delighted to achieve satisfactory vital signs and to keep the patient's haemoglobin above 5.0, until the group-checked blood arrived fifty minutes later.

The surgery took ninety minutes and then efforts were made to wake the patient up. Realising that recovery appeared delayed, the doctor did a blood sugar test and was horrified to find that it was dangerously low, less than 0.5 mmol/L. She had sustained irreversible brain damage from which she died ten days later.

The glucose and insulin regimen had become a distant memory, displaced by other immediate pressures. Mention had been made in the briefing, but no GKI chart (for glucose–potassium–insulin infusion) had been started in Accident and Emergency, and the case notes were unclear on the doses given, so there were no obvious reminders.

The scenario in **Vignette 2.5** above shows a weakness of analytic decision-making.

In this situation, the consultant's single analytic channel was committed to the problem of replacing blood loss and this blocked it to all other issues. The more relaxed regular situation awareness checks that she would have performed otherwise were missed, so she missed the glucose issue. Not an easy problem to avoid. If the patient had been a known diabetic patient on insulin, automatic decision-making would probably have led her to check the glucose earlier.

If during the briefing she had made a mental note like '*Chemical state: potassium, insulin, glucose – risks! Actions may be needed*' then her automatic mind would have been 'primed'.

Experimental evidence shows that automatic thinking can be primed. People notice things they are told to look out for, even if they do not remember being told. Warning inexperienced staff of potential risks to be aware of is worth it, even if they do not appear to take the information on board!

The advantages and disadvantages of analytic decisions are summarised in **Table 2.1** in the next section, which deals with rule-based decisions.

Rule-based decisions

Some of the most basic teaching in the healthcare specialties amounts to survival rules for avoiding and dealing with common everyday issues. Rule-based decisions are often included as a category separate to either analytic decisions or the automatic decisions considered below. They consist of the conscious application of a rule that is usually imposed from outside, rather than derived by the individual. The decision process involves fitting the situation to the appropriate rule and then applying it.

An example of rule-based decision-making in healthcare would be a ward doctor's prescription of the anticoagulant tinzaparin after an operation. This is given to prevent deep venous thrombosis (DVT) which leads to a risk of potentially lethal pulmonary embolus (often a clot detaches from the leg, travels to the lung and blocks the circulation).

Table 2.1 *Advantages and disadvantages of analytic decisions*

Advantages ✓	Disadvantages ✗
■ Uses all the evidence	■ Slow and expensive
■ Fully compares the alternatives	■ Breaks down under pressure
■ Uses expertise of others	■ Unsuited to noisy, distracting and dysfunctional environments
■ Most likely to produce an optimal solution (when long on time and short on information)	■ Affected by stress and fatigue
■ Can be justified	■ May produce overload and stall the decision maker
■ Can be audited	■ May ignore local good practice
■ Many techniques available (e.g. from business)	

The problem with rule-based decision-making is a lack of flexibility. A rule that all post-operative patients must receive an anticoagulant will lead to it being given inappropriately to people who are allergic to it or prone to bleeding, such as those with stomach ulcers. A dramatic example of this problem of inflexibility is given in **Vignette 2.6**.

Vignette 2.6 Derailment on Turkey Creek Bridge [9]

A Union Pacific coal train comprising a hundred trucks was travelling from Denver to Chicago on 12 April 2002. The fifty-seventh truck had an axle-bearing fail and overheat, which caused it to derail. The crew noticed smoke and sparks and stopped the train to investigate. The faulty truck was about half a mile behind the engine, and by the time they got to it the wooden bridge that the train had stopped on was on fire.

They uncoupled as many of the trucks as they could from the burning section, leaving six trucks to fall into the creek as the bridge burned. No-one was hurt, but total losses were estimated at over two million dollars (a quarter of a million for the trucks and more than one and a half million for the bridge).

Union Pacific had a rule to stop a train immediately if an axle bearing failed. A very sensible rule, but following it to the letter with a white-hot bearing over a timber-constructed bridge that had been recently creosoted was not a good decision.

Both the axle-bearing (**Vignette 2.6**) and tinzaparin situations (on the previous page) can be accommodated in rule-based decisions by incorporating exceptions into more complex protocols, but this is not ideal either as rules then become cumbersome, slow to apply and difficult to remember [10].

Never the less, rules, guidelines, policies and protocols have found increasing favour since the 1990s and now exist in abundance in healthcare [11], at least on paper, bringing two further problems: a gap between the rules on paper and what happens in practice; and making protocols flexible enough to allow for varying situations (such as the stomach ulcer mentioned above). Furthermore, managing, understanding and accessing all the rules that may apply has become something of a minefield [12].

A particular risk to be wary of in rule-based decisions is applying the high-minded platitude. These are phrases like *Safety first*; *Honesty is the best policy*; *The patient comes first*; and *Look before you leap*.

Difficult analytical decisions are hard to make and it is tempting to reach for a platitude as a shortcut to an answer. Platitudes do not represent universal truths but rather frequent opinions in fairly straightforward situations. Situations to which they are directly applicable are generally easy to resolve. If you are reaching for a platitude because the decision is hard, it is probably not appropriate!

The advantages and disadvantages of rule-based decisions are summarised in **Table 2.2**. These limitations of rule-based decisions lead us to suggest that they should be seen not as a separate category of decision, but rather as options for analytical decision-making.

Table 2.2 *Advantages and disadvantages of rule-based decisions*

Advantages ✓	Disadvantages ✗
■ Good for novices	■ May not suit new situations
■ No need to understand reasoning behind each step	■ There is not a rule for every situation
■ Rapid, (if the rule is known)	■ A rule that does exist may not be known or not be found
■ Course of action has expert backing	■ If interrupted, may miss a vital step
■ Uses available evidence of good practice	■ May not understand reasoning, leading to risk of wrong procedure being selected
■ Produces consistency	■ Can produce unthinking compliance
■ Easy to justify	■ May stifle creativity
■ Allows managerial control and audit	■ Can be time-consuming
■ Many good decisions come from following rules	

When presented with a rule-based decision consider the steps of assessment, options checking (applying the rule is one option), project and decide, and review. With frequent practice, simple rule-based decisions become automatic decisions, to which we now turn.

Automatic decisions

Automatic decisions are also referred to as *recognition-primed*, *pattern recognition* or *intuitive decisions*. They depend on prior knowledge. We recognise a situation, refer to our prior knowledge of it, and use that knowledge to decide what to do. With familiarity, such decisions normally become both automatic and unconscious. When we drive to work, we may be completely preoccupied with matters unrelated to navigation, yet at each road junction we still drive with due care and attention and *decide* to go the correct way.

Automatic decisions are our default way of managing everyday activities, and much of our routine – getting up, dressing, breakfasting, driving, and greeting people as we get to work, for example. The processes are normally simple, and use existing situation awareness rather than relying on the situation awareness-related steps of assessment, option checking and review that are part of analytic decision-making. It would be too laborious to assess and option check every tiny choice in life, and we would become ineffectual. Engaged in such multiple analytic decisions, we would paradoxically appear to be paralysed by indecision.

One situation in which automatic decision-making does not apply is a typical psychological laboratory experiment! These experiments were designed to investigate issues such as ethical, career or purchasing decisions for market research and they used students as subjects. Venkatesan's experiment on the effect of peer pressure on decisions is one example [13]. These experiments were not about decision-making models, but when students are asked to make decisions about unfamiliar situations, they make them analytically.

The model of analytic decision-making outlined above was derived from this body of results, and when researchers started to study real-life decisions made by experienced personnel they found the model did not fit. This lead to the terms *classical* decision theory for the experimental analytic type, and *naturalistic* decision theory for the real-life automatic type.

Most real-life decision-making is based on unconscious, automatic pattern recognition, which is helpful and accurate. A stream of automatic decisions is essential to keep a complex organisation like a hospital working at all. **Vignette 2.7** is a reminder that a stream of decision-making can also let you down badly. Healthcare workers often attend to stories or mishaps of the '*There but for the grace of God go I*' variety. These usually involve automatic decision-making.

Vignette 2.7   Misleading asthma severity

The doctor's first day in Accident and Emergency was a bit of a shock. A male patient in the resuscitation bay had had four recent admissions with severe asthma and this time when he arrived he was unable to speak. A quick chest examination revealed very little wheezing, which comforted the doctor somewhat. He then tried, with some difficulty, to get the rest of the patient's history and examination done, just as he had been taught at medical school.

The patient's consciousness level suddenly deteriorated and his heart monitor showed a slow rate with bizarre ECG complexes. Cardiac arrest was imminent, so the doctor summoned help.

After a few minutes of hectic activity, the patient was safely anaesthetised and ventilated, receiving treatment for severe asthma and a precipitating chest infection, and was on the way to being rehydrated.

The doctor's problem here was the use of faulty automatic decision-making and a failure to redress this using analytic thinking. He matched a simplistic pattern (asthma makes people wheeze; more wheeze equals worse asthma; less wheeze equals less severe asthma) and the patient's relatively quiet chest made him match it to the mild attack pattern, which he managed accordingly. He could not pattern match correctly because he had no prior experience of this type of case, but he was told of it during his training. If he had changed to analytic mode and assessed the situation with other guides to attack severity, such as measurement of peak airflow or blood gases, he would have got it right. If someone lacks experience, analytic decision-making can compensate, but it has to be engaged.

Experienced doctors in consultation with patients rapidly narrow a diagnosis down to two or three likely possibilities. They interrupt patients early in a consultation (on average after only eighteen seconds) to ask specific questions that help them distinguish between these possibilities. This rapid and effective system depends on much automatic decision-making and little analytic. It contrasts with the way these same senior doctors teach diagnostic skills, and a far longer list of diagnostic options would be on the classroom blackboard. The contrast is because teaching can only inform an analytic approach – automatic requires experience.

Automatic pattern recognition is also used in high-pressure situations where experience counts. Experienced decision-makers may take only seconds to recognise a pattern and take action, while a novice is still trying to understand the problem analytically.

This can be illustrated in the field of anaesthesiology, whereby there can be a drop in blood pressure llowing induction of anaesthesia. This is more common in elderly people, people with hypertension (especially when inadequately treated), and people on drugs that reduce the heart's ability to compensate. Detecting and managing this situation becomes so routine, that an experienced anaesthetist will see the pattern and proactively treat with corrective drugs, while a novice will still analyse and wonder whether to call for help or delay the start of surgery.

When the pace quickens and the perceived riskiness of the situation increases, those in healthcare's front-line still make most decisions rapidly, with automatically pattern recognition and little or no reflection. Look at **Vignette 2.8** for an example of what happens.

Vignette 2.8 Ruptured heart valve

An experienced cardiologist who happened to be in Accident and Emergency came to the assistance of a young doctor. The young doctor's heart patient had suddenly become very sick, and within just a few seconds the cardiologist's stethoscope revealed the distinctive heart murmur sound of a ruptured heart valve.

Immediate open heart surgery saved the patient, following this rapid and accurate decision.

In this scenario, the cardiologist was unaware of any thought processes in his decision.

The next scenario, **Vignette 2.9**, is another example of what happens when the pace quickens and the perception of the level of risk goes up. This time, the situation is drawn from a real incident in the field of aviation.

> **Vignette 2.9   No fuel at 41,000 feet—The Gimli glider [14]**
>
> In 1983, an Air Canada Boeing 767, ran out of fuel at 41,000 feet on the way to Edmonton. This followed an error by ground crew error, in which fuel volumes had been converted from US gallons to metric litres, but it appears ground crews had not been adequately briefed or trained on this change. Both engines consequently failed. The flight manual contained no instructions for this situation. The nearest airfield was Gimli, a former Canadian Air Force base, which was at that time being used as an airfield for small aeroplanes. It has a greatly shortened runway. On approach to Gimli, the powerless Boeing was too high, but aiming lower would make the aircraft gain speed. The crew considered performing a full 360 degree turn in order to lose height but projected that they would lose too much height.
>
> The pilot had past gliding experience. One gliding technique used in this situation is a 'slide-slip' manoeuvre, in which the glider is flown slightly side on to the wind to increase drag and lose height without gaining speed before landing. This is not taught to commercial pilots, and was not in the rules or the manual. The pilot successfully side-slipped and landed accurately. The plane was damaged and later repaired, but none of the sixty-one passengers or crew were significantly injured. When the manoeuvre was later tried on a simulator it failed to model the behaviour of the Boeing accurately.

The oblique, innovative thinking demonstrated above resulted in markedly less damage to the plane and avoided injury and loss of life to the passengers and crew [14]. The decision to use side-slipping was analytic with decisive options checking! Once side-slipping had been decided upon, the necessary actions were taken automatically from the captain's previous experience of a different situation.

The danger of pattern matching is picking the *wrong* pattern. Once in a while, a drop in blood pressur e will be the first sign of a serious situation that cannot be easily corrected – for example, an unfolding drug allergy. Then if the pattern is not corrected to the right one, and no change to analytic decision-making is made, a wrong decision is likely!

Increasing experience makes us better at recognising more patterns and so increases our use of this method, but at the same time it reduces our opportunities for analytic decision-making. The advantages and disadvantages of automatic decisions are summarised in **Table 2.3**.

Table 2.3 *Advantages and disadvantages of automatic decisions*

Advantages ✔	Disadvantages ✘
■ Very fast	■ Requires experience
■ Robust (most of the time)	■ Often is (or becomes) unconscious
■ Useful in routine situations	■ Does not deal well with the unfamiliar
■ Little conscious thought required	■ May not prompt a situation awareness check when things change or should be reviewed
■ Overloaded less easily than other modes	■ Hard to explain or justify later
	■ Prone to the limitations of heuristics

Rule-based automatic decisions

Rule-based decisions become automatic when we are practised at them. An example is stopping at a red traffic light. Experienced drivers do it automatically with a high, but not perfect, degree of consistency. Such automatic decision-making is also resistant to change and may be made inappropriate by contextual changes. Driving in other countries with alternative traffic signals provides an example of this, where original learning interferes with new learning. Here, in general, the more experienced you are with one system the more interference there will be with new learning.

Additionally, not all rule-based automatic decisions are good (deciding to have another cigarette, for example) and they can be particularly difficult when policy changes are planned. Recent concerns about hospital-acquired infections in the UK have prompted policy changes on dress and hand-washing by staff on wards.

It sounds easy, but what was needed was changing an automatic decision on actions on entering a ward to another one. Just telling staff was not enough; they were acting automatically and it was difficult for them to override their decisions analytically. After considerable exposure, discussion and effort, the new policy became an automatic rule-based behaviour, and healthcare managers could use the term 'embedded' with unwitting truthfulness.

Unconscious decision-making

The above section on *automatic* decision-making implied there is a significant role for *unconscious* processing that leads to an action plan appearing in consciousness without apparently having been considered. This is one manifestation of unconscious decision-making. It is informed by *implicit learning* where subjects learn non-episodic complex information in an incidental manner, without any awareness of what has been learned. Research suggests that such learning may require minimal attention and dependence on attentional and working memory mechanisms.

The result of *implicit learning* is *implicit knowledge* in the form of abstract representations, rather than verbatim or aggregate representations. Implicit learning appears largely non-intentional and incidental to consciousness and deliberate learning.

Implicit knowledge refers to the facilitation or change in performance that is attributable to information or skills acquired from prior experience, even though individuals do not need to (and may even be unable to) recollect the original learning. Implicit memory is the non-intentional recourse to this knowledge. This implicit knowledge base influences our decision-making.

Two theories in contemporary psychology address the question of unconscious decision-making. These are the *somatic marker theory* and the *unconscious thought theory*, which were touched on briefly in *Module 2*.

Somatic marker hypothesis

The somatic marker hypothesis is that unconscious cognitive processing leads to conscious correlates such as 'gut feelings' which influence decision-making, as well as to physiological somatic changes. The name *somatic marker* is a consequence of the experimental background to the theory.

Heart rate is an example of a somatic marker. It can be easily and unambiguously measured and so is a hard end-point for experimentalists. By contrast, *gut feelings* are difficult and ambiguous to record and quantify, so they give no hard end-points. They are, however, the most prevalent and important component of the somatic marker hypothesis!

The proposed somatic marker effect is mediated by the ventromedial prefrontal cortex (VMPFC) of the brain, where associations between factual knowledge and bioregulatory processes are processed and stored, largely unconsciously. Learning starts with an association between a perceived situation and an emotion with or without a physical bodily response.

The theory about the VMPFC arose because patients who had suffered damage to this area of the brain were found to have no abnormality of intellectual cognitive performance, but they did have profoundly disrupted social behaviour, often leading to disastrous decision-making.

The somatic marker hypothesis has been studied using the psychological experimental paradigm known as the *Iowa gambling task*. This task involves selecting cards from four decks, two of which are 'good' and yield more winning cards than the other two 'bad' decks. At the start of the experiment, subjects do not know that there are good and bad decks. As they proceed they begin to recognise that winning cards are more liable to be found in the 'good' decks. Subjects with damage to the VMPFC perform poorly at this task. More importantly, the performance of normal subjects indicated a preference for the 'good' decks, even before they had a 'hunch' that the there was a difference between decks, and, 30% of normal participants never became aware of the difference between the decks, yet they still favoured the 'good' decks in their decisions.

Real-life examples that we can recognise as somatic marker effects are not hard to find. The uneasy feeling of impending trouble is familiar. An experienced fire chief called all his troops out of a burning building just seconds before it collapsed. When asked to explain, he said he really did not know why he had called them out and denied even making a specific decision; he just did it. In this case an automatic decision was influenced by an unconscious marker. It seems likely that it was based on previous experience of incidents and unconscious learning of relevant cues about imminent collapse.

Such decisions can be hard to explain to observers and hard to justify to superiors when they pay off badly. They are possibly hard to justify even when they go well, since they may appear to divert from rules and subvert the main purpose (e.g. stopping a building from burning down).

Unconscious thought theory

Unconscious thought theory actually concerns decision-making with information that is consciously accessible. The theory is that the analytical solution of problems can be done in the conscious or the unconscious mind. In the latter case, the solution starts with conscious consideration of the problem. Conscious attention is then transferred elsewhere while unconscious analysis continues. The solution then re-emerges into consciousness, usually at times of relaxation.

This phenomenon led to the 'Three Bs' of creative innovation – the Bus, the Bath and the Bed. The unconscious thought theory holds that with highly complex situations and involved decisions, the quality of decisions is improved if the cognitive processing is unconscious. The reverse is true of simple decisions. **Figure 1.3** illustrates this theory.

Group decisions

Making decisions with multiple people is common in healthcare and is becoming commoner with the increasing use of multidisciplinary teams, subspecialisation, and human factors training (such as this course). Much of the literature on the subject emphasises the role of key decision-makers and their skills. However, the identity of the key decision-makers is not usually a prominent issue.

Group decisions require the conscious linguistic expression of issues by group members so that others can follow them, and this requires that such decisions are analytic in nature. The basic components of group decision-making are those discussed in depth under analytical decisions above.

These components are:

- Situation assessment
- Option checking
- Projecting and deciding
- Reviewing.

Situation assessment

Group assessment has the advantage that different people have different knowledge of the relevant issues and facts. One point to note about group decisions is that individuals who are aware of pertinent information have a duty to express it, if it is not already in discussion. This professional responsibility can be difficult for introverted people. Conversely, other members of the group have a duty not to impede the expression of such pertinent information by being unduly overbearing or dismissive.

Option checking

Effective option checking is key to the very best decisions. In group situations, suggesting imaginative and favourable options can be a loaded activity whereby the person who makes the suggestion often attracts credit as well as hostility from those who may feel under threat.

Group leaders have a duty to identify such options when suggested and facilitate accurate projection of them in the next step.

Projecting and deciding

In option projection, the likely results of implementing the various options are averred. A particular issue with multidisciplinary teams is that different specialists will be in a position to accurately project different options.

In the scenario described previously in **Vignette 2.3**, the decision was made by a group consisting of an anaesthetist and a surgeon. The anaesthetist was accurately able to project on the oral intubation option; the surgeon was accurately able to project on the surgical option; and between them they agreed that neither was attractive. Neither of them had previously done 'trans-wound guide-wire-assisted tracheal intubation' but both projected that it would be feasible.

When the projected results of all the options are considered, the decision usually becomes an easy one. In group situations, the skill in choosing lies in assessing the quality and accuracy of the projections, particularly the projections of creative suggestions that may have great advantages but which group members are likely to have little experience of.

The role of the group leader is not generally to *make* the decision, but rather to elicit the best quality options and projections possible from the rest of the group and then to fine-tune these options and projections until one winner is clear. If the group leader makes the decision prematurely – before this process is complete – he or she is likely to alienate other group members and lose personal credibility.

Reviewing

The nature of group decision-making in healthcare means that reviewing is often not done by the same group that made the decision. Commonly when a decision about patient treatment has been made by a group, individual treating clinicians will be present when further information becomes available, allowing projections to be updated and possibly new options to be considered. It may not be feasible to take the new information back to the original group, but the same decision-making processes is gone through again.

Problems with group working

There are a number of potential adverse effects associated with working in groups.

Groups can develop and sustain inappropriate practice. In a study of the 'teams' responsible for the use of X-ray screening to detect microscopic cracks in aircraft wings, there were highly effective and less effective teams. New members joining a high performing team tend to quickly gravitate to high levels of performance. In contrast in the poorer teams, new members tend to quickly gravitate towards the group norms for performance. Interestingly some who performed well in effective teams also gravitate towards the group norms in poor-performing teams [15].

In summary, for effective teams their performance tends to rise and bring all up to high levels of performance but in poor teams nearly all tended to drift down to poorer levels of performance.

Conclusions

Decision theory, cognitive processing, and situation awareness are all intimately linked to each other. Many of the aspects covered in this Module overlap with parallel aspects of the other Modules, and it is suggested that topics such as the triggered situation awareness check, analytic thinking, automatic thinking and unconscious processing are revised at the same time as presenting this topic. Further options are to combine Modules to provide the course in a reduced number of sessions.

References

1 Groopman J. *How Doctors Think*. New York: Houghton Mifflin, 2008.

2 Callum KG (ed.). *Functioning as a team? The 2002 Report of The National Confidential Enquiry into Perioperative Deaths*. London: UK Department of Health, 2002.

3 Flin R, O'Connor P, Chrichton M. *Safety at the Sharp End: A Guide to Non-Technical Skills*. Aldershot: Ashgate, 2008.

4 Gaba DM, Fish KJ, Howard SK. *Crisis Management in Anaesthesiology*. New York: Churchill Livingstone, 1994.

5 Swets JA. Separating discrimination and decision in detection, recognition, and matters of life and death. In: Scarborough D, Sternberg S (eds) *An Invitation to Cognitive Science, Volume 4*, 2nd edn. Amherst, MA: MIT Press, 1998; pp. 635–702.

6 Klein G. *Streetlights and Shadows: Searching for the Keys to Adaptive Decision-making*. Amherst, MA: MIT Press, 2011.

7 Wallace WA. Managing in-flight emergencies. *British Medical Journal*, 1995; 311: 374–76.

8 Swets JA, Dawes RM, Monahan J. Psychological science can improve diagnostic decisions. *Psychological Science in the Public Interest*, 2000; 1(1): 1–26.

9 Samuelson J. U*nion Pacific loses bridge to fire. The Western Times, 18 April 2002*. Available at: http:// www.arizonarails.com/bad_day.html (last accessed January 2013).

10 Zsambok CE, Klein G. *Naturalistic Decision-making*. Mahwah, NJ: Lawrence Erlbaum, 1996.

11 Aveling W, Armstrong RF, Grundy EM. An*aesthetic Algorithms*. New York: Oxford Univeristy Press, 1996.

12 Gawande A. *The Checklist Manifesto: How to Get Things Right*. London: Picador, 2010.

13 Venkatesan M. Experimental study of consumer behavior conformity and independence. *Journal of Marketing Research,* 1966; 3(4): 384–87.

14 Nelson WH. The Gimli glider. *Soaring Magazine*, October 1997.

15 Connolly T, Arkes HR, Hammond KR. *Judgement and Decision-making: An Interdisciplinary Reader,* 2nd edn. Cambridge: Cambridge University Press, 1999.

Situation Awareness

Key points for reflection

❶ We sometimes struggle to see evidence which does not support our initial hypotheses. It is important to actively note such evidence as part of a continuous process of diagnostic formulation.

❷ You cannot stop fixation happening and it is often appropriate, but be aware of it in other people and the potential for it in yourself.

Situation awareness (SA) is the idea of our mental picture of what is happening around us, as well as the implications of what is happening, and what is about to happen. This mental picture – or mental *model* – is formed and maintained from information received via the five senses, and cognitive analysis of that information. SA is important because of how easily it can become upset or dangerously faulty. Simply stating a definition of SA to course participants does not have much impact. They will understand the importance of the subject much more readily if, right at the beginning, they are presented with actual or hypothetical scenarios in which the loss of SA led (or could have led) to adverse events. A video clip showing loss of SA is available for showing on the course [1]. It is suggested that you use this and the appropriate vignettes (or substitute your own) to highlight the importance of SA. The scenario in **Vignette 3.1** is one example.

Vignette 3.1 The lost car

After work one evening, a man went to the multistorey car park where his car was parked. It was a tall people-carrier with a roof-box on the top, so was easy to spot. He searched the car park from top to bottom and finally began to consider other options for getting home and informing the police that it had been stolen. However, the reason he couldn't find the people-carrier was because he had driven to work in his wife's car that day; hers was a dark blue Subaru Legacy estate.

Slides of the cars in **Vignette 3.1** are included in the teaching material. This vignette (or another that you substitute) shows that being an experienced and competent driver does not prevent situation awareness problems like this. The driver was not distracted, but concentrating hard on the issue. A lack of driving experience would not have stopped his six-year-old daughter from solving the problem.

Origination of the term

The term 'situation awareness' originated in the training of military air-crew in the latter half of the twentieth century. Soon after, it entered the language of air accident investigators. In a large survey of aircraft accidents in which human error was to blame, nearly 90% were due to faulty SA [2]. This finding, and subsequent corrective actions, brought the term into the everyday language of pilots and air traffic controllers the world over. In the 1990s, the concept was adopted by psychologists who applied it to the more general study of human performance and limitations.

To illustrate SA-related adverse events in medicine we will look at a familiar type of error, namely the *wrong diagnosis*, in **Vignette 3.2**. These events took place in the early 1990s when there was a greater emphasis on x-ray examinations (as opposed to endoscopy) in the investigation of bowel disease.

Vignette 3.2 Crohn's or appendicitis?

An eight-year-old boy presented to an accident and emergency department with a three-day history of worsening abdominal pain and mild diarrhoea. The first doctor to examine him was a junior casualty officer. This doctor found non-specific abdominal tenderness without distension and mild fever. Blood tests showed evidence of an acute inflammatory reaction (leucocytosis and raised erythrocyte sedimentation rate, ESR). The patient's notes stated: *'Possible appendicitis but not typical. Inflammatory bowel disease? Enteritis?'*

The boy was referred to the paediatricians who, among other things, arranged a barium enema. This showed an area of irregularity in the mucosa of the large bowel consistent with Crohn's disease. In a clinical meeting the case was discussed and the radiologist deemed the diagnosis 'uncertain'. A trial of treatment was commenced with the intention of reviewing the diagnosis in the light of the boy's response. Crohn's disease is an autoimmune condition, in which the immune system attacks the body's own tissues (in this case, the bowel). Treatment is with drugs that suppress the patients' immunity, both their autoimmunity and their natural defence against infection.

Treatment was started and the child appeared to improve for two days before relapsing. A second immunosuppressive drug was added. His condition stabilised over the next few days, then again deteriorated. A week after the first clinical meeting the case was discussed again. The original plan had somehow been forgotten and discussion focused on how to manage refractory (i.e. not responding to treatment) Crohn's disease.

Immunosuppressive treatment was again escalated. This went on for a total of three weeks with trials of different doses of different drugs. Surgical resection of the bowel is an option for the treatment of Crohn's disease that is not responding to other measures, but it only done very reluctantly. This is particularly so in children, because the procedure does not cure the disease which may appear in other parts of the gastrointestinal tract and leads to a permanent loss of bowel and possibly a colostomy. In this case there seemed to be no alternative, so surgical bowel resection was planned. The surgeon found not Crohn's disease but appendicitis! After three weeks of immunosuppressing treatment with no antibiotics to control the infection, it was rampant – the worst case of appendicitis the surgeon had seen.

All doctors can all recall cases like this. They start with an assessment of the situation that may be tentative. The focus then shifts onto dealing with the situation as perceived, without returning to the assessment. If that assessment is incorrect, things can go badly wrong.

Notice the features of this situation:

- The problem was a mistaken mental model of the situation – the wrong diagnosis.
- It arose because critical information was presented in a manner that is prone to error.
- Before the operation the boy was sick, but the doctors were calm; there was no hint that they were part of the problem.
- During this time the problem would have been easy to correct if it had been recognised.

The way to fix the problem is to return to the assessment stage and do an 'SA check'. **Vignette 3.3** is another example of SA in surgery.

Vignette 3.3   Wrong-side eye surgery

Malignant melanoma is a form of cancer that originates in pigment-forming cells called melanocytes. It has received mediaattention because sunbathing and the use of sun-lamps are risk factors. The eye contains a dark layer (for the same reason that a camera is painted black inside) formed by melanocytes and this makes the inside of the eye a common site for malignant melanoma. It causes blindness in the affected eye and, like other cancers, it is fatal if not controlled. The diagnosis of ophthalmic melanoma is made by ophthalmoscopic examination or on scans. The eye is often normal to look at from the outside. The condition is treated with surgical removal of the eyeball and later fitting of a glass eye.

This operation was planned on a 52-year-old man with a melanoma in his left eye, which had to be removed to save his life. He was already blind in the left eye so the operation would not mean any additional disability. He was marked for the operation, then anaesthetised. In theatre he was prepared and draped. The first drape covered the mark on his left eye. When the scrub nurse went to pick up the second drape, the stack of drapes fell to the floor. There was a short delay while a new set of drapes was opened. The draping continued but around the right eye. Everything seemed calm and normal, and stress levels were low, but the team was heading for a disaster.

Notice the parallels between this and the previous case:

- The problem is a mistaken mental model that the surgeons were proceeding with the correct eye.
- It arose because circumstances made the presentation of crucial information error prone.
- All remained calm in theatre.
- The problem could have been easily be corrected if had been recognised in time.

The following adds more perspective to the scenario described in **Vignette 3.3**:

Two years previously the Medical Director of the hospital became exasperated when the neurosurgery department drilled a burr hole on the wrong side of a patient's skull. He introduced a strict checking system to all theatres before any scrub nurse handed a scalpel to a surgeon. The scrub nurse, anaesthetist and surgeon were then to consult the consent form and imaging to confirm the correct operation was being performed.

Thus, the procedure *was* carried out in **Vignette 3.3** which meant that the error was realised. All it meant was that the surgeon looked green for a minute or two. Then the patient was re-draped and the correct operation was done. Another example is given in **Vignette 3.4** (overpage)

Vignette 3.4 Conscious ankle manipulation

A patient with an ankle fracture was having it manipulated and splinted under general anaesthetic at the end of a long orthopaedic list. Time was short. The patient came to theatre in a wheelchair. To save time, the anaesthetist decided to transfer the patient to the operating table and anaesthetise her there rather than involve another transfer to a bed or trolley. The surgeon was called away before this decision was made. While the anaesthetists were oxygenating the patient on the operating table, the surgeon re-appeared and started to manipulate the ankle *before* the patient was asleep!

For reducing SA-related errors, it is essential to maintain accurate SA and recognise any SA errors in good time. To work out how to do this, various models of SA have been proposed. The commonest model is that of Endsley [2] or a variant of it. In Endsley's this model, SA is divided into three levels (**Figure 3.1**).

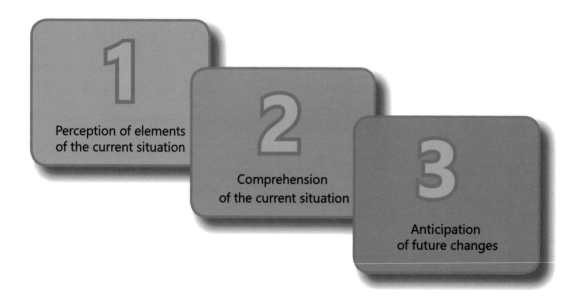

Figure 3.1 *The three levels of situation awareness (based on Endsley M.R. Towards a theory of situation awareness in dynamic systems. Human Factors, 1995; 37(1): 32–64 [3]).*

When SA-related mishaps are analysed according to this breakdown of levels, the overwhelming majority (78% in one study [2]) are caused by failure of *perception* – or failure to notice clues. Fewer (only 17%) are caused by failure of *comprehension* or understanding. Least (5%) are caused by failure to *anticipate*. Since Endsley's model was introduced, the study of SA has been categorised into two areas: *personal SA*, which is about how individuals gain and maintain their own SA; and *group SA*, which is about how SA influences the performance of whole groups. We will return to Endsley's model later when discussing 'group SA' but now we will turn to the principle tool for improving 'personal SA': the triggered check.

The triggered check

Triggered checks are an approach to the problem of maintaining accurate personal SA. They comprise:

- The SA check.
- The things that trigger it.

The situation awareness (SA) check

The SA check is a diagnostic cognitive process, comprising three steps (as in the process illustrated in **Figure 3.2**):

- **Step 1:** The check begins with a deliberate, conscious identification of the features of current SA, and stepping back from them to consider other possible hypotheses about the situation.
- **Step 2:** This is a conscious (ideally *spoken*) review of alternative hypotheses.
- **Step 3:** This involves seeking external evidence to decide between those alternatives.

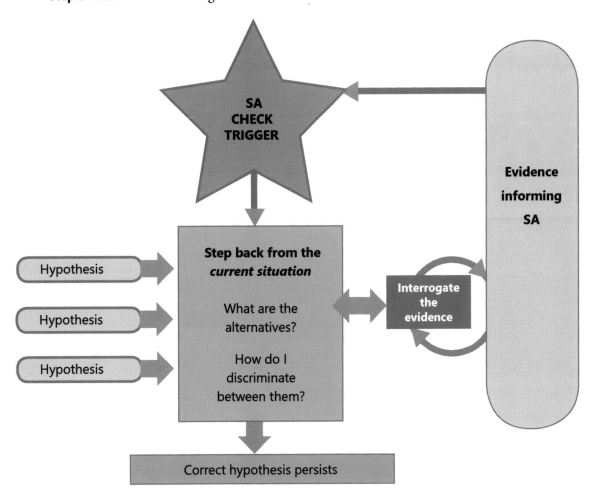

Figure 3.2 *The situation awareness (SA) check.*

One difficulty with the SA check is knowing just how far to step back in the first stage. The point to step back to is the last one when the SA was correct. The most recent point that passes the SA check is no help if the SA was faulty before then! If time permits, start questioning whether, for the task in hand, the SA could *always* have been wrong. Then review the alternatives and the evidence to choose between them. If the SA started out correct, it presumably has not changed, but the *situation* may have.

Work sequentially through past events, doing the same check for each point until reaching the present. Work from the *known* to the *unknown*. This sounds more difficult than it is in reality. As with all checks that fail, in the large majority of cases it is not because they were not done correctly, but because they were not done at all.

The SA check serves the following useful functions:

- **Break fixation:** This is the less common but possibly most important function. It is discussed in more detail below.

- **Update thinking:** This second – more common – function is to update thinking in the light of newly available evidence. In a dynamic environment, the SA of team members will inevitably drift away from reality on occasion, simply because they have had to concentrate on 'their bit' or go to get some equipment, or similar, so they are unaware of a situational change.

- **Update SA:** Repeated SA checks and mini-briefs (the updating of a group about a changing situation) are used to bring everyone's SA up to date.

What SA checks will *not* do is correct faulty SA if the evidence to do so is not there!

Triggers for SA checks

SA checks do not just happen – they are triggered, either by a checking schedule or by unscheduled prompting. Some checks are needed at particular points in a process, or after particular time intervals. The human brain is poor at remembering to do these checks, so we use checklists and automated warnings to trigger them. What our brains are better at is responding to events, or vague feelings of unease. These triggers cannot be automated, so our responses to them are all the more critical. Reliable and accurate SA depends on maintaining a low threshold for SA checks and accepting that, however skilled and experienced we may be, it is still possible that we have an incorrect understanding of the situation.

Awareness of clues

CLUES THAT MUST BE LOOKED FOR

This applies to clues that are *not* events, so they tend not to attract our conscious attention. Steady unchanging or slowly changing features (or changes in inconspicuous instruments) are among these. Others are things that *should* be there but are not, or things that *should not* be there but are. In the melanoma example in **Vignette 3.3**, clues were missed because of not checking. There were always things there (the side was noted on the consent form) but they were not referred to. These are lapses and errors that we humans are particularly prone to and need help to avoid reliably. That help is provided by checklists and by turning these features into *events*. In the case of operations, checks can prevent disasters and many monitored factors are turned into events by warning bleeps or lights, particularly in anaesthetics.

FIXATION AND CLUES THAT ARE NOTICED

These are clues that *are* events, so they tend to, or could, attract our conscious attention. Our ability to notice them is variable and human SA fails most often at the *notice* level, an example of the general rule that when checks fail, it is usually because they are *not done* rather than being done wrongly. The more familiar we are with how things *should* be, the more sensitive we become to things that are not expected; this familiarity comes with experience, but whatever our level of experience there are other factors that also determine our sensitivity to clues in a changing situation. These include fatigue, stress, and the degree to which our attention is occupied elsewhere. The more engaged we are with a particular task, the less we tend to notice other things, and the more obvious they have to be before we do notice them. In the extreme, this is called *fixation*, where one task or issue so engrosses us that we remain totally unaware of a change in the situation that is of greater significance than whatever we are concentrating on.

In a study of anaesthetist trainees in simulated situations, 20% of adverse events were due to fixation [4], and it occurs irrespective of the level of technical skill that someone has [5]. There have been several well-publicised disasters in medicine that occurred because of fixation. For example, fixation on the task of intubation of a patient (while serious hypoxia develops that should have prompted a surgical airway) [6]; fixation on repairing a bleeding vein (while a patient exsanguinates and should have been packed pending haemodynamic stabilisation); or fixation on gaining intravenous access (when the situation demanded administration of drugs via any route).

Several video clips are available that try to engage attention while slipping something 'obvious' past the observer that is designed to be missed. These have a remarkable impact the first time they are viewed and give great insight into the effects of fixation. Some examples of these that are well worth seeing are a series of advertisements made by Transport for London to promote awareness of cyclists among drivers [7–10]. The experiments behind these films showed that fixation is made less likely once we are made aware of it [11]. The value of showing these adverts to the course participants is that once people have experienced fixation, they become more wary of it and more likely to break it when it occurs. No other explanation is necessary.

The relevance of fixation to surgery can be relatively well demonstrated, for example, in a study of problems in bile duct surgery. An important factor in misidentification seemed to involve an unconscious superimposition of a preconceived mental map of a 'normal' duct system on a different ductal arrangement, constructed at operation by the processes of traction, duct dissection and display Other psychological factors in this study that were felt to be likely influences in the genesis and recognition of the injury were underestimation of risk, cue ambiguity, cognitive fixation and confirmation bias (discussed in more detail below) [12].

Confirmation bias and missed SA checks

Sometimes clues that would be expected to trigger an SA check do not, so that faulty SA continues. One type of missed trigger is so common and problematic that it has its own name – confirmation bias. The human brain resists changing its mental model. When new facts arrive that challenge our model, the instinct is to rationalise the facts to fit the model, rather than change the model to fit the facts. SA checks take cognitive effort and we avoid them by dismissing clues.

If a clue fits our model, we are more likely to notice it, to interpret it correctly, and to consider it important than if it does not [13]. When clues are open to more than one interpretation, we almost invariably pick the one that fits our current model, rather than look for alternative models and deciding which model the clues fit best. In the following scenario, **Vignette 3.5**, confirmation bias nearly led to disaster.

> ### Vignette 3.5   Tumour-related brain swelling [14]
>
> A 21-year-old woman presented with a single epileptic seizure. A scan revealed a tumour that was fairly small, appeared benign, and deep-seated in the right side of her brain. An operation was planned to remove it. The surgeons chose to use ultrasound scanning during the operation because the tumour was not on the surface; this was a fortunate choice as it turned out. They planned to open the space between the two sides of the brain to approach the tumour.
>
> To begin with, the operation was uneventful. However, when the surgeons began dissecting the plane between the two sides of the brain, they found the brain swelling was too severe *(cont ...)*

to allow it. There are a number of causes of the swelling that occurs during operations, of which the presence of a tumour is one. In this case it had not been expected because the tumour was relatively small. However, the surgeons thought that tumour-related swelling was the likeliest explanation, so they changed the operative approach. Marked brain swelling still impeded their progress, so some cerebrospinal fluid was removed. This reduced the swelling and the tumour was successfully removed.

Tumour-related swelling will recede when the tumour is removed, but in this case it became worse. Signs of life-threatening brain compression developed in the patient. The ultrasound scanner was used to look for a haemorrhage in the tumour bed that might be causing the swelling, but none was seen. The depth of the scanner was set to six centimetres, appropriate for the tumour, but at such a depth it could not visualise the whole brain. It was therefore reset to twelve centimetres. At this depth, something could be seen that should not have been there – a blood clot pressing on the left side of the brain.

The team suddenly realised that the swelling had been due to this clot developing on the other side. The situation was critical; there were only minutes to spare. The operative wound was hastily closed and the patient was re-draped for a craniotomy on the other side. An extensive extradural clot was removed. The swelling disappeared and the patient's pulse and blood pressure returned to normal. She made a full recovery, but the situation had been very stressful.

In this case the surgeon's mental model was that the swelling was most likely caused by the volume of the tumour and its irritant effect on surrounding brain. As time went by, however, other clues accumulated that were less and less consistent with this model.

The surgeons did nothing wrong, but inevitably the clues were all interpreted as confirming the *faulty* model, and their SA became dangerously wrong. Evidence then emerged that did not fit their mental model and the SA was corrected in time – but it was a close thing.

Now look at **Vignette 3.6**.

Vignette 3.6 Continuing intravenous drug abuse

On a maternity ward, an intravenous drug user had a difficult term delivery, experiencing greater than expected blood loss. Over the next few days, fourteen different team members reviewed her case and concluded that her lack of progress and fainting episodes were due to her continuing to feed her drug habit on frequent disappearances from the ward.

Three days later she deteriorated rapidly, and an ultrasound revealed retained products of conception. This was an obvious cause, but it was overlooked by judgmental fixation.

Specific SA check triggers

Investigations of accidents and disasters from many walks of life have found a small number of stereotypical patterns that repeatedly precede SA-related adverse events, and precede them by enough time that the adverse event could have been avoided if the stereotypical pattern had been recognised and triggered an SA check.

These stereotypical patterns are listed below:

- An action does not have the expected effect.
- Confusion or uncertainty not resolved.
- Disagreement between two sources of information.
- Fixation on a single task to the exclusion of all else.
- Leading questions.
- Displacement activities.
- Failure to adhere to accepted practice.
- Failure to react appropriately to warning signs.
- Failure to communicate effectively.
- When taking over.
- The vague feeling of unease.

These will now be considered in turn.

1. AN ACTION DOES NOT HAVE THE EXPECTED EFFECT

A familiar clue to the wrong diagnosis is that the patient does not respond as expected to treatment.

2. CONFUSION OR UNCERTAINTY NOT RESOLVED

Uncertainty is common with junior staff or staff seeking clarity on issues outside their specialist fields (such as anaesthetists or junior surgeons seeking clarification about aspects of an operation from a senior surgeon). The habit of doing an SA check if there is uncertainty is clearly a good one, but there is a more important message: if someone is in a senior position with others looking up to them for clarification, they should get into the habit of doing an SA check whenever they detect uncertainty in *others*. This habit alone would have prevented countless disasters (e.g. the wrong-side surgery event of **Vignette 3.7**).

3. DISAGREEMENT BETWEEN TWO SOURCES OF INFORMATION

Two conflicting sources of information cannot both be right. If the operating list and the consent form do not agree, one of them has to be wrong. Work out which before starting!

4. FIXATION ON A SINGLE TASK TO THE EXCLUSION OF ALL ELSE

This is hard to spot in oneself, and easier to see in others, especially if they are not responding to questions. Hearing is the first sense to go when fixating. If someone else thinks you are fixating, they are probably right.

5. LEADING QUESTIONS

With respect to fixation, this means repeatedly seeking confirmation of one interpretation of the situation, rather than looking for other interpretations. Leading questions are a symptom of this (e.g. 'The blood pressure is stable isn't it?' is leading, but 'Is the blood pressure stable?' is not).

6. DISPLACEMENT ACTIVITIES

These are a well-researched behavioural phenomenon seen in animals and humans [15]. They are behaviour patterns that seem out of context with the situation, or at odds with behaviour occurring immediately before or after them. They occur when people are in situations they cannot control or cope with. Typical displacement activities are scratching of the head, humming a tune, doodling on paper, or fiddling with small objects.

7. FAILURE TO ADHERE TO ACCEPTED PRACTICE

For example, in many surgical procedures it is normal practice to have a specified number of units of blood cross-matched for blood group. Where this is not done, a simple question such as *'Don't we usually cross-match four units for this operation?'* will suffice. If a team member appears to be deviating from standard practice it may be because they are not aware what standard practice is in the situation, because they have reason to believe standard practice is sub-optimal, or because either they or you have read the situation wrongly.

8. FAILURE TO REACT APPROPRIATELY TO WARNING SIGNS

Both fixation and confirmation bias stop people from critically interpreting warning signs and incline them to dismiss them as aberrations or as irrelevant. Blood pressure monitors do sometimes under-read, but equally they can be ignored because of fixation on something else, or dismissed because of confirmation bias.

9. FAILURE TO COMMUNICATE EFFECTIVELY

Deteriorating communication is a classic sign of overload or confusion. Signs include silence, difficulty speaking clearly, leaving sentences unfinished or questions hanging, asking for a 'whatsit', or rambling off the point and asking leading questions.

10. WHEN TAKING OVER

The change of staff or shift involves briefing from outgoing to incoming personnel. This is a potential source of SA failure for two reasons: first, the outgoing staff may have faulty SA; second, the communication process during briefing is prone to errors and omissions. People have limited memory capacity and fluctuating levels of attention. Issues of motivation may also be significant, particularly where individuals are not being actively involved. In the scenario outlined in the Silva advertisement (see www.safercare.eu/human/), the captain of the *USS Montana* missed this trigger.

11. THE VAGUE FEELING OF UNEASE

So far, we have described things that have been observed from an *external* viewpoint in team members before incidents occurred involving the loss of SA. The next point is something that is familiar to us all, but cannot be directly observed, namely the *vague feeling of unease*. This is an important SA check trigger, but to understand it we need to understand its unconscious origin. The 'unconscious' gets a bad press because early doyens, such as Freud and Jung, speculated freely about it in the absence of the rigorous scientific methods we used today. More recent experiments have clearly demonstrated that unconscious processing does occur, however, and that it is rational. The aspect relevant to the 'vague feeling of unease' is unconscious learning.

Two memorable, though not very well controlled, experimental demonstrations are instructive. In one study, students in a psychology class in America in the 1960s were asked to compliment any girl on the college campus who was wearing something coloured red. Within one week the college was a blaze of red. When girls wearing red were questioned they could not state the reason why they were wearing red. In another study, a psychology class received a lecture on unconscious learning and conspired to try some of it out on a lecturer at a later date. They paid close attention to him and laughed at his jokes *only* when he was standing on the right-hand side of the lecture theatre. They almost trained him right out of the door! When questioned later, he was completely unconscious of this [16].

Both cases are graphic illustrations of a large body of psychological research that shows how we learn unconsciously and how that learning influences our actions. The conscious manifestations of this process are vague feelings. In particular, unconscious recognition of patterns containing conflict or threat lead to feelings of unease. This means that if someone feels uneasy about a situation, it is likely to be a rational reaction to something being wrong.

> *The message from these clues is simple:*
> *Make the habit of keeping a low threshold for SA checks in response to any of them.*

Examples of SA checks

The exact mental process of an SA check is hard to explain in words so here we show it with the examples we have been presented in the individual vignettes.

- **The lost car (Vignette 3.1):** Searching did not have the expected result of finding the car. The SA check could have been 'Is this the right car park? Am I looking for the right car?'

- **Crohn's or appendicitis (Vignette 3.2):** The first-time treatment failure was discussed, an SA check could have been triggered. It would have been an action that did not have the expected result. The SA check should have been 'Is the treatment correct? Is the diagnosis correct?'

- **Wrong-side eye surgery (Vignette 3.3):** A timely SA check was triggered by a checklist.

- **Ankle manipulation (Vignette 3.4):** The surgeon was taking over the patient so should have done an SA check before taking any action.

- ***USS Montana* (www.safercare.eu/human/):** In the Silva advertisement about the fictional *USS Montana*, Captain Hancock misses the taking over SA check. This should have been along the lines of: *Where are we? Where is he? Are the voice and the radar dot coming from the same place?*

Group (team) SA

In healthcare delivery we generally work not as individuals, but in teams, though in reality it could be suggested that work is often undertaken in groups, with little sense of being members of a team! The conventional models of SA are based on individuals and how they gain, maintain or lose personal SA. **Vignette 3.7** gives a simple example of how personal SA and team SA can interact.

Vignette 3.7   Vena cava injury

During many abdominal and pelvic operations there is a risk of injury to the inferior vena cava. This is a large blood vessel that can bleed torrentially. Such bleeds are easy to control temporarily with packing because of the vessel's low pressure, but they are hard to repair permanently with sutures because of the vessel's thin wall. Surgeons have been known to continually attempt to suture vena cava injuries, oblivious of how many pints of blood are going up the sucker – that is, until the patient has bled out (exsanguinated), which does not take long! This has been the cause of two relatively recent deaths in theatre in the UK.

In this scenario, a patient was undergoing right hemicolectomy when the inferior vena cava was injured. The surgeon pressed a pack over the area and calmly explained what had happened to the team as he briefed them. He called in extra assistance and asked for the correct suture, extra suction, extra lighting and extra blood supplies before releasing the flow and repairing the tear. The team apparently worked like a well-oiled machine! The successful outcome was down to the surgeon having accurate personal SA, but more importantly he brought the team SA up with him.

Models of personal SA are adapted to teams with common goals as in Gorman *et al's Team SA* model [17], which models how the performance of a whole team depends on each member's personal SA and how they interact. More recently, the model of *Distributed SA* has been proposed [18], which extends *team SA* to include the whole system of team members, task, equipment and environment. Distributed SA has been adapted to cardiothoracic theatres [19] and anaesthetics [20].

Endsley's model [3] was not aimed at team SA, but it is in the team setting that the model has its greatest educational value. It was developed primarily to describe the SA process, rather than to improve it through training. The perception step is about noticing things. We notice things when they impinge on our consciousness. With experience, we more readily notice things of relevance to our speciality. An experienced coastguard, for example, will notice the faintest flare on the horizon that other people might miss. The mother of a large family looking after a number of children, whether her own or somebody else's, will notice when one disappears when other people might not. The same principle applies to comprehension and anticipation of future events. These stem from noticing things and they become more thorough and accurate with relevant experience. There is not much we can personally do to improve our performance at these things in general. Exhortations to notice more, comprehend more, and anticipate more accurately, will not improve a team's performance.

The educational value of Endsley's model is not in how we apply it to ourselves, but in how we apply to those around us. Everyone's ability to perceive, comprehend and anticipate is reduced by stress, fixation, distraction and preoccupation. Team members who are preoccupied will underperform at all three steps in the model. If we need to alert a preoccupied team member to a situation change, it is not good enough just to point out the relevant evidence. We need to probe further to ensure they have understood it, and understood what it means for the future.

Occasionally whole teams can lose SA, but usually only individual members lose it. A remarkable thing about this common situation is that whole teams can fail because of loss of SA by individuals, even though other members of the team continue to have accurate SA. The field of aviation provides several extreme examples. Loss of SA in just one member of an aircraft's crew has led to accidents with the loss of everyone on board. In several of these incidents, the cockpit voice-recorder revealed that other members of the crew had not lost SA; they could see what was happening and what needed to be done, but failed to correct the problem until it was too late, losing their lives as a consequence. **Vignette 3.8** is an example of a comparable SA problem from surgery.

Vignette 3.8 Wrong-side kidney surgery

A 70-year-old man was admitted for a right nephrectomy. Due to a clerical error the admission slip stated 'left'. The operating list was transcribed from the admission slips. The patient was not woken up to check the correct side on the pre-operative ward round, and the side was not checked from the notes or consent form. The side was questioned by the consultant surgeon when the patient arrived in theatre, but was not confirmed either way. The consultant instructed the senior registrar to carry out the operation, but mistakenly put the correctly labelled x-rays on the viewing box back to front. The consultant supervised the positioning.

The senior registrar did not check the side and did not notice the normal pulsation in the renal artery of the kidney he was removing – a clue to it being the wrong one. A medical student observing the operation suggested to the senior registrar that he was removing the incorrect kidney, but he told her that she was wrong. The mistake was discovered but not until two hours after the operation. The patient was left with no functioning kidney and died five weeks later [21].

Loss of SA by individual team members can lead the whole team to disaster, even though other team members keep good SA. This situation is the most common way in which loss of team SA leads to errors. It specifically happens when SA is lost by the team leader or a senior member of the team. The passive behaviour of other team members who maintain SA is related to their reluctance to challenge authority and insecurity in their own judgements. Such situations are avoidable, however, with appropriate communication training, as discussed in the next section.

Whole teams can lose SA together. It can happen that all members of a team miss or misinterpret clues to a changing situation and they all lose SA as a consequence. It can arise if the clues are particularly subtle or obtuse but it is rare. A more common cause of loss of team SA is when the attention of team members who are not directly involved in the task drifts. They gradually lose SA, but normally this does not matter because they can regain it when they need to by reference to other team members who are directly involved and thus maintaining accurate SA. If the people maintaining SA then lose it, the whole team can easily go down.

Another way in which whole teams lose SA is with group think, also called the *bandwagon effect*. This is when some team members take one view and others go along with it, *not* because it is correct but because of the number or seniority of those who hold that view. There is substantial evidence that most individuals will conform to such social pressures, which may range from subtle expectations through to overt aggression [22]. There is also evidence that a proportion of individuals are highly resistant to such effects (the medical student referred to above is an example). Imagine the position of the medical student in the wrong-side kidney operation in **Vignette 3.8**. She was the most junior there and the only one saying it was the wrong side. The team as a whole did not listen; instead they went along with the team leaders.

The Asch conformity experiments

The group think or *bandwagon effect* was the subject of a famous series of experiments conducted in the middle of the twentieth century by Solomon Asch, a psychologist working at a Philadelphia college in the United States [23]. He was prompted by the Nuremberg trials of Nazi war criminals to investigate why people could be complicit in projects they felt to be wrong. He asked groups of students to participate in a vision test. In reality, all of the students – except *one* in each group – were collaborating with the experimenter. The one student did not know that the others were collaborating, or that he or she was the subject of the experiment. In a classroom setting the students were presented with cards like those in **Figure 3.3** and asked a series of questions about the cards, such as how the single line compared in length with other lines labelled A, B and C.

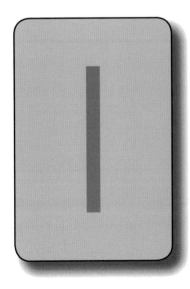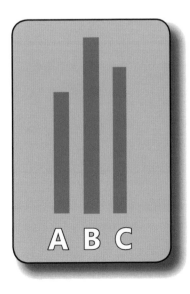

Figure 3.3 *Examples of the cards used in the Asch experiments into group conformity.*

These questions were easy; in a series of control runs, the rate at which the subject made erroneous answer was under 1%. In the experimental runs, the students collaborating with the experimenter were briefed about what answers to give. In cases where the answer was incorrect, and the same incorrect answer was given by *all* collaborating students, the single subject of the experiment gave the same incorrect answer 32% of the time. For example, the line on the left card in **Figure 3.3** is clearly the same length as that labelled C on the right card. When subjects were asked – without peer pressure – they said C more than 99% of the time. When all members of the group *except* the subject said A, the subject also said A 32% of the time. The point was that Asch was not testing vision or spacial awareness; it was just a device to allow him to ask questions with obvious answers. He was testing to see if the desire to conform to a group view was strong enough for people to reverse obvious rational judgements. He found that in many cases it was.

Communication for SA

Communication for situation awareness is highly dependent on the prevailing authority gradient. Theatre teams have authority gradients that depend on the seniority of staff and on the subject at issue. At the top of the authority gradient is the senior member of staff in the relevant discipline [24]. In issues of anaesthesia, the consultant anaesthetist is at the top of the authority gradient. Other members of the team rank below them, depending on their expertise in anaesthesia. Typically immediately below them will be the junior anaesthetic staff, followed by other staff such as operating department practitioners (ODPs), surgeons and nurses. Similarly the senior surgeons, nurses, and ODPs will be at the top of the authority gradient with issues in their own specialist fields. As far as SA is concerned, communicating *down* these gradients is a totally different issue from communicating *up* them.

Communicating down the authority gradient

Team members at the top of the authority gradient generally have better SA than those lower down because of their experience and expertise. Perhaps more important is that they have better SA because they make the plans about what is to be done. They therefore know what is to be done without anyone telling them, unlike members lower down the authority gradient who cannot read the boss's mind!

Staff at the top of the authority gradient are best placed to improve team SA. As loss of their own SA is likely to be a serious threat to the team's goal, the leaders have a duty to minimise the chance of it happening and minimise the impact of it if it does. To do this, they must optimise team members' SA and make it easy for team members to correct their own SA if they lose it.

Two mechanism by which this can be achieved are *display* and *talk*.

- **Display:** Leaders must not keep clues and displays of their part of the task private [25,26]. If there are facilities such as a video-monitoring of a surgical operative field, or a microscope, then they should be used, set up for all the team to see. It costs nothing in time and improves everyone's SA. In one study, a video-monitor of the theatre was used to update recovery staff of progress [27], allowing them to anticipate patient arrivals and improve their preparedness.

- **Talk:** Communication by briefing and verbal updates was found to be key to improved team SA in a study of delivery suites performance [28]. The habit of team talk in easy low-stress cases should be formed, with verbal updates or mini-briefs on issues as they arise. Thinking out loud is another method of verbal communication that can be appropriate, especially for introverted people who do not tend to do it naturally. Regular verbal updates serve two purposes: they inform the team of what is going on, and they give conversational cues where more junior members can engage, clarify and gain common SA, whether by changing their own or the leader's, without the barrier of a spontaneous challenge to authority. A problem with 'talk' is that it may be stopped by the stress or fixation that often goes with loss of SA. On the occasion when we lose SA and cannot understand why things are not going right, communication will not come naturally. For it to work under pressure it has to be a habit formed at times of low stress.

It may also be useful to think through any briefings given in terms of:

- *What is my intent or purpose for briefing?*
- *Who am I briefing?*
- *How well does the audience know the subject?*
- *What does the audience expect from me?*
- *What information do audience members need?*

Communicating up the authority gradient

Communication aimed at improving situation awareness *up* the authority gradient is rarer than down it, but when communication failure leads to disaster it is almost always a failure of communication up the gradient. The wrong kidney episode described in **Vignette 3.8** is a typical example.

It is obviously an advantage if people higher up the gradient take steps to make upward communication with themselves easier, but this alone is not enough. We can all think of people high up the authority gradient who are unreceptive to the issues of human factors management. While this may be regrettable, it does not absolve us from doing our best to avoid errors that involve them.

> Two issues impede up-gradient communication:
> *lack of confidence* and *fear*.

If a team member low down on the authority gradient thinks something is amiss they are likely to be unsure if there really is something wrong, or think they just do not understand what is happening. We all fear challenging authority, not only because we think we may be wrong and look foolish, but also because we fear the consequences of upsetting or alienating powerful people.

No amount of training will make these basic features of up-gradient communication go away, so instead a system of communication is used that allows confidence and challenge to authority to be escalated in a gradual, progressive fashion until the uncertainty is resolved. Frequently this will be achieved by improving the SA of the team member lower down the authority gradient, although a crucial part of the strategy is to ensure that all team members are equipped with skills to help them to raise concerns in an appropriate way and so, in one way or another, make sure their concerns are addressed.

The first people with whom someone lower down on the authority gradient should generally air a concern, assuming that time permits, are those immediately above on the authority gradient. The medical student in **Vignette 3.8** would have fared better if she had not gone quiet, but pursued the matter with the junior medical or nursing staff.

An intermediate person in the authority gradient when questioned by somebody below them may be able to resolve the issue or seek clarification from someone above them. If a junior team member does not get a satisfactory response from their immediate superior, taking the matter up another level is an option.

The other strategy for up-gradient communication in staged escalation is in the nature of the message.

- At the *lowest* level it starts with a request for information or clarification. If this does not resolve the issue, communication becomes more focused and urgent with specific conflicting information being pointed out.

- The acronym INCH stands for *I Need Clarity Here* and this fits in this second level of escalation. It is rare for issues to go beyond this level, but unfortunately further levels of escalation must be considered, because as the frequency falls, the stakes rise, and on those rare occasions when they *are* needed, they are *really* needed to avoid disaster.

- The third level of escalation is a direct challenge to authority – irrespective of the level authority or the authority gradient.

- The fourth and final level is *emergency* action to prevent disaster.

These steps of escalation in communication make up the acronym PACE.

Probe
Alert
Challenge
Emergency

The fictional scenario in **Vignette 3.9** can be used to illustrate how the steps are applied in practice.

Vignette 3.9   Lignocaine and adrenaline?

You are watching a procedure to suture a laceration of a patient's dominant index finger. A local anaesthetic digital block is to be used. This is done with plain lignocaine – never with lignocaine *and* adrenaline (epinephrine) because adrenaline causes spasm of the digital arteries that can lead to infarction and loss of the digit. The scrub nurse draws up the local anaesthetic from a vial held by the floor nurse, who then puts the empty vial in the sharps bin. As she does, you think you see red writing on the vial, but do not see what the writing says. Red on a local anaesthetic vial means adrenaline. *What do you do?*

In this kind of situation, PACE can be used to trigger a series of interventions:

P robe—You could take a discrete look into the sharps bin to see if the vial contained adrenaline. Then ask the floor nurse what was in the vial. Does this resolve the problem? If adrenaline is confirmed, or you still do not know, go to **Alert**.

A lert—Say to the floor and scrub nurse: '*I thought I saw red on that vial? I did not think adrenaline was used for digital blocks*'. If there is no response, go to **Challenge**.

C hallenge—Say to the surgeon: '*I think that is lignocaine with adrenaline*'. If there is still no response go up another stage to **Emergency**.

E mergency—Contrive to remove the syringe. This is not easy because it is in the sterile field and you are not scrubbed. Have you got time to scrub? Probably not. Pick up the syringe with a sterile Rampley's or similar, or contrive to contaminate the syringe itself or the trolley.

Conclusions

At the end of this teaching session, the things to emphasise are the lessons that can be realistically applied in the workplace rather than the theoretical models. These are what situation awareness is; how to do an SA check, when to do it, and how to enhance SA in a team with up-gradient and down-gradient communication.

References

1 Silva GPS. *Captain of the USS Montana* (television advertisment), 2004. Available at: http://www.youtube.com/watch?feature=fvwp&NR=1&v=EBwNwoDVT8E (last accessed January 2013).

2 Jones DG, Endsley MR. Sources of situation awareness errors in aviation. *Aviation, Space and Environmental Medicine*, 1996; 67(6): 507–12 (epub 1996/06/01).

3 Endsley MR. Towards a theory of situation awareness in dynamic systems. *Human Factors*, 1995; 37(1): 32–64.

4 De Anda A, Gaba DM. Unplanned incidents during comprehensive anesthesia simulation. *Anesthesia and Analgesia*, 1990; 71(1): 77–82 (epub 1990/07/01).

5 De Anda A, Gaba DM. Role of experience in the response to simulated critical incidents. *Anesthesia and Analgesia*, 1991; 72(3): 308–15 (epub 1991/03/01).

6 Bromiley M. Have you ever made a mistake? *Royal College of Anaesthetists Bulletin*, 2008; 48: 2442–45.

7 Transport for London. *Test Your Awareness: Do the Test.* London: Transport for London, 2008.

8 Transport for London. *Test Your Awareness : Whodunnit?* London: Transport for London, 2008.

9 Transport for London. *Test Your Awareness: Cyclist test.* London: Transport for London, 2008.

10 Transport for London. *The Bank Job London Cycling Campaign.* London: Transport for London, 2010.

11 Chabris CF, Simons DJ. *The Invisible Gorilla : And Other Ways Our Intuitions Deceive Us.* New York: Crown, 2010.

12 Hugh TB. *The Psychology and Heuristics of Cholecystectomy-Related Bile Duct Injury.* Lund, Sweden: Lund University, 2008.

13 Nickerson RS. Confirmation bias: A ubiquitous phenomenon in many guises. *Review of General Psychology*, 1998; 2(**2**): 175–220.

14 Tsermoulas G, Mitchell P. Unusual life saving application of intra-operative ultrasound: Case report. *British Journal of Neurosurgery*, 2011; 25(3): 341–42 (epub 2011/03/02).

15 Delius JD. Use of tools by wild macaque monkeys in Singapore. *Nature*, 1967; 214(5094): 1259–60 (epub 1967/06/17).

16 Gardiner WL. *Psychology: A Story of a Search,* 2nd edn. Monterey, CA: Brooks/Cole, 1974.

17 Gorman JC, Cooke NJ, Winner JL. Measuring team situation awareness in decentralized command and control environments. *Ergonomics*, 2006; 49(12/13): 1312–25 (epub 2006/09/30).

18 Stanton NA, Stewart R, Harris D, Houghton RJ, Baber C, McMaster R, *et al.* Distributed situation awareness in dynamic systems: Theoretical development and application of an ergonomics methodology. *Ergonomics*, 2006; 49(12/13): 1288–311 (epub 2006/09/30).

19 Hazlehurst B, McMullen CK, Gorman PN. Distributed cognition in the heart room: How situation awareness arises from coordinated communications during cardiac surgery. *Journal of Biomedical Informatics*, 2007; 40(5): 539–51 (epub 2007/03/21).

20 Fioratou E, Flin R, Glavin R, Patey R. Beyond monitoring: Distributed situation awareness in anaesthesia. *British Journal of Anaesthesia*, 2010; 105(1): 83–90 (epub 2010/06/17).

21 Alleyne R. Wrong kidney removed after X-ray mix-up. *Daily Telegraph*, 14 June 2002.

22 Milgram S. Group pressure and action against a person. *Journal of Abnormal Psychology*, 1964; 69: 137–43 (epub 1964/08/01).

23 Asch SE. Studies of independence and conformity: A minority of one against a unanimous majority. *Psychological Monographs*, 1956; 70(9).

24 Kohn LT, Corrigan JM, Donaldson MS (eds) *To Err is Human: Building a Safer Health System.* Washington, DC: National Academies Press, 2000.

25 Lai F, Spitz G, Brzezinski P. Gestalt operating room display design for perioperative team situation awareness. *Studies in Health Technology and Informatics*, 2006; 119: 282–84 (epub 2006/01/13).

26 Parush A, Kramer C, Foster-Hunt T, Momtahan K, Hunter A, Sohmer B. Communication and team situation awareness in the OR: Implications for augmentative information display. *Journal of Biomedical Information*, 2011; 44(3): 477–85 (epub 2010/04/13).

27 Kim YJ, Xiao Y, Hu P, Dutton R. Staff acceptance of video monitoring for coordination: A video system to support perioperative situation awareness. *Journal of Clinical Nursing*, 2009; 18(**16**): 2366–71 (epub 2009/07/09).

29 Mackintosh N, Berridge EJ, Freeth D. Supporting structures for team situation awareness and decision-making: Insights from four delivery suites. *Journal of Evaluation in Clinical Practice*, 2009; 15(1): 46–54 (epub 2009/02/26).

Personality Type

4

Key points for reflection

❶ If we better understand our personality characteristics, we will have insights into how we may behave under stress.

❷ An understanding of personality types can help us understand which roles we are good at and which do not play to our strengths.

❸ There are characteristic errors made by those with different personality types.

Understanding personality typing has applications in most aspects of team-working and leadership. The message to communicate to course participants is that we differ in thought, awareness and motivation, and each one of us has stronger and weaker areas. Without studying personality typing, we tend to judge others according to how they compare with us in our *strong* areas, not realising that they may perform better than us in our *weak* areas.

The purpose of this module is to allow participants to recognise their own and others' strengths and weaknesses to allow them to work well together, deploy each other effectively, and lead more intelligently. To do this, it is helpful to use a personality classification system on which to base explanations of the different personality types and demonstrate the differences between them. Several of these are described below. Some of them are not suitable for the present purpose but are included here because they are widely known about and course teachers may be asked about them. Two in particular, the *Five Factor Model* and the *Keirsey Temperament Sorter* (KTS), are described in detail. It is suggested that one or other of these is used as a basis for this module.

The terms *temperament* and *personality type* refer to a person's underlying nature, rather than their behaviour or assumed *persona*. Each personality type exhibits various characteristics in differing amounts, and personality classification schemes identify a number of such characteristics.

There are two broad categories of personality classifications: *type* theories and *trait* theories:

● **Type theories**—these suggest that we prefer to either think or behave in one way or in another; they classify people as being on one side or the other of a dichotomy (e.g. introverts or extroverts).

● **Trait theories**—these suggest that each of us lies somewhere along a spectrum (e.g. paying more or less attention to detail).

Historical perspective

The study of personality type is ancient. It was an aspect of the theory often ascribed to Hippocrates (460–370 BC) which held that the human body was composed of four basic substances, called humours. These humours were associated with the dichotomies of hot/cold and wet/dry: blood (hot and wet), yellow bile (hot and dry), phlegm (cold and wet) and black bile (cold and dry). In healthy people, these were in balance; in disease they were out of balance. Fever and sweating were evidence of an excess of blood, hence the medical profession's obsession at that time with blood-letting. **Figure 4.1** shows the detail from a woodcut that illustrates the four classical temperaments.

| *Phlegmaticus* | *Cholericus* | *Sanguinis* | *Melancholius* |
| RATIONAL | IDEALIST | ARTISAN | GUARDIAN |

Figure 4.1 *Images taken from a woodcut by Johann Kaspar Lavater in 1775 (from Physiognomische Fragmente) depicting the four classical temperaments: phlegmatic, choleric, sanguine, and melancholic.*

After Hippocrates, Galen (AD 131–200) developed this into a theory of four basic temperament traits, each one governed by one of the humours. In this theory:

- **Blood** promotes a sanguine temperament which is extrovert, friendly, talkative, sociable and passionate but has a tendency towards exaggeration and unreliable reporting.
- **Phlegm** promotes a phlegmatic temperament which is content, kind and affectionate, but is accepting rather than driven and motivated.
- **Yellow bile** promotes a choleric temperament which is ambitious, motivated and energetic, but quick to anger, and irritable.
- **Black bile** promotes a melancholic temperament which is thoughtful, quiet and creative, but given to nervousness, anxiety, and depression.

Unlike the four-humours theory of physiology and disease, aspects of the theory that relate to temperament have survived to the present day; their influence can be seen in current personality classification schemes.

Personality typing and associated management consultancy services have become a big industry and bold claims are often made, often poorly justified, of how such schemes can optimise personnel deployment.

In this module, our use of personality classification is less demanding because we are not concerned with long-term extrapolation or prediction of performance. The point we want to make is that other people have different personalities from ourselves and have viewpoints that are correspondingly different. While different, they may be equally reasonable. Good teams capitalise on these differences, ensuring that the roles people have in teams play to their particular strengths.

We now turn to describing some of the available systems of personality classification.

Type A and B personalities

One of the simplest and best known personality classification systems was not devised by psychologists, but by two cardiologists – Friedman and Rosenman – who studied a link between behaviour and the risk of coronary artery disease in the middle years of the twentieth century.

They shared a cardiology practice in San Francisco in the 1950s, and first made this observation when their waiting room chairs needed re-upholstering. The pattern of wear was not typical, being worst at the front edges of the chairs' arms and seats, rather than further back. The worn chairs were used by patients with coronary artery disease, who tended to sit on the edge of the seat and often jumped up to ask how much longer they were going to have to wait. They divided people into two groups – type A and type B – and estimated that type As had roughly twice the risk of developing coronary artery disease than type Bs.

This finding was controversial, but the phrase 'type A personality' is now commonly understood to be someone who tends to be aggressive, competitive, ambitious, impatient and highly strung. Type Bs are the opposite – patient passive and accepting [1].

The Five Factor Model

A large amount of data has been collected on many characteristics that have enabled broad statistical correlations to be determined. Of the many classification schemes that have been proposed, the Five Factor Model [2] has a significant following among academic psychologists and is currently used by the National Clinical Assessment Service to assess doctors about whom there are concerns.

According to this model, the numerous characteristics that have been studied fall into five groups that tend to combine in any one individual. So, for example, the traits for ease of making friends, comfort level in a busy social setting, and frustration with solitude, all tend to occur together in the same person; rarely does someone who makes friends easily feel uncomfortable in a social setting and prefer solitude.

On the other hand, laziness occurs together with friendliness no more often than would be expected by chance. This places friendliness, sociability and dislike of solitude in the same 'factor', and laziness in a different 'factor'.

The Five Factor Model is only one of many, and it has its detractors [3], but it is an important tool in mainstream psychological research and is the most firmly evidence-based system. However, it is relatively insensitive to the subtle nuances of personality that a keen observer might note and record. Other systems, perhaps scientifically less rigorous ones, come with more engaging, narrative descriptions of personality types.

The five factors described in the model are still summarised by the acronym OCEAN and their main features are described in **Table 4.1** overpage.

O penness
C onscientiousness
E xtraversion
A greeableness
N euroticism

Table 4.1 *The main features of OCEAN*

Character trait	Features of the trait
Openness	■ Openness to experience ■ Iinventive and curious vs consistent and cautious ■ Appreciate art and adventure ■ Have novel ideas ■ Responsive to emotion ■ Enquiring ■ Seek variety of experience
Conscientiousness	■ Efficient and organised vs easy-going (sometimes careless) ■ Tendency toward self-discipline ■ Act dutifully ■ Aim for achievement ■ Planned rather than spontaneous behaviour
Extraversion	■ Outgoing and energetic vs solitary and reserved ■ Have positive emotions ■ Energised by the company of others
Agreeableness	■ Friendly and compassionate vs cold and unkind ■ Tendency towards being compassionate and cooperative, rather than suspicious and antagonistic towards others
Neuroticism	■ Sensitive and nervous vs secure and confident ■ Tend to have low threshold for unpleasant emotions such as anger, anxiety and depression

Note that the neuroticism factor is sometimes called 'emotional stability' and the openness factor is sometimes labelled 'intellect' rather than openness to experience.

These five factors, often called the 'Big Five', describe five broad underlying dimensions that are thought to represent the basic structure behind all personality traits. Within each factor, a cluster of correlated specific traits are identified (for example, extraversion includes related qualities such as gregariousness, assertiveness, excitement seeking, warmth, activity and positive emotions [4].

Sir Francis Galton first recognised that significant and socially relevant differences in people's personalities become encoded into language, and that by sampling language it is possible to derive a classification or taxonomy of human personality traits. Known as the *Lexical Hypothesis*, this was put into practice by

Allport and Odbert [5] who extracted 17,953 personality-describing words from English dictionaries. These were refined through testing by Tupes and Christal [6], Cattell *et al.* [7] and others [8,9] so that sixteen major personality factors were identified, and this led to the development of the Sixteen-Item Personality Questionnaire (16-PF) [10] from which five groupings of characteristics were derived.

Lewis Goldberg found the same five factors independently [11] using language analysis, and later coined the term 'Big Five' as a label for the factors.

However, predicting behaviour by testing for these elements of personality was considered to be impossible. Mischel asserted that personality tests could not predict behaviour with a correlation of more than 0.3, and argued that attitudes and behaviour were not stable, but varied with the situation. This view was challenged during the 1980s when researchers found that they could predict patterns of behaviour by aggregating large numbers of observations. As a result, correlations between personality and behaviour increased substantially, and psychologists concluded that 'personality' could be described with a moderate degree of reliability using the five factors. Personality and social psychologists now generally agree that both personal and situational variables are needed to account for human behaviour.

Two questionnaires are now widely used to identify the Big Five; these are the *Neo-Five Factor Personality Inventory* (Neo-PI) [12], and the *Hogan Personality Inventory* (HPI) [13]. Both are designed specifically for use in occupational assessments, and are used widely in industry and in the public sector. The Neo-PI is used by the National Clinical Assessment service in its psychological assessment of doctors and dentists who get into difficulties.

Evidence for the Big Five

Since psychologists came to support the Big Five (in the 1990s), there has been a growing body of research surrounding these personality traits [14]. Longitudinal data that correlate people's test scores over time, and cross-sectional data that compare personality levels across different age groups, show a high degree of stability in personality traits during adulthood [15]. However more recent research and meta-analyses of previous studies indicate that change occurs in *all* five traits at various points in the lifespan. There is now evidence for a *maturation effect*, with levels of Agreeableness and Conscientiousness typically increasing with time, while Extraversion, Neuroticism and Openness tend to decrease [16].

The Five Factor Personality Inventory—Children [17] can be used for assessment between the ages of 9 and 18 years, because the Big Five traits have been found to correlate with children's social and emotional adjustment and academic achievement. John and colleagues [18] found two new factors – Irritability and Activity – in adolescent boys, and in studies of Dutch children of both sexes.

All five factors show the influence of both heredity and environment. Twin studies suggest that these factors contribute in roughly equal proportions [19]. In addition to group effects, there are individual differences too, whereby different people demonstrate unique patterns of change at all stages of life [20].

Barrick and Mount found that conscientiousness in the workplace showed consistent correlation with all job performance criteria for all occupational groups, and Extraversion was a valid predictor for good performance in occupations involving high levels of social interaction (e.g. management and sales). Extraversion and Openness to experience were valid predictors of training proficiency [21,22]. Sinclair and Barrow, in a study of 202 branch managers from a leading British Bank, found significant correlations (ranging from 0.21 to 0.33) with job performance across three of the five scales: High Extraversion, Low Neuroticism and High Openness to experience [23]

The Big Five have been replicated in a variety of different languages and cultures [24], including German [25], Chinese [26] and Indian [27]. Thompson has demonstrated the Big Five structure across several cultures using an international English language scale [28]. The degree to which a country values individualism correlates with its average level of Extraversion, while cultures that are accepting of large inequalities in their power structures tend to score higher on Conscientiousness. The *reasons* for these differences are as yet unknown, but this is an active area of research. Attempts to replicate the Big Five using the local language dictionaries of some countries have not succeeded; for instance, people in Hungary appear not to have a simple Agreeableness factor [29]. Other researchers find evidence of Agreeableness but not of other factors [30].

Cross-cultural research from fifty-five nations (on 17,637 people) has shown a universal pattern of gender difference on responses to the Big Five Inventory. Women consistently report higher levels of Neuroticism and Agreeableness, and men often report higher Extraversion and Conscientiousness. Gender differences in personality traits are most obvious in prosperous, healthy and egalitarian cultures in which men and women have more equal opportunities. Both men and women tend to grow more extraverted and conscientious and less neurotic and agreeable as their cultures grow more prosperous and egalitarian, but the effect is stronger for men [31,32].

Criticisms of the Big Five

A frequent criticism is that the Big Five personality traits are group-based *empirical* observations, rather than a theory; these observations remain to be explained. While this does not mean that the five factors do not exist, the underlying causes behind them are unknown. For example, sensation-seeking and cheerfulness are not linked to Extraversion because of an underlying theory; this relationship is an empirical correlation and the finding remains to be explained.

Additionally, the correlations observed suggest group trends. For groups of people, sensation-seeking and extraversion tends to correlate. For individuals, sensation seeking will, less frequently, be observed in more introverted individuals. Furthermore, the Big Five do not explain all aspects of human personality. Some psychologists have dissented from the model because it neglects other domains of personality, such as religiosity, manipulativeness, machiavellianism, honesty, self-awareness, thriftiness and conservativeness, critical judgement, masculinity and femininity, snobbishness, sense of humour, identity and self-concept, and motivation. Correlations have been found between some of these variables and the Big Five, such as the inverse relationship between political conservatism and Openness [33], although variation in these traits is not well explained by the Big Five themselves.

Methodological issues

The methodology used to identify the dimensional structure of personality traits – known as factor analysis – depends on some degree of interpretation by the analyst. It is often challenged for not having a universally recognised basis for choosing among solutions with different numbers of factors. A larger number of factors may, in fact, underlie the Big Five. This has led to disputes about the 'true' number of factors. In an attempt to explain variance in personality traits more fully, some have found seven factors [34], some eighteen [35], and some only three [36]. Proponents of the Big Five respond that although other solutions may be viable in a single dataset, only the five-factor structure consistently replicates across different studies. What determines the eventual number of factors is essentially the kind of information that is put into the factor analysis in the first place.

Since theory often implicitly precedes empirical science (such as factor analysis), the Big Five and other proposed factor structures should be judged according to the items that went into the factor analytic algorithm. In many studies, the five factors are not fully independent (orthogonal) of one another.

Negative correlations often appear between Neuroticism and Extraversion, indicating that those who are more prone to experiencing negative emotions tend to be less talkative and outgoing. Thus the Five Factor Model may not provide a comprehensive description of personality with the minimum number of variables; there may be some redundancy between the dimensions.

Another methodological criticism is that much of the evidence relies on self-report questionnaires. Self-report bias and falsification of responses are difficult to deal with and account for. Thus differences in scores may represent genuine underlying personality differences, or they may simply be an artefact of the way in which subjects answer the questions. Despite this, the five-factor structure has been replicated in peer reports [37].

Jungian models of personality

The early doyens of personality typing were psychotherapists who developed theories based primarily on narrative explanations of thought, with a particular interest in speculative subconscious processes. They tested their ideas using introspection and anecdotal personal observations of others. The most influential of these was Carl G. Jung.

In his book *Psychological Types* of 1921 [38] he proposed that there are two psychological 'attitudes' – *extraversion* and *introversion* (E/I) and four psychological 'functions'. The functions are divided into two *perceiving* functions – sensation and iNtuition (S/N) – and two decision-making or *judging* functions – thinking and feeling (T/F). He theorised that people have a preference for one or the other attitude, and for one of the four functions, thus forming their personality type. This gives *eight* personality types, namely E/S, E/N, E/T, E/F, I/S, I/N, I/T and I/F. Jung also theorised that the opposite attitudes and functions to those preferred were 'suppressed' and determined the behaviour of the 'subconscious'.

Jung believed that someone's personality type is fixed from an early age and cannot be altered other than by extreme psychological events, or brain disease. He considered that the different personality types have good and bad features. In everyday life we present to the world a persona that attempts to conceal the shortcomings of our own personality, while allowing our strengths to be seen. This process of maintaining a different persona from our underlying personality requires a degree of psychological effort. According to Jung, our mental capacity is strictly limited and when we are under stress we have little spare mental capacity to maintain our persona and outward behaviour reverts to that native of our personality.

Jung's complex model of personality involving hierarchical attitudes and functions, and their operation in subconscious and conscious domains as determinants of behaviour, is now largely of historical interest but the dichotomies he proposed and the idea of reversion to type under stress have proved a rich source of theory and experiment as well as being more durable. Outside of psychology, some common personality classifications used today are based on derivatives of Jung's model which is shown overpage (**Figure 4.2**). The four dichotomies then lead to sixteen possible combinations with sixteen corresponding personality types. The best known among these schemes are the *Myers–Briggs Type Indicator* (MBTI) and the *Keirsey Temperament Sorter* (KTS) which are discussed in turn below.

Myers–Briggs Type Indicator (MBTI)

The MBTI is an adaptation of Jung's classification developed by Katherine Cook Briggs and her daughter Isabel Briggs Meyers to assist in the placement of women into industry during the Second World War. It was first published in 1962 [39].

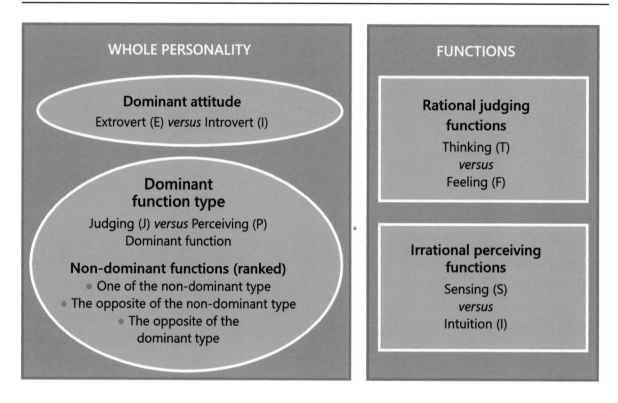

Figure 4.2 *Carl Jung's model of personality (incluing the four dichotomies T, F, S, I).*

Briggs and Myers took Jung's four dichotomies to produce sixteen types. While using the same function names used by Jung, they had slightly different meanings in mind.

E-I	**E**xtrovert	*versus*	**I**ntrovert
S-N	**S**ensing	*versus*	i**N**tuitive
T-F	**T**hinking	*versus*	**F**eeling
J-P	**J**udging	*versus*	**P**erceiving

The MBTI is a commercial product [40] aimed to develop understanding of differences. Much of the information on its performance is controlled by the company that sells it. It has been criticised in academic discourse, but remains one of the most frequently used tools throughout industry and in the public sector. It can be used in two ways, formal and informal.

● The *formal* way involves completing the commercial questionnaires in a facilitated session with an approved trainer, which can be quite expensive. There are forty-seven forced questions (i.e. none are to be left blank) that are then combined to give the four preferences and an index of the certainty of each preference.

● The *informal* way involves a test that describes what is meant by the four dichotomies and then asks respondents to classify themselves. They then read summaries of their, and other, personality types. Respondents often find these summaries to be insightful and accurate descriptions of themselves.

Keirsey Temperament Sorter (KTS)

David Keirsey is an American psychologist who developed this personality classification system that uses a hierarchical structure with four main temperaments, eight roles and sixteen role variants. It classifies people according to how they deal with four aspects of life, namely:

- Thought
- Order
- Feelings
- Other people.

Keirsey coordinated and developed previous ideas of personality typing and, as with Jung and the MBTI, used four dichotomies. For historical consistency, he retained the same words as Jung for these dichotomies, but he developed their meanings so that the words no longer seem well chosen, although they are entrenched in the literature and thus remain in use.

The KTS is available in a book entitled *Please Understand Me II*. It is well observed and written in a non-scientific style [41]. Various associated commercial products are available via the Keirsey website [42].

Thought (*Sensing vs Intuitive*)

This is the top dichotomy in Keirsey's hierarchy. It is better described as observing detail *vs* deriving general principles or concrete *vs* abstract.

We all have a mental model of ourselves and our environment that form the basis of all we think and do. Building this model involves two things: sensing our environment, and cognitive processing of the sensed information to allow us to determine things we cannot sense (such as what we cannot see or what will happen in the future). We all do both of these – but not equally.

The majority of people, maybe 75%, are Sensing. Their mental model is primarily built on experiences (sight, taste, sounds, etc.) and these inputs impact their mental model easily and without effort. They do as much cognitive processing as they need to, but no more because it does not come easily to them. They are observers, looking for specific relevant facts and details. They notice prominent things in their environment without effort and visualise issues and problems in the same way – with detailed observation. Under pressure, they tend to prioritise gathering and assessing this data over the general task in hand and can fail to see the wood for the trees.

The minority of people are Intuitive. For them, cognitive processing comes easily and without effort, but sensing does not. They sense only what they need to in order to inform the development of the general principles that occupy most of their thought. They notice things that carry significance for improving their understanding of principles, but outside of this context sensory input tends to be ignored, and only registered with effort. They gloss over details once they have grasped general ideas and do not notice things around them just because they are there. They conceptualise issues and problems through general principles rather than building up a picture from observation of data and detail. They spend time developing these ideas and are specifically observant of things that allow them to discriminate between different possible theories or scenarios. They appreciate general principles, systems, elegant logical arguments and debates between possible explanations of what is observed. Their riskiest tendency is to jump to conclusions.

Order (*Judging vs Perceiving*)

The KTS follows Jung in that J–P refers primarily to how we deal with information and observations. For those with a preference for data and detail (Sensing people) this is the second most important dichotomy. It refers to a need for order. People described as having a preference for Judging seek order in their lives and what they do. They are schedulers who prefer organised lives with tasks completed one by one. They resist changes they see as unnecessary. They can appear as rigid and inflexible. Perceiving people do not need order and they resist it when it is externally imposed. They keep several tasks going at once, moving from one to another as the need arises, the need often being a looming deadline! They prefer to leave options open in case things change. They become bored with routine and seek change out of curiosity. They are seen by Judging people as chaotic and disorganised, but cope well with change and are flexible and adaptable. They can appear to be indecisive. This dichotomy can lead to conflict between people of opposite types. Perceivers may regard Judging colleagues or bosses as rigid, inflexible and controlling. Judgers may view Perceiving people as disorganised and chaotic.

Feelings (*Thinking vs Feeling*)

For people with a preference for general principles over detailed observations (iNtuitives) this is the second most important dichotomy. Thinking types favour making decisions based on logical thought over consideration of the effect that an action may have on themselves and others. They may not trust their feelings and particularly dislike feelings that conflict with reason or make them vulnerable to appearing illogical. Thinkers do not like to show emotion and are inclined to be embarrassed by displays of feeling in others. They may suppress the influence that emotion has on what they say and do. Consequently they make tough-minded logical and analytical decisions. They may then give some thought to the likely effect of their decision on others, or they may not – particularly if under stress. If they do express feelings under stress, they may do it in an unskilled and unrestrained manner.

Feeling people are the opposite. They make decisions based on their set of core values, taking into account the impact any action may have on themselves and others. They trust their feelings and attend to them. They may not have the same inhibitions as Thinkers about showing emotions or allow them to influence what they say and do. They make decisions based on their effect on themselves and others and may then give some thought to whether the decision makes any sense, or they may not – particularly if under stress.

Like Judging vs Perceiving, this dichotomy can lead to conflict between people of opposite types, whereby Thinkers view Feelers as illogical and inconsistent and Feelers view Thinkers as insensitive, cold and even cruel.

Other people (*Extraversion vs Introversion*)

This is how a person deals with other people, and how sociable that person is.

Extroverts prefer to relax with others, and interact with others. They are refreshed by social interaction. Under pressure or stress they tend to become talkative, and rapidly become frustrated and lonely with solitude.

Introverts prefer to keep their thoughts and feelings more private. They need time alone or with just a few close associates to re-energise, relax, and organise their thoughts. Introverts are fatigued by social interaction. Under pressure or stress they tend to become silent.

Jung and the MBTI mention this dichotomy first because it is the most obvious difference between people and the one with which we can most easily classify others. Keirsey made it the least important because, unlike the others, its value in predicting how people behave goes no further than the dichotomy itself, so being an extrovert says nothing more about someone than that when they are in contact with other people they are extroverted.

The structure of the KTS classification system is shown in **Table 4.2**. The central idea is that of four temperaments – Guardian, Artisan, Idealist and Rational – that are analogous to the four-way classification system of Galen discussed previously. People of different temperaments are quite different from each other, whereas different roles and role variants within the same temperament are quite similar.

Table 4.2 *The KTS personality classification system*

	Temperament	**Role**	**Role variant**
SENSING	Guardian (SJ)	Administrator (STJ)	Supervisor (ESTJ)
			Inspector (ISTJ)
		Conservator (SFJ)	Provider (ESFJ)
			Protector (ISFJ)
	Artisan (SP)	Operator (STP)	Promotor (ESTP)
			Crafter (ISTP)
		Entertainer (SFP)	Performer (ESFP)
			Composer (ISFP)
INTUITIVE	Idealist (NF)	Mentor (NFJ)	Teacher (ENFJ)
			Counsellor (INFJ)
		Advocate (NFP)	Champion ENFP)
			Healer (INFP)
	Rational (NT)	Coordinator (NTJ)	Field-marshall (ENTJ)
			Mastermind (INTJ)
		Engineer (NTP)	Inventor (ENTP)
			Architect (INTP)

The descriptions in the following text relate to **Table 4.2.** Some of the different traits of the four temperaments are shown in **Table 4.3** (overpage).

Temperaments and roles of KTS personality types

Guardian temperament and roles (S-J)

Guardians favour observation over introspection and order over novelty. Jung and the MBTI classify them as S-J and Galen as melancholic, being solemn and prepared for the worst. Their strength is in responsibility. They have an innate sense of how things should be and are sensitive to situations when matters are not going according to plan. They are the pillars of society, ensuring that things run smoothly, supplies are available, everyone's physical needs are met, transport runs on time, shops remain supplied, and staff turn up to work and do what they are supposed to. They take responsibility seriously and are diligent and reliable. The things at which they excel are vital for the smooth running of organisations and their skills are much in demand. They are often asked to help out and their sense of responsibility makes it difficult for them to decline a request. Consequently they tend to end up over-worked and over-committed socially, working long hours for their employers and helping out with school functions, charitable events, and voluntary work in their spare time.

Logistics is the skill for which Guardians have the greatest aptitude – compared to tactics for the Artisans, strategy for the Rationals and diplomacy for the Idealists. Logistics is about making material goods and services available where and when they are needed. They can be less skilled at strategy, with tactics and diplomacy in between – the exact opposite of the Rationals. They respect authority, believe in hierarchical structures of authority, and trust people in authority or recognised experts. They see rules as being there for a purpose; even if they do not fully understand what that purpose is, they assume someone else does and are prepared to trust them; this is quite the opposite of the Rationals' default position that rules they do not see as necessary were made with self-interest or stupidity (or both).

Table 4.3 *Personailty traits of the KTS (see text for explanation)*

Personality trait	Temperament			
	SENSORS		INTUITIVES	
	Guardian (SJ)	Artisan (SP)	Idealist (NF)	Rational (NT)
Education	Commerce	Artefacts	Humanities	Science
Aptitude	Logistics	Tactics	Diplomacy	Strategy
Attitude	Stoical	Hedonistic	Altruistic	Pragmatic
Future views	Pessimistic	Optimistic	Credulous	Sceptical
Looks for	Security	Stimulation	Identity	Knowledge
Most values	Gratitude	Generosity	Recognition	Deference
Preoccupied with	Morality	Techniques	Morale	Technology
Vocation	Material	Equipment	Personnel	Systems
Vices	Controlling	Feckless	Gullible	Cruel
Virtues	Respectable	Resolute	Authentic	Adaptable
Wants to be	Dependable	Artistic	Empathic	Ingenious
Tends to be	Concerned	Excited	Enthusiastic	Calm
Trusts	Authority	Impulse	Intuition	Reason
Longs for	Belonging	Impact	Romance	Achievement

Guardians expend their own time and effort to create and enforce the rules that ensure societies and organisations run smoothly. They are good at making wise and effective rules that benefit everyone. Other types may not care much for rules but are thankful someone is making and enforcing them. They have a strong moral sense of what is right and wrong and of personal duty to those around them. They are concerned about numerous social, professional, family or environmental issues and take a stoical outlook, particularly in areas such as hard work and saving. They feel a duty of service, not through joy so much as obligation. They need to feel respectable and self-confidence can be a problem for Guardians who are averse to showing off. They are proud of, and collect, awards and qualifications in the pursuit of respectability.

Guardians are given to pessimism about the future, believing in Murphy's law '*Whatever can go wrong, will go wrong*' – and adding '*It will be my fault if I let it*'. They seek security and enjoy 'belonging' so they join clubs and groups. Their conversation is about concrete things like jobs, housing, credit, debt, prices and so on, rather than abstractions and generalisations. In discussion they change topic easily by association, the price of petrol may prompt a change to types of car, whereas for Rationals this would more likely prompt discussion of the factors influencing price. This ability to cover wide ranges of subjects makes Guardians good at holding everyone's interest. They also have an impressive memory for socially important facts. They easily remember names, faces, family ties, whose children are doing what, and so on, giving them the best social skills of all temperaments. They are cooperative in achieving common goals, so they are natural team players.

Guardians like routine and resist change for its own sake (or if they cannot see its purpose). They trust tradition and tend to think things are not as good as they used to be. They are people of regular habits, following the same routines day after day. They value durable items like heirlooms, collections and family photographs. They do not like to see old building demolished or old trees cut down.

They like to see themselves as beneficent to others, particularly when it comes to food, clothing, shelter and transport. They are good hosts but get upset if they are not appreciated and like to receive offers of help even though they are reluctant to accept them. They prize gratitude and find it galling when others exploit their self-sacrifice without showing any, but of all types they are the least able to ask for it. Furthermore, the tasks they take on tend to be thankless. If a Guardian is hosting dinner party, they will ensure supplies are available, will be concerned that there is enough food and wine, will set the table and wash up, often helped by Guardian guests. They will attend to the guests, making sure all are provided for, and will be quick to notice if anyone is feeling left out and so take corrective action. These efforts are essential for a successful evening, but only attract attention when they are not done – not when they are. Guardian roles include the Administrator and the Conservator.

ADMINISTRATOR (STJ)

Thinking Guardians are more results-oriented than friendly, and are interested in ensuring procedures and tasks are done properly to agreed standards by all those involved. They are divided in two role variants, the extroverted *Supervisor* and the introverted *Inspector*.

Role variant: Supervisor (E-STJ)

- Account for around 9% of the population.
- Confident and assertive, and are drawn towards leadership roles in which they do well.
- Enforce agreed procedures and monitor the performance of others, making sure they observe regulations and acceptable conduct or face the agreed consequences if they do not.
- Can be demanding and intolerant of dissent but are honest and not given to bearing secret and dangerous grudges. They are good at planning and prioritising.

- Can be insensitive to the feelings of others who they can upset by applying their fixed values without regard to those of associates.
- Have a sense of responsibility that drives them to decide what is required of them in any situation and do it irrespective of whether others think it necessary, or even know about it. This means they need little supervision but their performance is dependent on the goal in hand fitting in with their sense of order.

Role variant: Inspector (I-TSJ)

- Account for around 12% of the population.
- Like predictable, organised and regulated lives and bring the same qualities to their work with painstaking diligence and a desire for a tidy conclusion or 'closure' to allotted tasks. This makes then good 'completer–finishers'.
- Their introversion means they prefer roles such as account keeping, auditing and stock control to the extrovert supervisor role.
- Logical and realistic and tend to have little time for abstract theorising.
- Loyal, being more responsive to the reasoning of people they trust, unlike other types who focus on what is said rather than who says it.
- Readily take responsibility and reach their own judgements as to what should be accomplished, then work steadily towards it, disregarding distractions and objections.

CONSERVATOR (SFJ)

Feeling Guardians are more friendly than results-oriented Thinking Guardians and are given to the Conservator's role, which ensures the security and material needs of others. They favour informing and providing over commanding and checking. They are people oriented, noticing details about other people for the purpose of supporting them. They like people and want to be liked. They are popular because they make others feel good about themselves, and tend to bring out the best in them. They are easily hurt by indifference towards them and do not comprehend unkindness or cruelty. They are reluctant to see the faults in others so are vulnerable to being deceived and disappointed. Their perceptiveness and keenness to please makes them good at adapting their own behaviour to please the person with whom they are communicating. They can appear logical to logical people, sensitive to sensitive people, enthusiastic to enthusiastic people, and so on. They avoid abstract thought, theoretical concepts and impersonal analysis. They respect authority, tradition and rules and think others should too, but without internal reference they are prone to insecurity caused by conflicting demands of others. Their role variants are the extroverted *Provider* and the introverted *Protector*.

Role variant: Provider (E-SFJ)

- Account for around 12% of the population.
- Reliable and good with detail.
- Can see clearly what is needed for everyone's benefit and are good at getting it done.
- Have clear views on how things should be, and freely express their opinions, although these are based on those around them, their community and consensus of others rather than any internal commitment. This means that they take on whatever value system surrounds them and may not have the capacity to change it without external input. This can lead to disasters if they change from a community with one value system to one with another.

Role variant: Protector (I-SFJ)

- Account for around 14% of the population.
- Quiet and shy, but oriented towards people skills, they are drawn to the role of protecting others from all that is harmful in the world.
- Sensitive, with keen observation and good recall of the needs of others.
- Prioritise keeping others secure but do not tend to seek credit for doing it.
- Do not usually have technical interests but are accurate and painstaking.
- People oriented, but shy, tending not to volunteer contributions when among strangers. This can paradoxically make them appear uninterested.
- Most comfortable among people they know well.

Artisan temperament and roles (SP)

Artisans are the sanguine temperaments of Galen. They think and communicate in vivid and closely observed detail, focusing on the here and now and their immediate environment rather than on generalisations or principles. They are interested in experiencing things, particularly if they are novel or different. For instance, when considering a fine car they are likely to be interested in its shape and colour, its smell, acceleration and handling. Other types are interested in the inner workings of the car – the Artisans less so. They rapidly get bored with routine tasks and seek change out of curiosity. They excel in short-term reactive situations such as entertainment, making objects, emergency response, and team tactics. Of the four KTS types they have the best ability to sense and exploit their immediate environment. This is called *tactical intelligence*. They are not so good at long-term strategic planning and sensitivity to others' feelings, having little interest in morality or morale.

Their educational interests are in the creative arts and crafts, including performance, music, cookery and aesthetic design. These are not regarded as high educational priorities in the Western world and Artisans are often frustrated, distracted and may under-achieve at school. Their learning interest is in perfecting skills, be they musical, artistic, technical or dramatic. They are attracted to instruments and machines, not because of their workings but because of what they do to their environment and the Artisan's desire to experience and master them. They want to drive the bulldozer, fly the plane, shoot the arrow, and wield the mallet and chisel. These properties combine to make them the greatest athletes, artists, sculptors or cooks.

The Artisans' attitude to the present is hedonistic. They do things for the fun of it and see no point in doing something they do not have to do if there is no enjoyment in it. They are optimistic about the short-term future and do not worry about the long-term.

Compared to the other KTS types, they have a casual, happy-go-lucky attitude to life that can lead them into trouble and tends towards boom and bust, rather than stability. They may be cynical and distrustful of the motives of others. They want to see themselves as creative, accomplished and graceful in action. Their keenest embarrassment is in being dull, unskilled or clumsy. They want to be bold and adventurous, feel guilt about cowardice or demurring adventure. They are the great risk takers. They also see themselves as adaptable to changing circumstances and as being good in a crisis. They are impulsive, frequently acting on impulse, including being impulsively generous. Their longing is to create a social or cultural impact, to be noticed and to attract wide attention.

Thinking Artisans are more oriented towards influencing the physical environment than other people, and take the role of Operator. Feeling Artisans are the other way round, seeking primarily to influence the people around them and less so their physical environment; they take the role of Entertainer. Both of these roles come in *extroverted* and *introverted* variants.

OPERATOR (STP)

Operators are interested in precision of definition and meaning, in how systems work and what the effects of changes could be. This gives them an understanding of systems, causes and effects, and makes them good with machines. They are interested in theories and concepts as far as is necessary for this understanding, but not for their own sake. They are adventurous, independent and fearless. They are often drawn to careers or sports and pastimes that are both technically demanding and unforgiving of mistakes such as flying, motorcycling and SCUBA diving, making them appear to be thrill seekers. They easily become bored when denied such opportunities. They are independent and resist being controlled by others, which can lead to conflict with establishments. They side with others to resist control of them also. They have a strong sense of fairness and justice. They get excited easily and can spread this excitement to others, but they are not good at completion or follow through. Their role variants are the extroverted *Promoter* and the introverted *Crafter*.

Role variant: Promoter (E-STP)

- Account for around 4% of the population.
- Outgoing people of action.
- Risk takers.
- Can be averse to externally imposed rules but have strong belief in what they see as right.
- Perceptive of attitudes and feelings of others, noticing subtleties of intonation and body language that other types may not. This makes them effective at getting their way.
- Good at improvisation, storytelling and drama and fun to have around, but they put little priority on the effects of their decisions on others, so can unwittingly offend.

Role variant: Crafter (I-STP)

- Account for around 5% of the population.
- Detached onlookers with a deep understanding of systems (concealed by their quiet reserve), but occasionally revealed by their profound insights and flashes of perceptive humour.
- Take little heed of feelings, either their own or those of others, and make decisions based on the facts of a situation.
- Their practical abilities and resistance to fear make them good in crisis situations.
- Good at completing a project and tidying up any loose ends.

ENTERTAINER (SFP)

Entertainers are spontaneous and like excitement and new experiences, but may have difficulty seeing or heeding the long-term consequences of their actions. They base their decisions on their effects on others, so they appear sensitive and sympathetic. They make good peacemakers. They are quick to spot when someone is upset and to offer solace, but the advice on problems they give may be off-target due to their dislike of theory and planning. They are popular and get on with most people, but if they fall out with someone they lack the capacity to rationalise the causes and consequences of a quarrel and can bear a deep, protracted and destructive grudge. They do tasks at their own pace and tend to live in the present. They are more sensitive to their surroundings than other Sensing types and readily notice small differences in their environment or other people. They are also sensitive to 'harmony', recognising what 'goes well' with what. They are emotionally stable and empathetic to other people. They do not care to lead but are pleased to follow others. Their role variants are the extroverted *Performer* and the introverted *Composer*.

Role variant: Performer (E-SFP)

- Account for around 9% of the population.
- The most people-oriented type.
- Love company, are fun to be with and like to be the centre of attention.
- Easily form bonds, not only with other adults, but also with animals and small children.
- Drawn to live entertainment-type careers and pastimes such as comedy, acting or presenting.

Role variant: Composer (I-SFP)

- Account for around 9% of the population.
- Quiet, conciliatory and easy to please.
- Pleasant and caring and devoted to the other people in their lives.
- Value their own views and opinions but are reluctant to air them.
- Their introversion leads them into more private creative interests such as art, sculpture or storytelling.

Intuitive temperaments

Three of the dichotomies in the KTS divide the population into two roughly equal groups. The exception is Sensor *vs* Intuitive. Sensors outnumber Intuitives who make up 15–25% of the population and this has a bearing on how Intuitives develop as well as how to present the subject. Because there are many fewer Intuitives to study, sub-typing them is more inaccurate with lower statistical resolution. The impact of the other dichotomies on the intuitive mind is partly extrapolated from their impact on the sensing mind.

The thought processes of Sensors and Intuitives can be inaccessible to each other. Sensors find themselves surrounded by other Sensors, with the occasional misfit they do not understand. Intuitives, on the other hand, find themselves surrounded by Sensors, who they do not understand, with the occasional soulmate. These develop into lifelong feelings of:

- inclusion, for the Sensor temperaments (Artisans and Guardians)
- detachment, for the Intuitive temperaments (Idealists and Rationals).

Idealist temperament and roles (NF)

The Intuitive Feelers are Galen's cholerics. Idealists talk not of what they observe but what is in their minds. They talk of strong feelings, love, hate, empathy and passion, symbols, fantasies, meanings. They are highly imaginative.

Like the other intuitive group, the Rationals, Idealists move rapidly from the particular to the general, the general being not abstract theories but abstract moralities and feelings. They are highly sensitive to nuance and meaning, making them the best at mind reading and reading between the lines. They want to understand their beliefs and uncover meaning. They have a desire to connect disparate ideas and concepts to a coherent whole. They are given to exaggeration and hyperbole: the dinner others find adequate, the idealist finds exquisite; the colleague others find marginally tolerable, the idealists finds to be from hell.

They dream of perfect interpersonal relationships and their first instinct is to promote them ahead of achieving material goals. They particularly dislike fighting can be deeply hurt by callous criticism. Their sensitivity to others, reluctance to upset, avoidance of conflict and keenness to please makes diplomacy their strong suit. They are altruistic, believing self-service is bad and service to others is good. They believe there is good in everyone and feel driven to find it.

Idealists are typically drawn to humanities and social sciences rather than hard sciences or commerce and are not great with technology. They prefer working with words and people to tools and things and in health care are found more frequently in mental health than in surgery. Idealists are pre-occupied with the morale of those around them, unlike the guardians who are preoccupied with the comfort and physical needs of those around them. They chose careers that involve teaching, caring, and guiding people.

Idealists see themselves as on a journey of discovery of meaning. They want to be empathic and involved in inter personal relationships with individuals or groups. They want to be benevolent towards people, things, the earth etc. They suppress feelings of malice, revenge, hatred and cruelty. They want to be genuine, authentic, with no false façade.

More than other types, idealists are self-conscious, feeling the eyes of others on them. They are highly sensitive to the way they are judged by others. They feel inadequate and lose self-confidence if they give a false impression of themselves and fear others are able to look straight through their contrived façade. They are credulous and given to metaphysical and religious beliefs. They believe in things and causes easily especially if they have faith in leading figures and can develop fixed ideas from which logical reasoning will not shake them. They are the most loyal of all types but will not stay with a cause if it does not give them a lasting sense of worth.

Idealists are usually positive so they like enthusiasm. When frustrated or treated harshly they show the Galen choleric properties of quickness to anger. They trust their intuition which is more developed that that of other types. They seek inner meaning and a sense of personal identity, or finding themselves, so much so that they have been called the identity-seeking personality; note seeking not finding! They can be incurable romantics and appreciate recognition for who they are rather than the roles they must play in society. They can go through life feeling misunderstood. They divide between the judging Mentor and the perceiving Advocate.

MENTOR (NFJ)

The KTS calls the scheduling idealists mentors as they are drawn to a directive role in developing others. The two mentor variants are the extraverted Teacher and introverted Councillor. Mentors expect and inspire the best in those around them. They tend to be popular, are good with language and take to occupations where sustained personal contact is required.

As idealists, mentors are motivated to make others happy. Their ability to please makes it easy to get what they want out of people and they can be manipulative. They change their behaviour according to what pleases who they are with so their real identity can be elusive even to themselves. Their need to give support comes with a similar need to receive it and their efforts are not reciprocated by most other types. This can lead them to feel lonely and unloved even when surrounded by people. This feeling is deepened by their reluctance to express it.

Their intuition is both accurate, and mysterious to them and others, which makes it uncanny. They may have strong concerns that appear to anticipate a real issue and give the impression of unnatural insight that they then have to conceal for fear of ridicule. They become selective of what they share and can be secretive and protective of much of their thought and feelings. They appear as deep, complex and difficult to penetrate. They tend towards perfectionism and are rarely entirely content with themselves. They like structure and organisation but with weak analytical skills their ability to prioritise what should be organised and what can be left may be poor making them appear fussy. They do not readily understand the reasoning of others and cannot see the point of it. They may perform poorly and appear irrational when forced to deal with analytical issues. In any planning situation they enjoy the interaction with others in the process more than solving problems and realising goals. Without other types they would never get off the planning stage of projects. They are drawn towards creative careers and are poor with accuracy in detail. They lack ability in deriving general principles from multiple observations and when forced to attend to detail, they are prone to do so to excess, failing to see the wood for the trees. The role variants are *Teacher* and *Counsellor*.

Role variant: Teacher (E-NFJ)

- Account for around 2% of the population.
- Charismatic and take it for granted that others will meet their expectations.
- Good at coming up with group activities and class participation in learning.
- Seek social contact and may become morose when forced into isolation.
- Tend to give higher priority to the importance of others than themselves so are more circumspect about expressing their views and feelings that other extraverted types, especially on personal matters.

Role variant: Counsellor (I-NFJ)

- Account for around 2% of the population.
- Enjoy one-one guidance more than class teaching.
- Reserved and difficult to get to know, only sharing themselves with those they trust.
- Sensitive, quiet and complex.
- Like order and follow systematic process in their external lives (and expend considerable effort perfecting their systems), but internally they are intuitive and spontaneous.
- Their intuitions are often correct and they usually know when their intuitions are reliable and when they are not. This instinctiveness tends to blunt the order of other judging types, so they typically have mid-spectrum desk tidiness.
- Care about other people's feelings and avoid upsetting them.
- Comparatively averse to conflict. When forced into it they may see personal attack where it is not intended and hit back viciously.

ADVOCATE (NFP)

As the Perceiving Idealists, advocates can become excited about one thing after another and appear to lack long-term consistent goals. They become aware of their susceptibility to new obsessions and emotional excitement and may be concerned for their own emotional stability, making them seem intense to onlookers. Remaining focused is a constant struggle for them with which they have variable success. They dislike and are poor at routine tasks and the mundane acts of daily living.

Their liking for excitement and neglect of the mundane makes them prone to poor judgements. They seek value and meaning in their lives and screen concepts and ideas they encounter looking for any that enhance their quest for personal fulfilment. They have a genuine interest in people and are motivated towards selfless caring. They are given to 'causes'. They are either detached and uninterested in an issue or adopt it as a cause to be vigorously defended and fought for. This means their attention to detail, follow through and completion of a task is dependent on whether or not they see it as their cause. This can lead to paradoxical priorities where important issues that are not part of the cause are ignored but trivia that are part of the cause are vigorously pursued. This tendency is compounded by their limitations in the areas of theory and logic. The two role variants are *Champion* and *Healer*.

Role variant: Champion (E-NFP)

- Account for around 8% of the population.
- Bright and enthusiastic.
- Easily become excited about things and their enthusiasm is infectious.
- Good at talking their way into or out of things.
- Strong people skills and a particular need to be liked.
- Understand others intuitively and use the understanding to promote friendship with them.
- Happy risk-takers who need independence and resist being controlled. Many are self-employed.
- Productive without supervision as long as they maintain enthusiasm in what they are doing.

Role variant: Healer (I-NFP)

- Account for around 4% of the population.
- Driven to serve the interests of Earth's animate inhabitants.
- Keenly motivated and go to great lengths to achieve their self-imposed goals.
- Demand high standards of themselves and others and can appear as 'control freaks' as a consequence.
- Particularly averse to conflict. When forced into it they may put more importance on how they feel than on being right or wrong. They resolve the conflict in the way that makes them feel less bad rather than puts them in the right. This can make them seem week or illogical.
- Good at mediating other people's conflicts because they are motivated to genuinely understand each side rather than impose another agenda.

Rational temperaments and roles (NT)

Introspective Thinkers are Galen's phlegmatics, whom he described as not easily excited into emotion or action; they are calm, apathetic, composed, distant and detached. Keirsey's corresponding temperament is the Rational. Galen's description remains accurate, particularly when they are involved in solving some problem, as they often are. They detach themselves from society until it is solved.

Rationals spend much of their lives in abstract thought, thinking in three-dimensional space, time, logical relationships, causes and effects. They think more prominently in language and less in feelings, desires and impressions than other temperaments. They become highly practised at this and have the best ability of all the types to comprehend the workings of the physical world and to predict the results of actions taken now. They prefer to think than to act and, when addressing a task, will give considerable thought to how the task can be done to achieve the maximum effect for the minimum effort. They nearly always do this and become highly proficient at it. This makes them the most efficient type in the use of time and resources. They are adaptable and tolerant, judging ideas and people on their merits alone.

They talk of what is imagined, not what is seen. They do not exaggerate and speak in terms of possible, probable and consistent with – rarely facts or proof. They like words and puns and are economical and exact with word usage, tending not to elaborate, assuming that others will understand as they do. Others may not follow, however, and Rationals are prone to losing their audience and becoming impatient with the stupidity of other people. This problem is compounded by their lack of small talk.

They are highly curious and seek knowledge for its own sake. They are sceptical of the ideas and claims of others. An important aspect of their temperament is their yearning for achievement which stays with them throughout their lives and is quite unlike the drivers of the other temperaments (belonging for Guardians; making an impact for Artisans; and romance for idealists).

The way they wish to influence others is by being asked to devise, implement or explain complex systems, preferably all three together. In education they have a lifelong desire to know how nature works and love building theories. They are drawn to the study of systems in science and mathematics. Today's largely clerical school curriculum bores them and they may under-perform at basic literacy, gaining success in secondary school and further education where their favoured subjects are available to study.

They are pragmatic, with an eye on the efficient achievement or results. They trust reason fully, intuition and impulse rarely, and external authority never. Rules and morals are of secondary importance if they cannot be used to get results. They are not socially or politically correct, but neither are they given to snobbishness or prejudice. They care little for status, position, qualifications, reputation, authority, prestige or other badges of social acceptability. They will heed devils whose ideas are valuable, and ignore angels whose ideas are not. They are highly autonomous and ignore any law or instruction that does not make sense to them. They think for themselves and want to govern themselves. Ideas must stand on their own merit; authority, title, reputation and so on count for nothing. Lack of respect for authority makes them seem irreverent and arrogant.

Other personality types can see Rationals as risk-takers, which they do tend to be, but for very different reasons from Artisans. Most people's view of a risk of something bad happening is based mainly on how bad it would be if it happened, and only secondarily on how likely it is to happen. The Rational's view is based in equal measure on the severity of the risk and the numerical probability of it happening. This makes them much more inclined to ignore a risk of disaster than other types, if they see it as being highly improbable, and their ability accurately to judge such probabilities is greater than that of other types. They become bored in meetings when they see the discussion as being of no consequence, and turn to their own thoughts, not caring who knows they are uninterested. They do not respect custom and history, which can lead to conflict with Guardians and Idealists. Of all the temperaments, they are the most critical of their own abilities but they allow no external criticism that is not carefully measured and warranted. Criticism they see as unjust or inaccurate can turn them into dangerous enemies, harbouring secret resentments for years and plotting efficient, vindictive revenge. They like to remain calm, particularly when under stress, and if they cannot keep calm they will try not to let it show.

Unlike Guardians and Idealists, Rationals are not drawn by temperament into healthcare. They have a similar frequency as Idealists in the whole population, but within healthcare they are likely to be under-represented and form the smallest group. Their autonomy and disregard for tradition and authority can make them potentially difficult to manage but the perceptive leader, when faced with a Rational who will not comply with their plans, will identify what the goal of those plans is, explain that goal to the Rational and ask him or her to come up with an alternative plan; the result is likely to be better than the original plan, with the added advantage that the Rational will comply. Rationals divide between judging Coordinators and perceiving Engineers.

COORDINATOR (NTJ)

Judging or scheduling Rationals choose a coordinating role over a more probing inventive role. They are quick to assimilate information, understand complex situations and make clear decisions. They like to identify and solve practical problems. They like predictable systems and organisation and dislike anything that is non-specific or unclear. These combine to give them aptitude for science and engineering. They are good at foreseeing long-term consequences, intended or otherwise, of measures taken now. They are intolerant of inefficiency and recurrent errors and are skilled at cutting unproductive bureaucracy. They are also career-minded, all of which makes them successful in the corporate world. They are insensitive to the feelings of others and have little time for those who disagree with them, so can appear overbearing. They are confident with good communication skills. They enjoy lively conversation and respect those who argue cogently against them. They favour order, tidiness and efficiency in their home and work lives. The role variants are *Field Marshal* and *Mastermind*.

Role variant: Field Marshall (E-NTJ)

- Account for around 2% of the population.
- Aptitude for marshalling large groups or organisations in the preparation and conduct of major complex undertakings.
- Natural leaders, decisive and forceful.
- Command respect with an aura of personal power that can help them achieve their aims, but can also appear as pride and lead to the alienation of others.
- Like to be in charge both at home and at work but their career focus makes them prone to neglect the former.

Role variant: Mastermind (I-NTJ)

- Account for around 2% of the population.
- Skilled at planning complex operations with the need for numerous contingency options against possible events.
- Respect intelligence and scholarship and will only make the effort to express their thoughts to people they see as possessing these qualities.
- Effective leaders, but do not seek leadership for its own sake, taking over only when others have demonstrated their inability to lead.
- Usually able people who meet their goals fairly easily.
- Objective, far-sighted and not bound by rules and traditions, which means they are flexible and able to change tack when a situation demands it. However, they have little patience for explaining the reasons for their decisions to others they see as dim, so they can be misunderstood.
- Communicate for a practical purpose, rather than to please, and can be seen as reserved and aloof.

ENGINEER (NTP)

Engineers are clever, innovative and flexible. They like detailed and indepth understanding of the world and are good at accurately identifying the key features of a situation or problem, and at dreaming up novel solutions to difficult problems by 'thinking outside the box'. They are poor at follow-through. They tend to flip from one interest to another and are good at devising plausible reasons for what they want. Once they have come up with the idea they prefer to move on to something else, rather than see through its implementation.

They are given to black humour and inclined to argue for fun, which can lead to misunderstandings and unintended offence. When properly deployed on a team, Engineers add thorough understanding, flexibility and problem-solving ability. They trust their ability to deal with situations as they arise and are not given to careful pre-planning which can be a limitation. They appear clever and objective to others and are excited by theoretical issues, longing to discuss them in detail with others, but this longing is commonly frustrated because Rationals are relatively rare and their train of thought can be inaccessible to most other types.

When expressing themselves, they aim to be exact rather than easily understood. Their ability to solve the most intricate problems makes them valuable but if they are not given tasks that interest them they rapidly disengage from a group or workplace, doing the minimum necessary while looking elsewhere for issues to engage them. Their role variants are the extroverted *Inventor* and the introverted *Architect*.

Role variant: Inventor (E-NTP)

- Account for around 3% of the population.
- Tend to be out-going and resourceful.
- Prize intelligence highly in themselves and others are inclined to dismiss out of hand the contributions of those they regard as stupid.
- More than any other type, they believe there is not such word as 'cannot' and if told that they cannot, they will go to lengths to show how they can.

Role variant: Architect (I-NTP)

- Account for around 3% of the population.
- Skilled at visualising and designing complex systems and structures.
- The least people-oriented type.
- Value abstract knowledge above human contact.
- Neither comprehend nor value feelings or subjectivity, so are poor at meeting the emotional needs of others, with obvious implications for social situations and relationships.
- Do not give much heed to what others think of them.
- Pay little attention to their appearance and may not bother with unnecessary courtesies.

Limitations of Jungian classification systems (MTBI/KTS)

Several criticisms are applied to these Jungian systems.

First, there is test–retest reliability. This refers to how well two tests done on the same person at different times produce similar results. For the MBTI, test–retest reliability varies from just over 80% to under 40%, the consistency declining with a longer time between tests. This suggests that contrary to Jung's beliefs such tests are not of unchanging life-long characteristics. Some have suggested that the tendency to identify such stable personality types is in itself part of a pervasive cognitive bias called the *fundamental attribution error*. This refers to a tendency to see others' actions as being internally driven and stable, while seeing our own actions as more dependent on circumstances. This pattern of attribution tends to become more pronounced where actions have adverse outcomes [43].

Second, there is dichotomy. A characteristic like extraversion is not an all-or-none phenomenon but it forms a continuous spectrum from extreme extraversion at one end to extreme introversion at the other. The distribution of the variable along this spectrum is typically Gaussian, with extreme cases being rare and the majority being nearer the middle. Modelling this as a dichotomy is not entirely satisfactory because it fails to distinguish between the extreme case, whose personality is dominated by that one trait, and the more typical intermediate case. One particular distribution issue is with Keirsey's use of the S–N (sensing *vs* intuitive) dichotomy which gives 75–85% of the population as Sensing. The UK norms based on the MBTI version of the dichotomies show that 76% of the general population and 53% of those involved in management are Sensing.

The problem of *definition* affects all personality classification systems to some extent, but particularly Jungian ones. What is meant by the eight terms is not the same from one system to another, nor is it the same as their common English meaning. Extra explanation, with potential for misunderstanding, is necessary in order to use these classification systems.

Limitations of personality testing

Evidence base

There are four methods of evidence generation in personality studies: one-to-one case studies, questionnaires from large numbers of respondents, observational studies and laboratory experiments. All have their strengths and weaknesses.

Jungian systems are primarily based on only one of these, namely one-to-one case studies. This method has the advantage of facilitating indepth detailed analysis, but the disadvantages of subjectivity, inter-observer variation and, consequently, limited repeatability. Mainstream psychology favours systems informed by repeatable lines of evidence generation, such as the *Five Factor Model*.

Predictive value

A common doubt raised by healthcare professionals about the value of personality testing is that it has little (or no) practical value. In the terms of academic psychology, this is referred to as the limitation of predictive value. Claims made for personality-typing systems often maintain that they can be used optimally to deploy people on a team, and predict responses to psychological treatment modalities, and so on. And these claims, particularly when made for commercial-typing products, are often unduly exaggerated. The predictive value of testing falls into two categories: *tautological* and *non-tautological*.

TAUTOLOGICAL PREDICTION

This means that if somebody reports a particular trait, that trait is likely to be true of them at the time of reporting and in the future. As an example, if a person has a Rational temperament and reports that they prefer abstract logical thought to detailed observation, this is highly predictive that they will give the same report if asked again a year later. This relatively successful tautological prediction of personality typing systems is a consequence of the relative constancy of people's personality types. Predictive value generally becomes weaker as the link between the reported trait and behaviour becomes more distant. For example, someone preferring order to novelty is likely to have a tidy desk but the link to desk tidiness is not as strong as it is to continuing to report a preference for order over novelty at a later date.

NON-TAUTOLOGICAL PREDICTION

As the link between reported characteristics and behaviour becomes weaker, the predictive value of all personality-typing systems also becomes weaker. A good example of this is the type A/B system in which type A personality characteristics are claimed to be predictive of the apparently totally unrelated risk of coronary artery disease. This claim is controversial and it is generally true that when tested, the ability of personality-typing systems to predict behaviour not directly related to the reported preferences is weak.

The predictive value of testing can also be seen in terms of group and individual prediction:

- **Group prediction** refers to the ability to predict performance on a group basis, for example, a group of 100 individuals scoring high on extraversion are likely to perform better in a sales role than a group of 100 individuals scoring high on introversion.

- **Individual prediction** refers to whether one person will perform better than another. This is clearly a more difficult task than group prediction, both statistically and practically. In the two groups mentioned, some of the 'introverts' will perform better than some of the 'extroverts'.

The criticism that personality typing has little useful application in healthcare systems is usually based on the failure of non-tautological prediction, but it is the tautological rather than non-tautological prediction that is of potential value. The hypothesis of the value of personality typing in a healthcare environment is nothing more than:

> A more detailed understanding of people's strengths, weaknesses, likes and dislikes enables us more effectively to allocate tasks in a way that optimises their efficient completion, as well as the engagement and satisfaction of team members.

References

1 Friedman M, Ulmer D. *Treating `Type A' Behavior and Your Heart.*0 New York: Fawcett, 2010.

2 Digman JM. Personality structure: Emergence of the five-factor model. *Annual Review of Psychology*, 1990; 41: 417–40.

3 Eysenck HJ. Four ways five factors are not basic. *Personality and Individual Differences*, 1992; 13(6): 667-73.

4 Matthews G, Deary IJ, Whiteman MC. *Personality Traits*. Cambridge: Cambridge University Press, 2003.

5 Allport GW, Odbert HS. *Psychological Monograph Trait Names: A Psycholexical Study*. Psychological Review Publications, 1936.

6 Tupes EC, Christal RE. *Recurrent Personality Factors Based on Trait Ratings*. Lackland Air Force Base Tupes, TX: Personnel Laboratory, Air Force Systems Command, 1961 Contract No.: ASD-TR-61–97.

7 Cattell RB, Marshall M, Georgiades S. Personality and motivation: Structure and measurement. *Journal of Personality Disorders*, 1957; 19(1): 53–67.

8 McCrae RR, Costa PTJ. Validation of the Five Factor model of personality across instruments and observers. *Journal of Personality and Social Psychology*, 1987; 52(1): 81–90.

9 Saucier G, Goldberg LR (eds) *The Language of Personality: Lexical Perspectives on the Five Factor Model*. New York: Guilford, 1996.

10 Cattell HEP, Mead AD. The 16 Personality Factor Questionnaire (16-PF). In: Boyle GJ, Matthews G, Saklofske DH (eds) *Handbook of Personality Theory and Testing*. London: Sage, 2007.

11 Goldberg LR. Language and individual differences: The search for universals in personality lexicons. In: Wheeler L (ed.) *Review of Personality and Social Psychology*. Beverly Hills: Sage, 1981; pp. 141–65.

12 Costa PT, McCrae RR. *The NEO Personality Inventory Manual*. Oxford: Hogrefe, 2011.

13 Hogan R. Hogan *Personality Inventory (HPI),* 2011 . Available at: http://www.hoganassessments.com/ hogan–personality–inventory (last accessed January 2013).

14 Hogan R. *Handbook of Personality Psychology.* San Diego: Academic Press, 1997

15 McCrae RR, Costa PT. *Personality in Adulthood.* New York: The Guildford Press, 1990.

16 Srivastava S, John OP, Gosling SD, Potter J. Development of personality in early and middle adulthood: Set like plaster or persistent change? *Journal of Personality and Social Psychology,* 2003; 84(5): 1041–53.

17 McGhee RM, Ehrler DJ, Buckhalt J. *Five Factor Personality Inventory – Children (FFPI-C).* Austin: Pro-Ed, 2007.

18 John OP, Srivastava S. The Big-Five trait taxonomy: History, measurement, and theoretical perspectives. *Handbook of Personality: Theory and Research.* New York: Guilford Press, 1999.

19 Jang K, Livesley WJ, Vemon PA. Heritability of the Big Five personality dimensions and their facets: A twin study. *Journal of Personality and Social Psychology,* 1996; 64(3): 577–91.

20 Roberts BW, Mroczek D. Personality trait change in adulthood. *Current Directions in Psychological Science,* 2008; 17(1): 31–35.

21 Barrick MR, Mount MK. The Big Five personality dimensions and job performance: A meta-analysis. *Personnel Psychology,* 1991; 44: 1–26.

22 Mount MK, Barrick MR. Five reasons why the 'Big Five' article has been frequently cited. *Personnel Psychology,* 1998; 51: 849–57.

23 Sinclair P, Barrow S. Identifying personality traits predictive of performance. *British Psychological Society Journal on Occupational Testing: Selection and Development Review,* 1992; 8(5).

24 McCrae RR. NEO-PI-R data from 36 cultures: Further Intercultural comparisons. In: McCrae RR, Alik J (eds) *The Five Factor Model of Personality Across Cultures.* New York: Kluwer Academic Publisher, 2002; pp. 105–25.

25 Ostendorf F. Sprache und Persoenlichkeitsstruktur: *Zur Validitaet des Funf-Factoren-Modells der Persoenlichkeit.* Regensburg, Germany: University of Regensburg, 1990.

26 Trull TJ, Geary DC. Comparison of the Big-Five Factor structure across samples of Chinese and American adults. *Journal of Personality Assessment,* 1997; 69(2): 324–41.

27 Lodhi PH, Deo S, Belhekar VM. The Five Factor model of personality in Indian context: Measurement and correlates. In: McCrae RR, Allik J (eds) *The Five Factor Model of Personality Across Cultures.* New York: Kluwer Academic, 2002; pp. 227–48.

28 Thompson ER. Development and validation of an international English Big-Five mini-markers. *Personality and Individual Differences,* 2008; 45(6): 542–48.

29 Szirmak Z, De Raad B. Taxonomy and structure of Hungarian personality traits. *European Journal of Personality,* 1994; 8: 95–117.

30 De Fruyt F, McCrae RR, Szirmák Z, Nagy J. The Five Factor personality inventory as a measure of the Five Factor Model: Belgian, American, and Hungarian comparisons with the NEO-PI-R. *Assessment,* 2004; 11(3): 207–15.

31 Costa PTJ, Terracciano A, McCrae RR. Gender differences in personality traits across cultures: Robust and surprising findings. *Journal of Personality and Social Psychology,* 2001; 81(2): 322–31.

32 Schmitt DP, Realo A, Voracek M, Allik J. Why can't a man be more like a woman? Sex differences in Big Five personality traits across 55 cultures. *Journal of Personality and Social Psychology,* 2008; 94(1): 168–82.

33 McCrae RR. Social consequences of experiential openness. *Psychological Bulletin*, 1996; 120(3): 323–37.

34 Cloninger CR, Svrakic DM, Przybeck TR. A psychobiological model of temperament and character. *Archives of General Psychiatry*, 1993; 50(12): 975–90.

35 Livesley WJ, Jackson DN. The internal consistency and factorial structure of behaviors judged to be associated with DSM-III personality disorders. *American Journal of Psychiatry*, 1986; 143(**11**): 1473.

36 Eysenck HJ. Dimensions of personality: 16, 5 or 3? Criteria for a taxonomic paradigm. *Personality and Individual Differences*, 1991; 12: 773–90.

37 Goldberg LR. An alternative "description of personality': The Big-Five Factor structure. *Journal of Personality and Social Psychology*, 1990; 59(6): 1216–29.

38 Jung CG. *Psychological Types*. London: Routledge, 1992 (first published 1921).

39 Myers IB, Myers PB. *Gifts Differing: Understanding Personality Type*. Palo Alto, CA: CPP Books, 1980, 1995.

40 Available from OPP in Europe (http://www.opp.eu.com) and from CPP in North America (http://www.cpp.com).

41 Keirsey D. *Please Understand Me II*. Topeka, KS: Topeka Bindery, 1998.

42 Keirsey D. *Please Understand Me II*. Available at: http://www.Keirsey.com (last accessed January 2013).

43 Jones EE, Davis KE, Gergen KJ. 1+Role playing variations and their informational value for person perception. *Journal of Abnormal and Social Psychology*, 1961; 63: 302–10 (epub 1961/09/01).

Team Working

5

Key points for reflection

❶ It is important to distinguish between 'groups' that are merely collections of individuals and 'teams' that optimise members deployment to make the whole better than the sum of individuals.

❷ There are various levels at which errors may be made or contributed to, namely organisational influences, unsafe supervision, preconditions for unsafe acts, and the unsafe acts themselves.

❸ For teams to be optimal, a number of roles need to be undertaken effectively.

Team working refers to the difference between the overall effectiveness of a team and the sum of the effectiveness of the individual members [1]. Team-working needs to be clearly distinguished from group-working:

- *Group-working* involves individuals coming together to perform a task or achieve a target; the group is as effective as the sum of its members.

- *Team-working* involves motivating and coordinating member's strengths and weaknesses to maximise the team's effectiveness as a whole; the team is more effective than the sum of its members.

People do not always value the importance of teamwork as much as the acquisition of technical skills and work places tend to default to group-working. To achieve team working requires a vision, and a leader who is able to develop that vision with the team and to use all the talents of the team to achieve the objective. In particular, it depends on the ability of all the members to align their own personal objectives with those of the team. They must also fill in for others in the team who lack skills or need help, and work flexibly between skill domains to achieve the agreed objective. Conflicting opinions are to be expected and the process of resolution enhances the strength of the team. Openness and honesty are essential. The main differences between teams and groups are summarised in **Table 5.1**. The UK's National Health Service (NHS) is the world's seventh largest employer with 1.4 million workers. The size of the organisation and its somewhat amorphous structure means that teams and interfaces are often indistinct and constantly changing. As the NHS has evolved to more sub-specialised care, and implemented European Working Time Directives, the numbers of teams and interfaces between them has mushroomed. Analysis by team inventory reveals that most of the time NHS staff work as groups rather than teams, an observation that will surprise few (see **Table 5.1**), and poor team working is a ubiquitous conclusion of investigations into adverse events.

Table 5.1 *Comparision of teams vs groups*

Teams	Groups
■ Decision by consensus	■ Decisions often not made
■ Disagreements discussed and resolved	■ Unresolved disagreements
■ Objectives well understood and agreed by members	■ Objectives often not agreed
■ All members contribute ideas	■ Personal feelings often hidden
■ Frequent team self examination	■ Discussions avoided regarding group functioning
■ Members understand their roles	■ Individuals protect their roles
■ Share leadership on as-needed basis	■ Leadership appointed

Healthcare is behind other industries in deploying teamwork training. In aviation, spectacular events such as the crash of a passenger plane onto the M6 motorway near Kegworth, the explosion of the Space Shuttle Columbia and the successful landing of a passenger jet on the Hudson river without loss of life, made it a priority. Aviation teamwork training has been developed over the last thirty years and is now into its fifth generation. The original concept was *error avoidance* and while that is a worthy goal, it is an impossible one. Academics concluded that the overarching goal for such training should be *error management*.

From the point of view of healthcare, other industries have given us teamwork training material and courses but not convincing evidence of their benefit. Some evidence has been gathered within health care and this is summarised below.

The benefits of teamwork

Evidence suggests that effective team-working brings the following benefits to patients:

- Reduction in mortality (by 5%) [2]
- Reduction in errors by positive contribution to performance [3]
- Reduction in patient time in hospital (shown to save more money than the cost of running the teams) [4]
- Improvement in service provision by streamlining services [5]
- Enhancement in patient satisfaction [6]
- Improved decision-making [7]

Evidence also suggests that effective team-working brings the following benefits to the staff:

- Decrease in sickness rates within the team (doctors in poor teams have nearly a two-fold increase in sickness rates) [8]
- Better decision-making, increased motivation and well-being; 21% of staff in real teams report above-threshold stress levels – compared to 30% of staff in loose teams or groups, and 35% of staff in no teams [9]

It is widely believed that effective teams produce improve patient outcomes, reduced hospital stays and costs, and improve the working lives of staff but these are not easy to prove. Whatever the science, there is no doubt about the politics of team working.

One of the strongest messages about the dangers of ineffective teamwork comes from the largest public enquiry into medicine in the UK. The Bristol Heart Scandal, as it has become known, ran from 1984 to 1995. During this time the death rate following complex paediatric heart operations in Bristol was higher than that in other units in the UK. The Public Inquiry that followed was chaired by Ian Kennedy. It ran from October 1998 to July 2001, considered 900,000 pages of documentation, and took witness oral evidence for 96 days. It found that performance had indeed been poor, and it had been principally due to poor team working. In his report [10], Kennedy made numerous significant references to the dangers of poor or ineffective team-working. One of his observations was that:

" ... it should be the norm for surgical teams (the surgeon, anaesthetist, theatre nurses, operating department assistants) to have time together and with other teams, such as those in the ITU, to review and develop their performance as a team."

The scandal and its enquiry had far-reaching consequences. Unlike other scandals and disasters, there was no single event or individual person behind it. Furthermore, the reason it came to public consciousness was not because of how uniquely bad the situation was, but the co-incidence of other circumstances:

- **A powerful outcome measure.** Paediatric heart surgery was the speciality, and even in the best of hands this specialty has a substantial mortality. This had two consequences: first, because paediatric deaths are highly emotive, they attract more public interest than an equivalent numbers of adult deaths; second, performance is easily and objectively measurable.

- **The presence of a whistle-blower.** Dr Stephen Bolsin, was appointed as a consultant anaesthetist in Bristol in 1989. He noted the high mortality rate, but unlike others was prepared to knowingly sacrifice his professional popularity, and his job, in order to correct the situation.

Without these two factors, it is probable that the events in Bristol would have gone on unchallenged. The relevance of this is that the failings seen in Bristol were – and are – not restricted to that unit, at that time! They are equally applicable to numerous other units in other specialties that have avoided the co-incidence of a powerful outcome measure and whistle-blower. Not surprisingly, the Kennedy report makes eerily familiar reading to other healthcare professionals.

Origin of the team approach

The emergence of the team approach can be traced back to the late 1920s and early 1930s with the now classic Hawthorne studies in the USA [11,12]. At the time there was a widespread fashion in the USA for *scientific management*, involving numerous time-and-motion experiments where things like workplace lighting, temperature, piped music, break patterns and pay systems were varied, and their effect on productivity was observed. The Western Electric Company conducted a study on lighting at their Hawthorne plant. They found that the lighting level made no difference to productivity, but doing the experiment did! When the factory was being studied, productivity improved; when the study ended, it fell back to previous levels. Keen to exploit this observed effect, managers set out better to define its cause and launched the now famous second Hawthorn study – the bank-wiring room [13].

The bank-wiring room

Bank wiring involved connecting wires to banks of terminals, in this case on telephone switching equipment. For the experiment, a special room was set up to do this. Working in the room were nine wirers who installed the wires, three solderers who soldered the connections, and two inspectors. A full-time observer was also in the room. Initially the workers would not talk freely when the observer was in earshot, but after three weeks, normal behaviours resumed including gossiping, game playing, quarrelling, teasing, helping and job trading. After the analysis, the researchers agreed that the most significant factor in the effectiveness of the bank-wiring room was the building of a sense of group identity, a feeling of social support and cohesion that came with increased worker interaction. Elton Mayo, one of the original researchers, pointed out the presence of certain critical conditions, which were identified for developing an effective work team [13,14]. These were:

- The manager had a personal interest in each person's achievements.
- He took pride in the record of the group.
- He helped the group work together to set its own conditions of work.
- He faithfully posted feedback on performance.
- The group took pride in its own achievement and had the satisfaction of outsiders showing interest in what they did.
- The group did not feel they were being pressured to change.
- Before changes were made, the group was consulted.
- The group developed a sense of confidence and candour.

These conditions can still be used to judge the effectiveness of any team in the twenty-first century.

Team motivation

We are all motivated throughout our waking hours. The problem is that the motivating factors we default to when valuable productive motivation is lacking read like a list of deadly sins – fear, greed, sloth, wrath, envy, and pride. Thus *demotivation* does not result from a 'passive absence' of motivation, but rather from an active negative force. Achieving *constructive* motivation is a central parts of team-working. Various methods can help achieve it.

Buy-in

Team members are motivated to perform if they agree that the team's goals are worthwhile. In order to agree with goals, team members must know what the goals are and why they matter. It obviously helps if they do matter! There are numerous examples of management schemes that failed largely because workers saw no point in them. Assuming that a team's goals do matter, then team members are motivated by clear explanations of where their particular task fits into the overall objective, and why it is important. The UK NHS is a large, high-profile public service in a mature democracy. This makes it more than averagely prone to one issue affecting 'buy in'. That issue is the conflict between *political* and *technical* motivation.

> **Political motivation** leads personnel to do things
> that improve the impression of the NHS's performance to the wider electorate.
>
> **Technical motivation** leads personnel to reduce
> the impact of disease on individual patients as far as possible.

As we all know, these motivations often come into conflict. There is an obvious tendency for front-line staff to be *technically* motivated and for administrators and managers to be *politically* motivated. Politically motivated people see technically motivated people as narrow and naive, while technically motivated people see politically motivated people as expedient and self-serving. Neither group is wholly right or wholly wrong.

The way to address the problem is for both sides to understand the other's position. If someone is trying to get over this kind of barrier to motivation with a fellow team member, it will generally be pretty obvious whether they are politically or technically motivated. First a conscious effort should be made to understand the colleague's point of view, before explaining their own – rather than the other way round.

Appreciation

Irrespective of how clearly a team member understands the importance of his or her role, they will be better motivated if their efforts are appreciated by their leaders and their fellow team members. Telling someone you appreciate what they are doing helps, as long as it is not over done. It is difficult to do this up the authority gradient. It is better, where possible, to *show* them that they are appreciated by involving them in tasks and decisions appropriate to their experience and skills.

Skill deployment

We acquire skills, both physical and mental, through frequent practice. We spend time on things we enjoy, so in all of us there is a close relationship between what we are good at and what we like doing.

Optimal team-working involves distributing tasks in a team so that each member has tasks that best match their skills. This has the obvious advantage that tasks given to people who are good at them will be done well, but also – and more importantly - it benefits the morale of the whole team. People are better motivated when they are doing something they are good at and enjoy, and are more likely to be appreciated and easier to 'buy in'.

Optimal skill deployment has major advantages but it is one of the things done less well within the NHS, This is because it takes a long time for team members to get to know what one another are good at. The process can be speeded up by encouraging more open discussion about what tasks need to be done and who would like to do what.

Team roles

Several attempts have been made to classify the roles people take in teams. The Belbin Team Inventory [15] is one of the better known ones. It overlaps with the personality types described in *Module 4* in that certain personalities tend towards certain roles. These are given overpage in **Table 5.2**.

When matching up tasks that *need* doing with what team members *like* doing, there will inevitably be routine, repetitive or tedious tasks that are not particularly popular with anyone. While these tasks are necessary and cannot be avoided, the boredom and consequent demotivation can be mitigated by variation so that individual team members do not always end up doing the same thing, but change roles within their capabilities.

The effects of varying roles and supervisor support have been extensively investigated in industrial settings [16]. However, the health service has been slower to implement such practices.

Table 5.2 *The Belbin Team Inventory*

Teams	Description of role
Plant	A creative generator of ideas
Resource investigator	Gets the necessary resources from outside the team
Coordinator	Overall coordinator or tasks
Shaper	Committed to achieving the team's goal and motivates others to do so
Monitor–evaluator	Detached and unbiased logical observer and judge of what is going on in the team
Team-worker	Diplomat who aids understanding, defuses aggression and resolves conflict
Implementer	Takes the suggestions of others and acts on them
Completer–finisher	A perfectionist who ensures all is as it should be
Specialist	Brings a details knowledge of the subject at hand, but tends to be disinterested in other things

Skill development

Related to skill deployment is skill *development*. People get familiar with the tasks they do regularly, so deployment affects the skills they develop. A particular issue with healthcare teams is continuity of service through changes in team membership. Many departments contain leading specialists in their fields, and consequently enjoy wide reputations for excellence. Too often, these departmental reputations collapse when key individuals retire or move. Another issue concerns provision of emergency services. This requires twenty-four-hour on-call teams with members working in shifts. A single highly skilled individual cannot provide such a service alone. These issues require development of team skills whereby the team members work together on particularly demanding tasks, partly to make the task easier and safer, but also to share the skill development between team members.

Use of time

If tasks were always given to those who are best at them and their skills were developed accordingly, the senior members of the team would end up doing more, and be busier and more stressed than the junior members. Redressing this situation involves recognising and optimising 'time use'. If a junior (or less able) team member is under-occupied, then identifying an area in which to develop their skills will improve their engagement with the team and relieve the busier members, allowing better use of their skills.

The optimal deployment of time and skills is something that requires team members to have a close working knowledge of each other. It is best done by the team and its immediate leader, but it is usually done by remote managers so it is rarely achieved in practice.

Briefing

Team briefing means to allocate time at the start of the day or shift for a team to meet and prepare themselves. It is routinely employed in many safety-critical industries. Briefing is a skill and it needs to be developed. It is more than an exchange of information. It also lowers authority or power–distance gradients and empowers more junior team members to bring up concerns or ask questions to clarify uncertainties. It also makes team members *people* rather than *roles!*

Although a pre-shift briefing should be encouraged in all clinical settings, the same skills are required to conduct 'mini-briefs' during the working day. These serve to alert all team members of alterations to plans or changes of situations. It is only by this form of communication that all team members can have the same mental model and situational awareness of their environment and challenges. In periods of lower workload, when the team have greater cognitive capacity, it is recommended that these briefings or updates should be encouraged.

People often fail to recognise that others with whom they interact have a totally different perception of the world around them. These differences are based on each individual's experience, role, background, personality types and numerous other factors. Every time there is a perception mismatch, there is the opportunity for misunderstanding and the potential for errors.

Process improvement

Process improvement refers to a particular team's performance being at least maintained and ideally showing steady improvement as the weeks, months and years pass. The single most important internal tool in process improvement is *feedback*. In many non-healthcare industries, such as aviation, navigation and the military, debriefing is a formalised process whereby team members meet at the completion of a task or shift to discuss any problems that arose in a situation (and could be avoided in the future) and anything that went well (and could be repeated in the future). System feedback – that is the adoption of beneficial actions and the avoidance of detrimental actions – is the mechanism by which debriefing has its effect.

The effectiveness of a standardised briefing and debriefing routine after surgical training was studied in a large research project, in which the theatre team routinely recorded misunderstandings and case delays and gave scores on case efficiency. Any problems that were identified were reviewed and rectified by a medical team training committee. A safety attitudes questionnaire was administered after training and one year later. The items identified at debriefing were analysed to see if they were better or worse one and two years after training. A total of 4863 debriefings were analysed.

One year after training, case delays decreased significantly from 23% to 10% and the mean case efficiency score increased from 4.07 to 4.87; both changes were sustained after two years. Data from one-year and two-year follow-up showed a decrease in preoperative delays (from 16% to 7%), equipment issues and case delays (from 24% to 7%), as well as a reduction (from 23% to 3%) of cases with low case efficiency scores (less than 3). Adherence to timing guidelines for administration of prophylactic antibiotics improved from 85% to 97. Participants also perceived improvements in both teamwork and patient safety, and a major systems issue regarding orders for perioperative medication was identified and corrected [17]. It is sensible to encourage debriefing where it is feasible to do so, but in many healthcare settings formalised debriefing meetings are not practicable because the shifts or tasks of individual team members finish at different times and there is no specific time point when everyone is available at once. As an example, consider a theatre team at the end of an operation. The surgeons finish closing the wound, de-scrub and start to write their notes. The scrub team are still busy assembling, checking, cleaning and packing up the equipment. The anaesthetist's workload increases during the wake-up phase. Then, when the anaesthetist's job is done, the surgeon goes to review the patient.

In situations like this, formal timetabled debriefing is unlikely to be convenient and therefore unlikely to be successful. It is worth bearing in mind, however, that (all else being equal) a team that uses a regular system of feedback will outperform a team that does not. Even if formal debriefing sessions are not practical, feedback should still be elicited and applied. This can be done using a 'hot debrief'. In a hot debrief, any issue – whether positive or negative – is discussed at the first available opportunity after it occurs [17].

Wrong-side surgery is a problem that particularly affects neurosurgical departments. This is the subject of **Vignette 5.1**.

Vignette 5.1 Wrong-side neurosurgery

One such department was working to avoid such errors and had implemented an apparently watertight checking system that seemed to have fixed the problem. Eventually however, a wrong-side error did occur.

A junior surgeon was operating and shortly after the operation began – on the wrong side – the senior (responsible) surgeon came into the theatre and recognised the error. The operation was immediately halted. Members of the theatre team who had been in theatre at the beginning of the operation and during the checking process were asked about what happened, with no implications of blame.

The issue was fresh in their minds and a number of causative factors emerged, the principal one being that the checks had been followed but the read-back system had used leading questions, including: *'This is the right side, isn't it?'* rather than *'What is the intended side?'* and *'What is the prepared side?'*. The checking system was changed accordingly. The senior surgeon completed the operation on the correct side. The harm was limited to an extra scar, about which the patient was graciously forgiving!

In this true story, 'hot' debriefing enabled an accurate, blame free, and decisive analysis of what had happened and how the system could be changed to prevent such occurrences in the future. It is doubtful that enough detail of the checking process would have been retained had the usual investigative processes been followed without a hot-debriefing.

Teamwork training systems

Safety-critical industries use a variety of teamwork training programs. Although the healthcare industry is probably more complex and patients are more idiosyncratic than aircraft, ships or power stations, they share a critical similarity in that they all rely on effective multiprofessional teamwork, and effective communication in stressful, fluctuating environments.

Medical practice is particularly challenging because critical decisions are often made with incomplete evidence. Personnel in other safety-critical industries have learned the 'hard way' about the introduction of human factors training and development of the skills needed to cope with these challenges during the last twenty-five years. By learning from their experiences, there may be an opportunity to shorten that journey in medicine.

During the formative years of human factors training in aviation, there was considerable opposition from some of the senior airline crew members. They felt it called into question their technical abilities and the way they had always conducted themselves and managed their on-board team, and also ran counter to much of their prior training. The earlier courses concentrated purely on the *behavioural* skills of the pilots. In the mid-1980s, working groups from airlines that had initiated Crew Resource Management (CRM) training programs concluded that the ultimate goal was to embed the principles of effective teamwork into all flight and general operational training. In other words, these new 'softer skills' were deemed to be as important as 'technical skills' and, as such, should be taught to all personnel who were part of the operational division of an airline, with updates throughout their careers.

NOTECHS

In order to implement CRM training in large organisations, there was a need to formalise teaching and vocabulary, and to assess the effectiveness of the training. In aviation, objective frameworks to measure the effectiveness of human interaction were developed. The currently used training system in aviation is called NOTECHS (Non-Technical Skills). The EC Directorate General of Energy and Transport and the Civil Aviation Authorities of France, the Netherlands, Germany and the UK sponsored the NOTECHS project which ran from March 1997 to March 1998.

The goal was to provide a feasible and efficient method of assessment of individual pilot's non-technical skills in a multi-crew environment. The behavioural marker system used by NOTECHS describes human interaction in four main categories:

- two cognitive categories (*situation awareness* and *decision-making*) and
- two social categories (*leadership* and *team-working*).

The NOTECHS category of teamwork is also referred to as *communication* and *cooperation*. It is divided into four *elements*, each of which has observable and teachable *behaviours* – both positive and negative (see **Table 5.3**). With this system, an experienced observer can pinpoint which elements of teamwork are effective or ineffective. If it is used in training or coaching, those same behaviours can be observed and then trained to contribute to a more effective team performance.

The two main attributes of the system are consistency of language and objectivity. Evaluation of such training has shown that it needs to be tailored to particular settings and cultures; it is not a 'one size fits all' approach [18]. An experienced coach should be able to use this framework to identify areas where teams need assistance and also to show teams how they are performing in an effective manner.

The NOTECHS system has been extrapolated for use in various studies within healthcare:

- Non-Technical Skills for Surgeons (NOTTS) [19]
- Anaesthetists' Non-Technical Skills (ANTS) [20]
- Oxford Notechs (ON) [21]
- Team Self-Review (TSR) [22]

Table 5.3 gives a generic example of the team-working category of a NOTECHS system that has been used successfully to train teams in operating theatres.

While the NOTECHS system is a great help in assessing teamwork skills on the ground (and in the sky!), it is short term and limited in its scope. In **Table 5.3** a number of significant issues are missing: motivation, skill development, skill deployment, time use, and process improvement, to name but some. These omissions reflect the origin and nature of the system, in as much as it was used by independent observers of flight-deck behaviour among airline crew over periods of a few hours. It was implemented after a number of aviation accidents in which poor team working was heavily implicated.

Table 5.3 *Generic example of the team-working category of a NOTECHS system used to train teams in operating theatres*

Team function	Traits and roles
Team building/maintaining	■ Relaxed ■ Supportive ■ Open ■ Inclusive ■ Polite ■ Friendly ■ Uses humour: ■ Does not compete
Support of others	■ Helps others ■ Offers assistance ■ Gives feedback
Understanding team needs	■ Listens to others ■ Recognizes ability of team ■ Considers condition of others ■ Gives personal feedback
Conflict solving	■ Keeps calm in conflicts ■ Suggests conflict solutions ■ Concentrates on what is right

Error management

This is a key concept in human factors management that has relevance to leadership, system design, stress management and situation awareness as well as team-working; it is included in this module, but could equally be considered with these other subjects, or on its own. That concept is that human error is unavoidable and must be *managed* rather than *prevented*.

Early human factors training programs concentrated on preventing human errors, but workers in the field came to the conclusion that this goal was unachievable. Human error is ubiquitous and inevitable, and teamwork training should be expanded to include error countermeasures.

Swiss Cheese Model

James Reason of Manchester University proposed the so-called Swiss Cheese Model of accident prevention, in which an organisation's defence against errors can be modelled as slices of cheese with randomly placed holes of different sizes [23]. When the holes in multiple slices line up, errors occur (**Figure 5.1**). This model has been used successfully in a range of safety critical settings ranging from aviation security to safety in nuclear facilities. To date, however, it has had little impact in medicine.

Most accidents are caused by one or more of four failure levels:

- Organisational influences.
- Unsafe supervision.
- Preconditions for unsafe acts.
- The unsafe acts themselves.

Protection in the Swiss Cheese Model is seen as a series of barriers, each with its own weaknesses, that vary in place and size. Some may be avoidable lapses or errors, some may be unavoidable hazards. Failures happen when weaknesses in all the barriers line up to give a 'trajectory of accident opportunity'. This fits in well with our experience of many accidents, whereby a series of errors is generally involved, and most potential accidents are caught in the early stages.

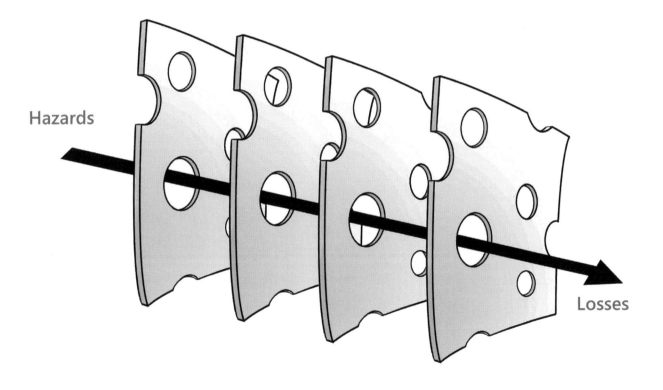

Hazards

Losses

Figure 5.1 *The Swiss cheese model (based on Reason, 1997 [23]).*

Threat and Error Management (TEM) Model

Accidents are fortunately rare but this means that simple accident rates are a highly insensitive statistical measure of safety, making it difficult to assess the effectiveness of different interventions. This limitation in error-avoidance research motivated the development of the University of Texas Threat and Error Management Model (TEM) [24,25] as shown in **Figure 5.2**. This classifies the causes of adverse outcomes into threats and errors. Threats are not errors – they are the circumstances that *provoke* them. The term *hazard* is also used in a similar manner in much of the evidence base on risk assessment and management. Consider the following examples:

- Ice on the road is a *threat* – but driving too fast is an *error*.
- Allergy to penicillin is a *threat* – but giving an allergic person penicillin is an *error*.
- A missing identity bracelet on a patient is a *threat* – but taking the wrong patient into theatre is an *error*.

The TEM uses three lines of defence against accidents: (i) avoid, (ii) trap and (iii) mitigate.

I. AVOID

Much of error avoidance is about recognising threats and, where possible, managing them. With respect to the examples above, ice on the roads can be managed by gritting where economically feasible, and modern cars can be fitted with low-temperature warning systems; hospital notes include prominently displayed warnings about allergy; when identity bracelets have to be removed from patients, they should be replaced, where practicable, on another limb as soon as possible.

II. TRAP

When errors do occur they do not always lead to disaster. The error can be 'trapped' with no bad consequences, for example, by slowing down on the icy road, or by returning the wrong patient to the ward (and getting the right one).

III. MITIGATE

The error can have bad consequences that can be mitigated, thus leading to a good outcome. Giving penicillin to an allergic patient can be mitigated by treating the patient with adrenaline (epinephrine), steroids and fluid.

An error can lead to a bad outcome because it is not – or cannot be – mitigated. This is illustrated in **Figure 5.2**, where threats and errors are managed by getting to the dashed boxes via the shortest possible route. The longer the route taken, the greater the risk of an adverse outcome and the greater the cost and stress for team members.

The TEM was developed in response to problems in the field of aviation. Accidents in commercial aviation are caused by series of coincident minor errors and misunderstandings – the so-called 'accident chain' [26]. These minor errors are very common but accidents are rare. People investigating accidents only had access to data on a small proportion of such incidents so, in order to reduce accident rates, more data was needed on the contributing factors.

This led to a number of initiatives aimed at gathering data outside the context of accidents. Voluntary reporting of near misses is now commonplace in aviation, as is professional observation of cockpit behaviour. Airlines have also adopted real-time monitoring and reporting of aircraft performance as a means of trapping and mitigating errors [27].

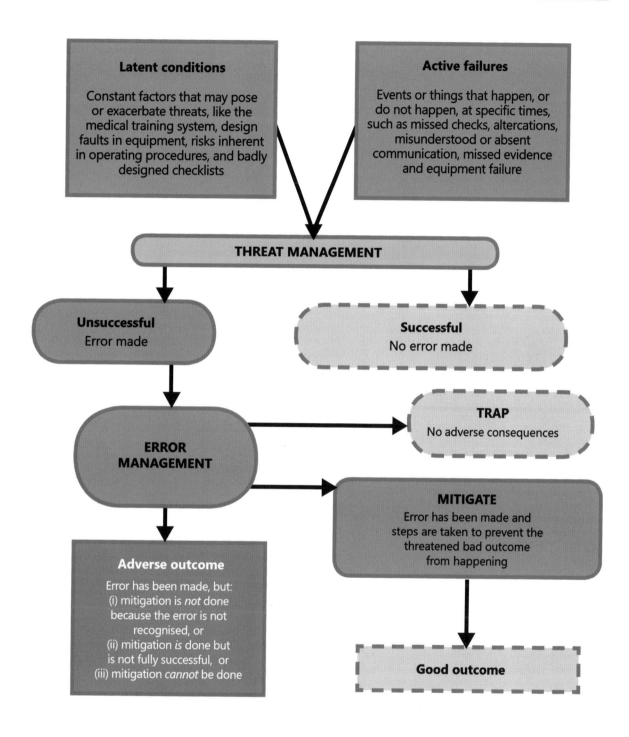

Figure 5.2 *The University of Texas Threat and Error Management (TEM) Model.*

The same applies to the field of medicine. Mortality rates and quality of life measures remain a goal of research, but they are insensitive, and require large and expensive studies. Surrogate markers are therefore used in the early stages of research into the effectiveness of interventions.

In the case of safety and human factors, these surrogates are *threats* and *errors*. They have been used in simulation and observation studies that look for minor errors and aim to reduce, trap or mitigate them [28]. As an example of the use of the TEM, consider the case in the true-life **Vignette 5.2**.

> ### Vignette 5.2   Intrathecal vincristine
>
> Wayne Jowett died in 2001 in a well-run oncology unit in Nottingham [29]. Chemotherapy for his leukaemia comprised two drugs: cytosine (to be given by the intrathecal (spinal) route which involved lumbar puncture) and vincristine (to be given intravenously). The senior registrar Dr Mulhem was supervising the senior house officer, Dr Morton, who was passed the cytosine, then the vincristine. He wrongly administered both to the patient intrathecally.
>
> It was a lethal error. It occurred despite product warnings, a body of literature that stresses the dangers, previous well-publicised cases, local protocols in addition to elaborate pharmacy defences that included procedures to ensure the drugs were never administered at the same time (or on the same day).

Numerous background threats and errors conspired to cause the disaster:

- The senior doctors assumed that the juniors knew their subject (it was later argued that the relevant induction and training systems had been faulty). A *threat*.
- In Dr Mulhem's previous workplace, two syringes containing different drugs were commonly given intrathecally and simultaneously. A *threat*.
- The patient had arrived late for his therapy and extra efforts had been made to accommodate him before the day-ward closed. A *threat*.
- The staff member who went to collect the drugs from the pharmacy did not know they should be separated, so they were transported together. An *error*.
- The nurse delivering them to the bedside also brought them together. An *error*.
- Dr Mulhem did not notice that the vincristine was to be given intravenously. An *error*.
- Or that it was prescribed for the following day. An *error*.
- The labelling and the general appearance of the two syringes was similar. A *threat*.
- Dr Mulhem said at one stage he wrongly thought the second drug was methotrexate, which is given intrathecally, partly because vincristine should not be available on the same day. An *error*.
- Dr Morton was surprised to be given a second syringe, so queried the drug and the route verbally, although not sufficiently challengingly to abort the disaster that followed. A *failed opportunity* to trap.
- Connectors for both the syringes – to either the lumbar puncture needle or to the intravenous cannula – were interchangeable (even in 2012). A *threat*.

As newcomers to the hospital, both of the junior doctors assumed a number of things (this was unreasonable – and is quite typical):

- First, that the organisation had all its procedures in place.
- Second, that the other doctor was competent to do what he was doing.
- Third, that the other doctor had read the patient's record.

Both doctors then overrode an all-important clue: *they were presented with something that was not routine and that they did not understand*. This last chance to protect the patient from harm was a prompt to decision-making, yet it was ignored. In mitigation, it was subtle – just one point buried in complexity –

and it was unexpected. Essentially this 'non-routine event' was the presentation of a second injectable drug, which neither doctor actually understood well enough to protect the patient. A more experienced and more safety-aware doctor might have taken this non-routine event as a sign to stop, to take stock, reflect and reassess the situation. The error, therefore, was caused by a long chain of latent conditions which created a threat, and active failures that could have been 'trapped'. In this case, mitigation was not possible.

The complex team structure that exists within the healthcare industry, as summarised in **Figure 5.3**, stands to benefit from human factors training.

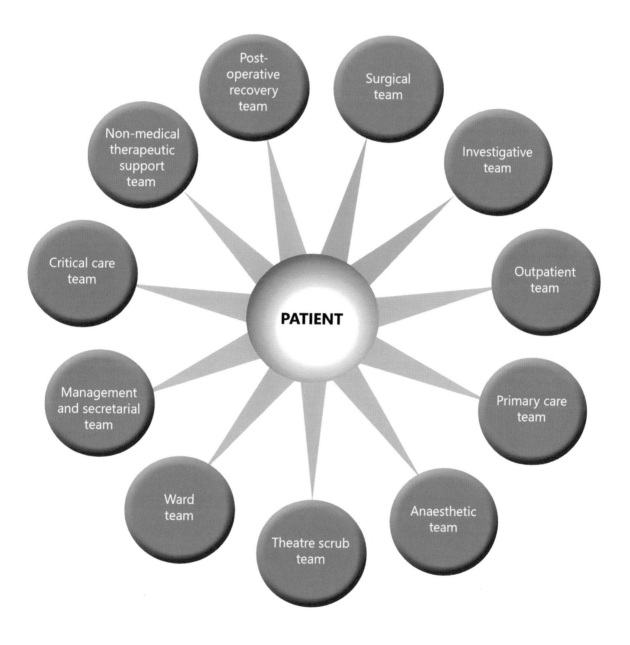

Figure 5.3 *Multiple Teams in the NHS (adapted from Giddings AEB, Williamson C. The Leadership and Management of Surgical Teams, Royal College of Surgeons, 2007 [30]).*

Conclusions

There is now good evidence that effective teamwork leads to improved patient outcomes, reduces costs and improves staff morale. Elements of human factors training developed in aviation over the past twenty-five years can be extrapolated to medical teams, provided that the key differences in medicine are recognised. It seems entirely sensible to learn from other safety-critical industries as appropriate and to adapt the successes from their programmes for making the healthcare system safer for patients. Wherever human factors training has been introduced, it has been met with cynicism from a number of people, but those numbers continue to dwindle as the programme develops and its advantages become clear. An understanding of ourselves and our colleagues leads to the ultimate goal of greater safety for our patients and has the added bonus of increasing efficiency and contentment at work.

In healthcare, human factors and teamwork training should be considered as important as technical training. The goal should be to introduce such training from the first day at medical school until the last day of an individual's career. The only way to embed such training into the culture is by including it in the curricula. The various regulatory bodies should require that the human factors elements of performance are assessed in the same way as the technical elements.

The content of human factors courses should include the understanding of authority gradients and how people behave, error management, communication, situation awareness, decision-making, and briefing and debriefing. One only has to read the report on any incident in healthcare, or any other safety-critical industry, to realise that the root causes of most incidents are the very topics mentioned in this paragraph. A football team would never take to the field without a briefing from its manager and an aircraft would never start to taxi without a full briefing of the crew by the captain.

It is clear that the healthcare industry is far more complex than other industries, but this only makes the case for human factors training stronger.

References

1 Wiener EL, Kanki BG, Helmreich RL. *Cockpit Resource Management*. San Diego, CA: Academic Press, 1995.

2 West MA, Borrill C, Dawson JF, Scully JW, Carter M, Anelay S, *et al.* The link between management of employees and patient mortality in acute hospitals. *International Journal of Human Resource Management*, 2002; 13(8): 1299–310.

3 Firth-Cozens J. Celebrating teamwork. *Quality in Health Care*, 1998; 7(Suppl.), S3–S7.

4 Sommers LS, Marton KI, Barbaccia JC, Randolph J. Physician, nurse and social worker collaboration in primary care for chronically ill seniors. *Archives of Internal Medicine*, 2000; 160(12): 1825–33.

5 Ross F, Rink E, Furne A. Integration or pragmatic coalition? An evaluation of nursing teams in primary care. *Journal of Inter-Professional Care*, 2000; 14(3): 259–67.

6 Hughes SL, Cummings J, Weaver F, Manheim L, Braun B, Conrad K. A randomised trial of the cost effectiveness of VA hospital-based home care for the terminally ill. *Health Services Research*, 1992; 26(6): 801–17.

7 West MA, Tjosvold D, Smith KG. *International Handbook of Organisational Teamwork and Co-operative Working*. Chichester: John Wiley and Sons, 2003.

8 Kivimäki M, Sutinen R, Elovainio M, Vahtera J, Räsänen K, Töyry S, *et al.* Sickness absence in hospital physicians: 2 year follow up study on determinants. *Occupational and Environmental Medicine*, 2001; 58: 361–66.

9 Carter AJ, West MA. Sharing the burden: Team-work in health care settings. In: Firth-Cozens J, Payne R (eds) *Stress in Health Professionals: Psychological and Organizational Causes and Interventions*. New York: Wiley, 1999; pp 191–202.

10 Kennedy I. *The Bristol Royal Infirmary Enquiry Final Report*, 2001.

11 Roethlisberger FJ, Dickson WJ, Wright HA, Pforzheimer CH. *Management and the Worker: An Account of a Research Program Conducted by the Western Electric Company*, Hawthorne Works, Chicago. Cambridge, MA: Harvard University Press, 1939.

12 Franke RH, Kaul JD. The Hawthorn Experiments: First statistical interpretation. *American Sociological Review*, 1978; 43(5): 623–43.

13 Mayo EG. *The Human Problems of an Industrialised Civilization*. New York: McMillan, 1933.

14 Dyer JL. Team research and team training: A state-of-the-art review. In: Muckler FA (ed.). *Human Factors Review*. Santa Monica, CA: Human Factors Society, 1984; pp. 285–332.

15 Belbin RM. *Team Roles at Work*, 2nd edn. Oxford: Butterworth-Heinemann, 2010.

16 Griffin MA, Patterson MG, West MA. Job satisfaction and teamwork: The role of supervisor support. *Journal of* Organizational Behaviour, 2001; 22(5): 537–50.

17 Wolf FA, Way LW, Stewart L. The efficacy of medical team training: Improved team performance and decreased operating room delays a detailed analysis of 4863 cases. *Annals of Surgery*, 2010; 252(3): 477–85.

18 Helmreich RL, Wilhelm JA, Klinect JR, Merritt AC. Culture, error and crew resource management. In: Salas E, Bowers CA, Edens E (eds) *Improving Teamwork in Organizations*. Hillsdale, NJ: Erlbaum, 2012.

19 Yule S, Maran N, Rowley D, Youngson G, Paterson-Brown S. Surgeons' non-technical skills in the operating room: Reliability testing of the NOTSS behavior rating system. *World Journal of Surgery*, 2008; 32(4): 548–56.

20 Fletcher G, Flin R, McGeorge P, Glavin R, Maran N, Patey R. Anaesthetists' non-technical skills (ANTS): Evaluation of a behavioural marker system. *British Journal of Anaesthesia*, 2003; 90(5): 580–88.

21 Mishra A, Catchpole K, Dale T, McCulloch P. The influence of non-technical performance on technical outcome in laparoscopic cholecystectomy. *Surgical Endoscopy*, 2008; 22(1): 68–73.

22 Henderson S, Mills M, Hobbs A, Bleakley A, Boyden J, Walsh L. Surgical team self-review: Enhancing organisational learning in the Royal Cornwell Hospital Trust. In: Cook M, Noyes J, Masakowski Y (eds) *Decision-making in Complex Environments*. Aldershot: Ashgate, 2007.

23 Reason J. Human error: models and management. *British Medical Journal*, 2000; 320(7237): 768–70 (epub 2000/03/17).

24 Helmreich RL. On error management: Lessons from aviation. *British Medical Journal*, 2000; 320(7237): 781–85 (epub 2000/03/17).

25 Helmreich RL, Klinect JR, Wilhelm JA. System safety and threat and error management: The line operational safety audit (LOSA). In: *Proceedings of the Eleventh International Symposium on Aviation Psychology*. Columbus, OH: Ohio State University, 2001; pp. 1–6.

26 Reason J. *Managing the Risks of Organizational Accidents*. Aldershot: Ashgate, 1997.

27 O'Leary M. The British Airways human factors reporting programme. *Reliability Engineering and System Safety*. London: British Airways, 2002; pp. 245–55.

28 Catchpole KR, Giddings AE, Wilkinson M, Hirst G, Dale T, De Leval MR. Improving patient safety by identifying latent failures in successful operations. *Surgery*, 2007; 142(1): 102–10 (epub 2007/07/17).

29 Toft B. *External Inquiry into the Adverse Incident that Occurred at Queen's Medical Centre, Nottingham, 4th January 2001*. UK Department of Health, 2001.

30 Giddings AEB, Williamson C. *The Leadership and Management of Surgical Teams*. London: The Royal College of Surgeons of England, 2007.

Leadership

6

Key points for reflection

❶ Different leadership styles will tend to deliver different outcomes for our staff and patients.

❷ There are some key features of effective leaders wherever they sit within an organisation.

❸ Different styles of leadership may be needed for different situations. The effective leader is able to recognise, acknowledge and act upon such contingencies.

The prominent position of leaders in society has made them a topic of study for centuries. Plato addressed the question in his writings and considered that leaders should be taken from the ruling class (of Athens at that time) and specifically educated to lead, then they should take personal responsibility for the common good and put this priority over issues such as honesty with the populace. Plato made a distinction between ruling by law and the art of ruling by persuasion [1].

These views were developed further and arguably modified by Niccolò Machiavelli (1469–1527), albeit with different terminology. He agreed that leadership could be taught. His book of 1532, *The Prince* [2], is an instruction manual on political leadership, and the use and retention of power. In it, his discussions of the use of 'fear' and 'love' are analogous to Plato's 'law' and 'persuasion'. He advises that leaders seek to appear to govern virtuously, but in reality act on expediency. They should be seen to be merciful, faithful, humane, frank and religious, but not actually *be* these things. He deals with this issues of generosity *vs* meanness, honesty *vs* reputation, and cruelty *vs* kindness with a similarly expedient rather than principled approach. Most famous is his belief that within certain limits it is better to be feared than loved because:

> *"Men worry less about doing an injury to one who makes himself loved than to one who makes himself feared."*

Machiavelli's ideas have been widely applied to leadership in general. His target audience was medieval Italian princes. The system in which they operated meant that they predominantly used one style of leadership, which we now call *autocratic*. Five hundred years after it was written, *The Prince* remains one of the most controversial – and widely read – books on leadership. Widely read, because his advice is seen as effective. Controversial, because it is also seen as immoral!

Nineteenth-century studies on leadership sought personal characteristics, or traits, that were common to effective leaders and led to the trait theories of Thomas Carlyle [3] and Francis Galton [4]. Carlisle assessed the traits of great historical figures, while Galton, in his 1869 book *Hereditary Genius: An Inquiry into its Laws and Consequences* studied the leadership skills of the blood relatives of powerful individuals. He found that they declined from first-degree to second-degree relationships, and concluded that leadership skills were *inherited* rather than learned. Galton reached this conclusion for most of the areas he studied, leading to his support for eugenics. This theory of inherited traits was accepted for many years, relating to such traits as intelligence, morality, self-confidence, adaptability and persistence and was highly influential in the development of psychology in England and indirectly in areas such as education policy [5].

Machiavelli aside, most models remained trait-based and descriptive, making little attempt to instruct on how to lead. By the middle of the twentieth century, trait theory faced severe criticism on the grounds that people who are good leaders in one situation are not necessarily good in another, so effectiveness must depend on some interaction between leaders and their environment [6]. This led to a backlash against trait theory from the 1950s to the 1970s. Improved methods of research and statistical analysis led to the more flexible idea that both the situation a leader finds him or herself in and his or her personality traits are predictive of their performance [7].

Leadership style

Leadership style is an alternative way of classifying leaders to their traits and situations. Styles refer to their behaviour patterns. The original experiments in leadership style were due to Kurt Lewin (1890–1947), who was a prominent applied psychologist in the mid-twentieth century. In 1939 he published the results of his leadership experiments [8]. He is best known for coining the term 'action research' meaning the process of planning action in an organisation, taking that action, and observing its effects before continuing with it or changing. He is also well-known for Lewin's equation which stated that behaviour is a function of a person in their immediate environment. When his equation was published in 1936 it defied the prevailing view that behaviour was purely determined by a person's past.

In one leadership study, Lewin identified several groups of ten-year-old boys from various boys' clubs, and gave them tasks of interest to boys such as making masks, model aeroplanes and soap carving. Each group had an adult leader and was professionally observed over a period of three months. The leaders presented a series of different leadership styles, so their effect on the groups could be compared. Lewin was particularly interested in their effects on the aggression expressed by the boys in each group. The styles and definitions he used are shown in **Table 6.1**.

A commonly misunderstood point about these experiments is that they were to compare democratic and autocratic styles. The laissez-faire group was simply included as a control and was intended to represent 'minimum leadership'. The authoritarian group was divided into two autocratic styles: *aggressive authoritarian* in which aggression among the boys was noted at a high level throughout the sessions, and *passive authoritarian* in which little aggression was shown with the leader present but once the leader left the room, aggression levels increased ten-fold. The main results of Lewin's experiments were:

- **Overt aggression** This was eight times greater between boys in the autocratic group than in the democratic group. None of this was directed towards the leader. The boys' reaction to the leader involved submission or attention seeking. In two cases, the general inter-member aggression condensed into aggression against an individual boy. In both cases the boys left the experiment, and in both cases the leader saw these 'victims' as natural group leaders.

- **Egocentric behaviour.** This occurred twice as much in the autocratic group than in the democratic group.

Table 6.1 *Styles and definitions used by leaders in Lewin's experiments on aggression among boys* [8]

Authoritarian	Democratic	Laissez-faire
■ Leader determined policy	■ Leader assisted group to determine policies and decisions	■ Leader did not participate in decisions ■ Group had complete freedom over group and individual decisions
■ Leader dictated techniques and steps one at a time ■ Future steps were unknown to a large degree	■ Activity was planned during the first discussion period with general steps sketched out ■ Leader suggested two or three alternatives from which the group chose, when technical advice was needed	■ Leader supplied materials and made it clear that information would be supplied when asked for ■ Leader took no other part in discussions
■ Leader dictated who did what task and who worked in which subgroup	■ Group members were free to work with whoever they chose ■ Whole group decided how tasks were divided	■ Leader did not participate
■ Leader was friendly or impersonal, but not openly hostile and did not participate in activities except to demonstrate	■ Leader was objective with both praise and criticism and tried to be a regular group member in spirit without doing too much of the work	■ Leader made infrequent comments on member's activities unless questioned ■ Leader made no attempt to participate or interfere with the course of events

Later experiments suggest that groups that are under stress perform better with authoritarian leadership, while groups that are not under stress are more productive with better quality when under democratic leadership [9].

Autocratic leadership

Autocratic leadership is at its best when the team members are under stress and the leader's judgement and decision-making is the best in the group. This implies that they have the highest level of competence at judging the task in hand, and it occurs when the leader has extensive direct experience of the tasks and situation of the group members. Military authority is a good example. In Lewin's experiments, which gave a clear endorsement of democratic leadership, the leaders were all adults and the group members were all boys. If a leader has greater seniority, experience and knowledge than their team, this does not alone imply that an autocratic style is the best style.

Autocratic leadership is at its worst in situations where a leader lacks direct experience of the front-line tasks of their team, and lacks the intelligence to recognise their own limitations.

Democratic leadership

Democratic leadership is at its best under relatively low stress conditions and with complex tasks, particularly if those tasks require the cooperation of a number of people working in different specialist areas. In such situations, the leader is not likely to have detailed knowledge of each person's specialty. They do not need detailed knowledge of any of the specialties if their democratic leadership skills are good. The widespread success of the democratic leadership style means that people with these skills tend to do well wherever they are.

Democratic leadership is at its worst in high stress situations with inexperienced teams that have leaders experienced in all aspects of the team's task, the same situation where autocratic leadership is at its best.

The basic styles in Lewin's experiments, and their associated group performances, have been repeatedly confirmed in other experiments. The laissez-faire style has been treated as an *actual* style rather than just a control group as was intended, and other styles have been added, including narcissistic and toxic styles. Lewin's democratic and autocratic styles have been developed into theories of situational leadership whereby individuals adapt their styles to suite their situation.

Situational models

Leadership style theories make *group performance* a function of style and the situation. Situational leadership theories make *style* a variable, as well as the situation and performance. Now style can be varied and optimised so that optimal leadership style is a function of the situation. Good leaders can suite many situations by adapting themselves to them. Situational theories of leadership arose as part of the backlash against trait theory. For example, Lewin's styles of autocratic, democratic and laissez-faire (**Table 6.1**) have been suggested to suit situations of urgent crisis, day-to-day management and creative problem solving respectively [10].

A number of theories of this type have been proposed, some using the term *contingency* instead of *situation*. The best known is that of Hersey and Blanchard, which proposes different leadership styles and different levels of what they call *follower maturity*. Effective leadership depends on matching the leadership style to both the task and the follower maturity (**Table 6.2**). A good leader's behaviour is then a function of the followers they are dealing with, as well as their personality and the situation [11]. A good leader balances the needs of the task in hand, the team as a whole, and the individuals within the team, and reviews and updates this optimal balance when the task or team members change. Hersey *et al.* (2008) proposed four leadership styles based on two behavioural domains – task driven and relationship driven (as shown in **Table 6.2**). None of these styles is thought to be the best one for all situations; good leaders are capable of adapting their style to different situations.

The other central part of their theory is their system of classifying followers into four levels of maturity, M1, M2, M3 and M4. Again these are derived from two domains – competence and commitment and they are shown in **Table 6.3**. People have different levels of maturity for different tasks, so that someone who is M4 for their job may be M1 if asked to do something they think is not worth bothering with.

Table 6.2 *Matrix of Hersey–Blanchard leadership styles S1, S2, S3, and S4 [11]*

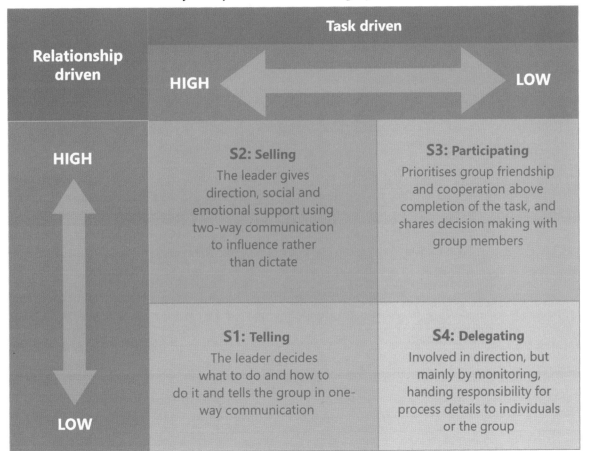

Table 6.3 *Hersey–Blanchard levels of maturity among followers [11]*

Level	Characteristics
M1	Incompetent or unwilling to do or take responsibility for the task in hand
M2	Not competent but willing to gain the necessary competence and do the task
M3	Competent to do the task but are not aware of this and think that they are not
M4	Can do the task, know they can and are willing to do it

Transactional/transformational model

Eric Berne developed the idea of transactional analysis in interpersonal dealings, whereby interactions are modelled as transactions in which people get what they want from others in exchange for giving the other person what they want. Applying this idea to the relationship between leaders and followers led to the concept of *transactional leadership*. A transactional leader has external reward or coercive power and their team follows them in exchange for reward or avoidance of punishment [12]. Transactional leaders therefore work on the rational conscious level of their followers.

A transformational leader, on the other hand, does not engage in deal-making to get a job done but motivates followers emotionally. They are visible, good communicators, conscious of the ultimate aims of what the group is doing, and use non-power based methods to achieve them.

Table 6.4 illustrates the differences between the transformational and transactional leaders [13].

Table 6.4 *Differences between transformational and transactional leaders* [13]

Transactional leadership	Transformational leadership
■ Head down	■ Head up
■ Focuses on the practical	■ Focuses on the possible
■ Coaches/directs	■ Inspires
■ Does the job right	■ Does the right job
■ Harnesses or directs energy	■ Creates energy
■ Turns ideas into reality	■ Has vision and ideas
■ Focuses on the next intermediate objective	■ Focuses on ultimate objectives
■ Performance oriented	■ People oriented
■ Sets objectives	■ Questions assumptions
■ Fixes problems	■ Creates problems

Toxic leaders

A toxic leader is one who leaves a group or organisation worse-off than they found it. Toxic leaders are not in positions of leadership because of their leadership skills! They must therefore be in these positions for other reasons, or because of a change in their leadership skills since their appointment.

The term was first coined by Marcia Lynn Whicker [14] and popularised by Jean Lipman-Blumen in her book *The Allure of Toxic Leaders* [15]. This was not about leadership styles, but about our willingness to follow beguiling but incompetent or corrupt leaders. The name stuck and is now widely used to refer to bad leaders.

The usual reason for leadership toxicity is for a leader's failure to be situational; that is, they are unable to change their style in response to a changed situation. The most common and most obvious is the so-called 'inflexible autocrat'. This is a pattern that is often rewarded and reinforced in large bureaucracies, as the failures of some UK banks and public sector organisations in recent years well illustrate. The failures of the toxic autocrat are as might be predicted for anyone using an autocratic approach where a democratic approach would be more appropriate. The mistakes they make are:

● **Poor decision-making.** This is because they fail to recognise that other group members have a more accurate view of what the appropriate decision should be than themselves and they do not elicit this.

- **Capriciousness.** Consultation and agreement tends to lead to moderate, stable decisions that are neither brilliant nor disastrous. Autocratic decisions are more liable to be brilliant or disastrous – disastrous in incompetent hands of course, but less stable, and prone to sudden unexpected reversal.

- **Alienation of the group.** This occurs because team members who do not feel dependent on the leader, and who are never consulted or involved in policy, quickly lose interest in the team and its aims.

- **Frequent aggression.** Lewin's original observation was of a higher rate of inter-member aggression within autocratically led groups than within democratically led groups.

The converse – a toxic democratic leader – is rare. The problem with the toxic democratic leader is that they fail to apply autocratic leadership when it is appropriate. This means that in situations where they have the knowledge and experience to determine what goes on – and those around them do not – they still dither and ask for further input into decision-making. One thing that saves democratic leaders in this situation is that they can readily recognise which group members are qualified to take an autocratic role when needed, and can use them to coordinate the required autocratic component of leadership while themselves maintaining group cohesion and motivation with a democratic style.

Apparatchik

In public services, a particularly common version of the toxic autocrat is the apparatchik. The term comes from the Russian description of middle-ranking Communist Party officials. Apparatchiks accept without question what their superiors ask of them, and then brook no opposition from their inferiors when carrying out these orders. They are poor at taking personal responsibility, they work to rules; when no rule can be found to address a problem, they ask those above them what to do.

Consequently they appear as compliant but needy and unimaginative functionaries to their superiors, and as inflexible pedantic autocrats to their inferiors. They are common in situations where middle-ranking managers are appointed by their superiors and in large rigidly bureaucratic organisations, where such behaviour is frequently rewarded.

Working under an apparatchik is, of course, no fun but their real danger to an organisation is in converting the two-way discourse between frontline staff and senior management into a one-way autocratic communication channel. Two-way discourse provides the feedback essential for optimum effectiveness, especially in an organisation like the NHS where efficiency is otherwise difficult to measure directly.

There are numerous examples where an apparatchik has presided over a service that disintegrated into chaos and disaster, to the point where it was too late to rescue, with neither senior management nor the apparatchik being aware of what was going on.

Inverse apparatchik

The *inverse* apparatchik is unshakably cynical about people above them in the command structure, believing them to be incompetent, self-serving and corrupt. They see themselves and those below them as dutiful, competent, down-trodden and exploited, and they vigorously defend the interests of their colleagues and subordinates or patients. They may have strongly held political views on economic and class divides in society. They are common in situations where middle-ranking managers are elected by their peers or juniors.

The problem is that they cannot – or will not – see issues from the strategic, expedient point of view of more senior leaders. When they succeed in their parochial aims, they can seriously undermine or even ruin the organisation.

Command structure in healthcare

The above theories and models are generic. As with most descriptions of leadership, they are primarily aimed at people who have been appointed to roles of leadership. Most contemporary research on the subject addresses the behaviour of appointed leaders in areas such as fire-fighting [16], policing [17] and the military [18]. In healthcare in general, and the UK's NHS in particular, such appointed leaders are not so apparent.

Organisations like the fire services, the police and the military use a single pyramidal command structure. At each level of the pyramid there is a leader who is in charge of usually between two and ten individuals. This structure is often reinforced by visible symbols. The Royal Navy, for example, has ranks for commodore, captain, commander and lieutenant; the uniform of each rank has clearly identified markings. Everyone knows who answers to whom. This kind of command structure is referred to by Henry Mintzberg as a 'machine-like'.

The NHS in the UK is different – with not one but at least *three* command pyramids. These relate to the medical staff, the nursing staff and the administrative staff. Therefore, in an operational team such as a theatre team, different members are answerable to different command lines rather than to a single team leader. Nurses are answerable ultimately to the nursing hierarchy, administrative staff to their own hierarchy, and medical staff to consultants. This often leads to conflicting expectations. For example, how does a senior nurse deal with a junior doctor who is not in her command line and wishes to do something contrary to instructions from above? This multiplicity of command lines leads to the many conflicts healthcare workers are familiar with [19].

The administrative and nursing command structures are similar to other organisations in that they have fairly clearly defined ranking. In the case of nursing staff, they also have identifying attire, making them machine-like, but the whole organisational structure has another character courtesy of the medical profession. The medical command structure in NHS acute Trusts consists of medical directors over clinical directors of directorates and heads of clinical departments, then consultants, specialist trainees and foundation trainees under them.

Actually, the rankings above consultant do not apply to the operational front line. Traditionally the operational structure was of teams, or firms, headed by consultants, under which were senior registrars, registrars, senior house officers and house officers. As with other organisations, there were more juniors than seniors. This is changing in the NHS, with a greater increase in numbers of consultants than in numbers of juniors, so that the numbers of consultants and juniors are more similar, and they are not organised into firms as they once were.

The result is a flat command structure with large numbers of consultants who are independent practitioners of equivalent seniority, and junior doctors who have numerous 'masters', each with their inevitable idiosyncratic differences. This is what Henry Mintzberg describes as a *professional bureaucracy* [20].

Thanks to the dominant role of the medical profession in healthcare, this makes the overall command structure a professional bureaucracy. According to Mintzberg they have predictable properties:

- Stability is prioritised over change.
- Work is organised in many multidisciplinary teams.
- The function of leadership is distributed to many professionals.
- Leadership skills training is important for many professional groups.
- Front-line staff have:
    o control over work content
    o more influence than appointed managers on day-to-day decisions.

- Leaders have to negotiate changes rather than impose them.
    - o Hierarchical directives have little effect.
    - o Positional power is not always followed or respected.
    - o Influence is more significant in achieving change.
    - o Professional networks and peer pressure are important.
    - o Professional credibility is important.

The result is that large numbers of NHS employees need particularly democratic leadership skills.

Leadership and power

There is considerable overlap between the common English meanings of the words 'authority', 'leadership', 'management' and 'administration' which often leads to confusion. For the present purpose we need to be more specific about these meanings.

'Authority' means having power over the actions of others by means of inducements and threats of sanction that are external to the immediate task – but the word has another meaning too. It also means being a respected expert on a subject. We refer to the ability to threaten punishment or offer reward as *power*, although even this is not totally specific because power comes in different forms:

- *Coercive* power (the power to punish).
- *Reward* power (the power to reward).
- *Legitimate* power (power by virtue of position).
- *Expert* power (power gained from experience and knowledge).
- *Referent* power (power of a follower's identification).

'Leadership' means the ability to bring a group of people to effective action. In most discussions of leadership this includes the administration of power. With the command structure in healthcare institutions, particularly in the UK's NHS, who has power for front-line operations is often ambiguous, and consequently recourse to power can lead to conflict; even if who has power is clear, it is often more effective for them not to exercise it overtly. For this reason we draw a distinction between leadership *with* and leadership *without* the exercise of power.

'Management' and 'administration' necessarily involve the use of leadership with power, and ideally of leadership without power as well, but they can, and often do, go on without it. While administrators are driven by process, achieving an objective or completing a task, leaders are people-driven. People in charge of others take on a role within a spectrum that extends from administration at one end to leadership at the other. The term 'management' does not of itself imply a specific position on the spectrum, and managers tend to take up a position that depends on their personality, interpersonal skills and foresight.

Not everyone has a job where they can exercise power, but leadership can be exercised in many ways, depending on a person's skills, making leadership training relevant to everyone. Leadership is also ultimately more effective than power. Power can take a horse to water but cannot make it drink; leadership takes a horse to water when it is thirsty. Leadership is 'better' than power. If something needs to be done, it will be done better, faster and more efficiently if it is coordinated by leadership than if it is coordinated by power. Only when leadership fails is it necessary to resort to power, and the frequency with which people do resort to power is inversely proportional to their leadership skill.

The defining quality of leadership is the ability to bring multiple people to a common purpose (that is, a *common* purpose, not the leader's purpose!). In the context of healthcare staff, it is generally the ability to motivate and direct those around them to achieve the best outcome for the patient. Clinical staff must be both managers and leaders. They need to form constructive relationships with other managers of the service, dealing with misunderstandings, giving information and developing a common purpose.

Credibility

Credibility is that quality in a leader which means that their team members respect their opinions about what actions and measures will successfully achieve the team's objectives. There are various aspects to it, such as reliability, honesty, respect, genuineness, empathy, intelligence and vision. If a leader is thought to be foolish or inconsistent then it is likely that when they make a suggestion or issue instructions, their team members will not be easily persuaded that they will prove successful.

Credibility is a vital but difficult area of leadership skill. It is impossible to go on a course and learn how to be credible, or to wake up one morning and decide to be a credible leader. Credibility is something that others observe in the leader; the leader has little direct short-term control over it. A leader's credibility in the eyes of others is based on the consistency of his or her behaviour over time. Most are able to put on a good impression for a short period of time with a new team – the honeymoon period – but the longer the time the team spends with the leader, the more accurate a view they will have of the leader. The leader will find it more difficult to persuade the team of credibility if he or she does not demonstrate it in everyday practice.

Credibility and personality type

People view the credibility of others differently, according to a range of factors including their own personality type. Guardians are inclined to assume that people in authority must be credible unless proven otherwise. They respect reliability, serious-mindedness and worthy objectives. Artisans give credibility to people with grace and taste. Idealists are inclined to afford credibility when it depends not so much on effectiveness but on creditable motivations. Rationals do not accept the credibility of leaders because of their position, but only because of their grasp and usage of reasoned explanations for their actions. Similarly, Feeling people find sensitivity credible, whereas Thinking people find logic credible.

The best leaders are able to engage all of these personality types by using characteristics that each of them look for in a leader. The good leader will not only have these characteristics on tap, but will also be able to identify the personality type of someone they are dealing with, and use an approach that is credible to them. This skill is not uncommon in effective leaders and is generally learned from experience and comes to be acted on automatically, rather than being taught. It is described in Daniel Goleman's *Emotional Intelligence* [21] and is part of the Hersey–Blanchard situational leadership theory [11].

Credibility and intelligence

In general the credibility of leaders increases with their level of intelligence and education, and it falls with increasing levels of intelligence and education among their followers. The issue is not the absolute level of intelligence but the difference between the intelligence and educational levels of leaders and followers.

This is particularly relevant in healthcare because the medical profession has been selected for training on the grounds of academic achievement and universally has a high level of education. It can be difficult for anyone to appear credible to the medical profession without having a similar level of intelligence, equivalent professional qualifications or a higher degree. This raises the bar rather high for members of healthcare organisations who have a lower level of education. It also means that the consultant bodies of healthcare organisations are among the most difficult to lead and influence. In general it is not possible to alter one's own educational level to suit that of the target audience but there are certain controllable factors as described under the heading *Training leadership* below,

.

Emotional intelligence (EI)

Leadership is an emotion-laden activity and various attempts have been made to model and measure people's performance with emotional issues, and derive measures of emotional intelligence (EI). Daniel Goleman measured the success of PhD students who graduated from Harvard University. He defined what he called the Emotional Intelligence Quota (EQ) to quantify these skills.

The quota consists of five domains – knowing one's own emotions; managing one's own emotions; motivating one's self; recognising and understanding other people's emotions; and managing relationships. He found EQ to be more closely correlated with success than the intelligence quotient (IQ) [21]. Since then the current tools of the Emotional and Social Competency Inventory (ESCI) and the Emotional Intelligence Appraisal (the latter for self reporting and 360-degree apraisal) have been developed from Goleman's model.

Several other measures of emotional inteligence have been proposed. Salovey and Mayer's Ability Model [12] is based on the ability to perceive, use, understand and manage emotions. It offers the Mayer–Salovey–Caruso Emotional Intelligence Test (MSCEIT) which is modelled on the IQ test but uses questions based on the model's four emotional domains, rather than on reasoning skills.

K.V. Petrides has developed a trait-based model of EI [22]. It models EI as observed characteristics rather than skills or abilities, and measures have been derived from it including the EQ-i, the Swinburne University Emotional Intelligence Test (SUEIT) and the Trait Emotional Intelligence Questionnaire (TEIQue) which is relatively widely used. Others, however, have questioned whether EI is really a distinct psychological entity as opposed to another way of expressing personality traits, and questioned its value in prediciting career success [23].

Training leadership

The published research tends to be descriptive of leadership characteristics and their consequences, rather than instructive on how to be a good leader. We turn to that matter now. Leaders of exceptional vision and skill are probably born rather than trained, but such natural leaders are few.

For most people, leadership skills can be taught in a two-phase process, and developed by guidance, experience and reflection. The first phase is in learning concepts and the tools of leadership; the second is practical implementation and refinement gained by dealing with changing situations and particular individuals. Learning from experience does improve leadership skills, but it is maximised by honest and respectful feedback from other people. The following are specific practical points of instruction.

1. SHOW — DON'T TELL

Increasing perceptiveness, especially in softer science, makes people increasingly sceptical about the conclusions of others. Therefore the more sophisticated audiences become, the more leaders or instructors should err towards showing evidence and allowing them to draw their own conclusions, rather than drawing conclusions from evidence and then expecting those conclusions to be accepted in the absence of the evidence itself. This particularly applies when it comes to human factors in healthcare! This is an area in which there is minimal evidence to support much of what is proposed, and that evidence seldom reaches the rigorous level expected by the medical profession. Medical personnel rarely *tell* each other what to do. They *ask* for advice; they *present* evidence; and they *discuss* the implications of that evidence.

2. LEAD BY EXAMPLE

This important principle is illustrated by the scenario described in **Vignette 6.1**.

Vignette 6.1   Choice of surgical technique

A specialist trainee in orthopaedics spent her first year with two consultants, both of whom were relatively recently appointed. She then rotated to a more senior consultant aged in his mid-fifties who had a more established reputation. Discectomy is a common orthopaedic operation and the registrar learned how to do this with the recently appointed consultants using a 'minimally invasive' small skin incision and specially designed retractors.

The more senior consultant used a traditional approach to the operation with a longer skin incision, no use of special minimally invasive retractors, and heavy dependence on bony surgical landmarks. The registrar thought this was old-fashioned, unnecessarily invasive and distinctly suboptimal. The authority gradient in the theatre made it difficult for the registrar to openly discuss this with the consultant so she probed with questions about whether more minimally invasive options were available.

The consultant had faced this situation before and recognised the direction of the registrar's thoughts. During the operation, he gave the following so that all the staff could hear:

'There are minimally invasive options. I have used them, and on occasion I still do. Every year, fifty discectomy operations are done under my care, of which I do twenty personally. The other thirty are done by traines such as yourself. It is my responsibility to ensure all fifty operations are done satisfactorily with minimal risk. The reason I do it this way is not for me, but for you. It can be done with minimally invasive techniques but it is more difficult, and consequently more prone to variation, depending on surgical skill. If you do it my way, it avoids a lot of variability due to surgical skill and availability of specialist equipment'.

The junior consultants had learned how to operate, but lacked experience in supervising and delegating surgery. The more senior consultant had this experience and had developed a method that could be easily and safely adopted by inexperienced registrars. He had also recognised the registrar's concerns before she had fully expressed them, and before she had expressed her opinion. He explained his reasons in front of the whole team. As the registrar had not expressed an opinion she had no face to lose if she changed it. This left her open-minded to his reasoning and she accepted it as sound. She began to use his technique herself.

People with credible leadership are closely watched and copied by those around them. The orthopaedic surgeon in this scenario thought and acted like a leader, choosing a method because it was easy and safe for others to copy. This is generally true, and is the reason why actions speak louder than words.

3. MOTIVATION

Motivation and credibility are clearly linked – people are poorly motivated to work with a team leader who lacks credibility – but they are not quite the same. Good leaders have an ability to add motivation to that intrinsic in the team's desire to complete the task effectively. They use this to bring the team through difficult times, to supplement the motivation of individual team members where this is lacking, and to direct efforts towards areas that are likely to be most productive. Unlike credibility, motivation is much easier to teach. There are specific actions that lead to motivation. It is no doubt true that some people have a natural gift for enthusing others, but while some people can never achieve credibility, most can learn how to motivate. Points 4–8 below promote motivation.

4. POSITIVE REINFORCEMENT

Positive reinforcement means responding to something another person does in a way that encourages them to do it again, generally by appreciating, thanking or praising them. For example, take a surgeon who occasionally holds a pre-list briefing; if, on those occasions, the other theatre staff thank him and say how the briefing helped the list run much more smoothly, then the surgeon is more likely to carry out briefings more often. Positive reinforcement is an effective technique [24] and, because it involves only praise, it is inexpensive!

5. BUY-IN

Team members should feel possession of the process. When a team member has an idea, that member should be identified with the idea. This will encourage them to make it succeed. When an idea has input from other team members, it is good to let them feel the idea is theirs.

6. USE OF BLAME

Just as crediting team members with success draws them to the leader and motivates them to perform, blaming them for failures drives them away and demotivates them. There are occasions when things go wrong and blaming is either obvious or could potentially be apportioned. The motivational approach is to *separate* the problems and issues from the people. Even if someone is clearly to blame, it is more likely to be due to their lack of training, poor team communication, or inappropriate personnel deployment (rather than deliberate sabotage). These issues can be handled without implying a personal judgement about an individual team member.

7. DELEGATION OF TASKS

The default position of task delegation in teams is for the same tasks to be given to the same people, or people in the same role, time and time again. These tasks are distributed from the most important or interesting to senior members, to the most straightforward, repetitive and dull to junior members. Changing this pattern of delegation can be highly motivational. Giving more junior team members tasks they are capable of, but do not generally get (and may not know they can do) both develops and motivates them.

8. COMMONALITY OF PURPOSE

Commonality of purpose is the leadership technique that can be improved most! it requires that all the people involved in a project agree with its ultimate goals, as well as the methods. Without commonality of purpose, the only way to get people to act is through the exercise of power. Achieving commonality requires leaders to see the situation from different points of view: their own, those of the team members, those of patients and those of the organisation as a whole. Leaders should be careful not to become parochial in their approach to the organisation. Conflicts between the interests of the team and the organisation do arise and require balanced judgement and background explanations to resolve; without this, the leader is liable to trend towards toxicity, in the form of the *inverse apparatchik*. From a balanced understanding of the needs of all involved, commonality of purpose is gained when the leader communicates to explain the aims, and is sufficiently flexible to change any proposals and methods of achieving them to concur with those of others. It is this last thing that is most often done poorly.

9. DEVELOPMENT OF TEAM MEMBERS

Very few leaders attract a significant following that endures long after their death. Those few that have achieved this, such as the founders of the world's great religions, were characterised by their tendency to prioritise the development of others over their own interests. Developing other team members is the way in which leaders secure the most lasting loyalty and respect.

10. VISIBILITY

The above-mentioned issues (commonality of purpose, credibility, leading by example, team member development and motivation) are all advanced by *visibility*. Visible leaders are easy to find and easy to approach; they have offices that are conveniently located in their departments, and spend time in and around the teams they lead. The degree of visibility is limited by the time constraints. Professional personnel are generally under time pressure and see activities like corridor chatting, so-called constructive meetings, social gatherings and visible supervision of competent team members as a less productive use of time than perhaps writing reports or doing research.

There is obviously a need for balance in this area, but there is no more effective way of achieving one's own objectives than by motivating others to share them and work towards them too.

11. HUMOUR

All organisations contain some serious-minded people who look down on humour as a frivolous and distracting waste of time. The conclusion of research on the subject is quite the opposite. Data from a wide range of working environments show that appropriate humour can improve productivity, teamwork, morale and work-related stress. It can defuse anger and soften reprimands. It allows things to be said that would be unacceptable in a serious context. It has utility in problem-solving, decision-making, and enhancing creativity [25]. These are all positive effects of humour.

The main disadvantage of humour is that humorous statements can be turned against the maker by opponents or enemies. Humour can easily be viewed as trivialising issues, denigrating, flippant or prejudiced. That is why official documents, protocols, manifestoes, medical records and correspondence and the like never contain humour. Another disadvantage is that not everyone is equally adept at humour, therefore blanket advice to use it cannot be followed by everyone. The right balance is something individuals must judge for themselves but, within these constraints, humour has some very serious benefits.

12. DIFFUSION OF RESPONSIBILITY

Diffusion of responsibility refers to a tendency for people to take less responsibility for their actions, or inactions, when other people are present. Individuals assume either that others will take necessary action or have already done so. Diffusion of responsibility is prone to occur in groups of three or more people and is more likely if tasks and responsibilities have not been specifically assigned. As such, it is a particular risk of the democratic leadership style.

The solution is clear allocation of responsibility. The autocratic style is also affected by diffusion of responsibility. Subordinates readily disengage themselves from everything except what they have been instructed to do, and do not make allowances for changing situations without new instructions.

When adverse events also occur, subordinates later claim to have been *'just following orders'*; supervisors claim their role was to *'give instructions, not carry them out'.* Such explanations have followed many crimes against humanity. The solution is more democratic engagement of group members with buy-in as in Point 5 above.

Medical Leadership Competency Framework (MLCF)

The NHS's leadership training program aimed at doctors was developed by the NHS Institute for Innovation and Improvement and the Academy of Medical Royal Colleges. The MLCF was published in 2008 with a second edition appearing in 2009 and a third in 2010 [26]. It has been adopted by other NHS policy documents including *Tomorrow's Doctors* [27], *Guidance for Undergraduate Medical Education* [28], and the *Medical Leadership Curriculum* [29] which is now part of the syllabus for training in the fifty-eight specialties of the Medical Royal Colleges and Faculties. It is intended to be taught to medical students, doctors in training, consultants and GPs. The main attributes of effective leaders in the NHS are shown in **Figure 6.1**.

Figure 6.1 *Key attributes of effective leaders in the NHS (courtesy of Professor Michael West of Aston Business School).*

The MLCF is a government-sponsored public document written with the consensus of numerous 'stakeholders' in mind. As such, it is subject to constraints. It is easy to criticise but these criticisms arise from the constraints its authors were working under – not from their performance! It uses one model of leadership, referred to as *shared leadership*, in which any doctor can perform acts of leadership whether or not they hold a designated leadership role. This position is adopted on this course, which is why leadership training is considered applicable to everyone.

The MLCF contains no discussion on leadership styles, but the style it promotes is strongly democratic. It is structured in five chapters on *Personal Qualities, Working with Others, Managing Services, Improving Services* and *Setting Directions*. These five tenets appear in the MLCF logo as shown overpage.

Figure 6.2 *The Medical Leadership Competency Framework logo.*

Strengths and weakness of the MLCF

Among strengths of the MLCF are that it has been officially accepted and therefore incorporated into undergraduate, postgraduate and continuing medical education in the UK. It is also clear and specific. Many similar official documents are full of non-specific aspirations for 'excellence', 'patient-centred care', 'continuing service improvement', and overused words like 'underpinning', but they lack specificity about what these terms mean. The MLCF is relatively unaffected by these failings.

Among its weaknesses are the fact that its promotion of a democratic style of leadership does not extend to teaching leadership skills, in which area it is autocratic. Each Module contains the statements 'Doctors show leadership by … (e.g. planning)' and 'Competent doctors … (e.g. take some action, for example, by minimising waste)'. These statements are made without justification or qualification. In most cases they are not controversial, but some cases, such as supporting the plans of what is termed the 'wider healthcare system', clearly require qualification. The document does not show, it *tells*; it cites no evidence and invites no debate on what is and is not acceptable teaching content. As such it provides a good example of how not to lead highly educated and informed audiences.

A further limitation is that the MLCF includes, as part of 'leadership', issues that are more about obedience to priorities and agendas that were current in NHS management at the time it was written, such as systems of appraisal, reflective practice and multidisciplinary team meetings (a current fashion in cancer care). These limitations damage the credibility of the MLCF, especially as its target audience is accustomed to weighing evidence and deriving, rather than accepting, knowledge.

Conclusions

The two basic styles of leadership are democratic and autocratic. Both have their strengths and weaknesses and suit different situations. The best leaders adopt the situational leadership approach; this is where the leadership style is adapted to suit the situation. Western societies in general, and healthcare in particular, have evolved over the last few generations from a primarily autocratic leadership style to a primarily democratic style which better suits the complex multidisciplinary demands of modern practice.

References

1 Takala T. Plato on leadership. *Journal of Business Ethics*, 1998; 17: 785–98.

2 Machiavelli N. *The Prince*. London: Penguin, 2003 (first published 1532).

3 Carlyle T. *On Heroes, Hero-Worship, and The Heroic in History*. New York: J. Wiley, 1841.

4 Galton F. *Hereditary Genius: An Inquiry Into its Laws and Consequences*. New York: D. Appleton, 1869.

5 Stodgill R. Person factors associated with leadership: A review of the literature. *Journal of Psychology*, 1948; 24: 35–71.

6 Mann RD. A review of the relationship between personality and performance in small groups. *Psychological Bulletin*, 1959; 56: 241–70.

7 Kenny DA, Zaccaro SJ. An estimate of variance due to traits in leadership. *Journal of Applied Psychology*, 1983; 68: 678–85.

8 Lewin K, Lippett R, White R. Patterns of aggressive behavior in experimentally created social climates. *Journal of Social Psychology*, 1939; 10: 271–99.

9 Rosenbaum LL, Rosenbaum WB. Morale and productivity consequences of group leadership style, stress, and type of task. *Journal of Applied Psychology*, 1971; 55(4): 343–48.

10 Van Wormer KS, Besthorn FH, Keefe T. *Human Behavior and the Social Environment: Macro Level: Groups, Communities, and Organizations*. New York: Oxford University Press, 2007.

11 Hersey PH, Blanchard KH, Johnson DE. *Management of Organizational Behavior: Leading Human Resources*, 9th edn. New Jersey: Prentice Hall, 2008.

12 Burns JM. *Leadership*. New York: Harper and Row, 1978.

13 Connor MP, Pokora JB. *Coaching and Mentoring at Work: Developing Effective Practice*, 2nd edn. Open University Press, 2012.

14 Whicker ML. *Toxic Leaders: When Organizations Go Bad*. Westport, CT: Greenwood Press, 1996.

15 Lipman-Blumen J. *The Allure of Toxic Leaders*. New York: Oxford University Press, 2005.

16 Salka J. *First In, Last Out: Leadership Lessons from the New York Fire Department*. New York: Portfolio, 2005.

17 Haberfeld MR. *Police Leadership: Organizational and Managerial Decision-making Process*, 2nd edn. Boston: Pearson, 2012.

18 Sweeney P, Matthews MD, Lester PB. *Leadership in Dangerous Situations: A Handbook for the Armed Forces, Emergency Services, and First Responders*. Annapolis, MD: Naval Institute Press, 2011.

19 Osterman K (ed.). *Indirect and Direct Aggression*. New York: Peter Lang, 2010.

20 Mintzberg H. *The Structuring of Organizations: A Synthesis of the Research*. New Jersey: Prentice Hall, 1978.

21 Goleman D. *Emotional Intelligence: Why it Can Matter More Than IQ*. London: Bloomsbury, 1996.

22 Petrides, K. V. Technical *Manual for the Trait Emotional Intelligence Questionnaires (TEIQue)*. London: London Psychometric Laboratory, 2009.

23 Landy FJ. Some historical and scientific issues related to research on emotional intelligence. *Journal of Organizational Behaviour*, 2005; 26(4): 411–24.

24 Lussier RN, Achua CF. *Leadership, Theory, Application and Skill Development*, 4th edn. Mason, OH: Cengage Learning, 2010.

25 Holmes J. Making humour work: Creativity on the job. *Applied Linguistics*, 2007; 28(4): 518–37.

26 Academy of Medical Royal Colleges. *Medical Leadership Competency Framework*. Coventry: NHS Institute for Innovation and Improvement, 2010.

27 General Medical Council. *Tomorrow's Doctors*. London: UK GMC, 2009.

28 Spurgeon P, Down I. *Guidance for Undergraduate Medical Education. NHS Institute for Innovation and Improvement, 2010*. Available at: http://www.institute.nhs.uk (last accessed January 2013).

29 Academy of Medical Royal Colleges. *Medical Leadership Curriculum*. Coventry: NHS Institute for Innovation and Improvement, 2009.

Communication

7

Key points for reflection

❶ Communications often benefit from particular structuring depending on the situation.

❷ Both 'sender' and 'receiver' characteristics are important in understanding effective communications.

❸ Do not be afraid to give colleagues a "good listening to".

The aim of this Module is to improve the accuracy and effectiveness of communication. It will cover the sender–message–channel–receiver (SMCR) model of communication, feedback and operational talk times, the role of sound bites and active listening, and the strength and weaknesses of written *vs* spoken communication. The difference between structured and narrative messages will be assessed, detailing the effect of impoverished communication channels and the limitations of serial and parallel communication. Advice is given on effective communication using the three-point rule and dedicated communication sessions (such as briefing and handover).

Communication skills are beneficial to team functioning, stress, efficiency, safety and personal performance. This is why an entire industry has developed to train them, resulting in numerous training courses and the production of thousands of books and articles every year. Healthcare has focused on patient communication for some time, but it has been comparatively slow to adopt team-based communication training. The 2008 UK consensus statement on communication training in undergraduate medical education focused almost exclusively on the doctor–patient clinical interview [1]. The balance is now changing, with increasing acceptance of the value of team communication [2].

Communication failures are well-documented contributors to medical mishaps [3]. Serious adverse events (SAE) occur in 5–20% of NHS patients; 20% of these are in acute care, with an estimated cost to the NHS of two billion pounds in 2003, which was when the estimate was made.

Analysis of SAEs shows that communication errors may contribute to as much as 80% of cases [4]. In the USA, the Joint Commission accredits and certifies healthcare providers. Its data indicate that in over 75% of sentinel events in healthcare, and a similar proportion of such events that resulted in the death of a patient, poor communication was among the root causes [5].

A 2010 review of perioperative communication concluded that it facilitates surgical safety [6]. Hostile or demanding communications in the operating theatre from senior team members have been shown to be stressors which lead to characteristic responses of mimicry and withdrawal [7].

A 2006 survey of Australian anaesthetists, looking at communication in the operating theatre between themselves and surgeons, found that the majority believed good communication lead to better patient outcomes; 99% said good communication reduced stress and 89% said they felt personally stressed when there was poor communication. Furthermore, 94% of them said that poor communication caused procedural delays, and only 23% felt that the current state of communication was acceptable [8].

Without thought or training, people tend to act on *impulse*. Impulsive reactions are primitive and simple, and focus on short-term self-interest. They are rarely appropriate when multidisciplinary teams are working towards complex goals.

The alternative to impulse is *reflection*. Reflective reactions require consideration, thought or training, without which impulse remains the default. This dichotomy pervades human behaviour and impulsive behaviour, despite years of training and education, is a common experience. Tasks that are particularly prone to impulsive behaviour are those that require little concentration or thought. First among these is speaking in one's mother tongue, which is why impulse *vs* reflection is such an issue in communication. Various aspects of communication skills follow below. But if there is one overriding message for improving our communication, it is this – think before speaking!

Communication theory

Communication theory is about developing generalised models in the hope that they explain more about a situation than the real-life and experimental observations from which they were derived. In this course, what we want to know is specifically how to improve communication in the healthcare service. Current models do not add to observational results in this regard so we do not spend a lot of time on them. We have used one model to classify communication issues into those of 'sender', 'message', 'channel' and 'receiver', or SMRC.

One of the first modern communication models was used for telephone research at Bell laboratories. In 1949, Shannon and Weaver divided communication into encoding, transmission and decoding of the message. The message is subject to noise (interference) during transmission [9]. The relevance to telephony is obvious, but the model can also be applied to non-telephonic communication where noise is one of many sources of inaccuracy. However, the model does not give a complete description. It was expanded by Berlo in 1960, therefore, into four component parts, creating the SMCR model of sender–message–channel–receiver [10]. All parts of this process are subject to noise, and errors arising at any stage are transmitted through the rest, so the final error rate is cumulative (see **Figure 7.1**).

The importance of feedback in communication was addressed by Schramm in 1954. He described a two-way model in which communication goes from the sender to the receiver and back [11]. This feedback can either confirm that the receiver has understood what the sender intended, or it can be corrective.

This was expanded upon in 1970 by Barnlund [12]. In his transactional model, the sender and receiver have fields of experience that depend on the individual's culture, background, past experience, attitudes and beliefs. When the fields are shared, communication is more effective. As communication proceeds, the shared fields expand. Both sender and receiver can adapt their mental models in the light of the message and its feedback, improving further communication. The signals sent between the sender and receiver include spoken words, tone of voice, facial expressions, gestures and body language, and props such as graphic aids.

There have been several variations on these models, often yielding flow charts and diagrams, but these should only be included in teaching material if practical points on how communication can be improved follow directly from them.

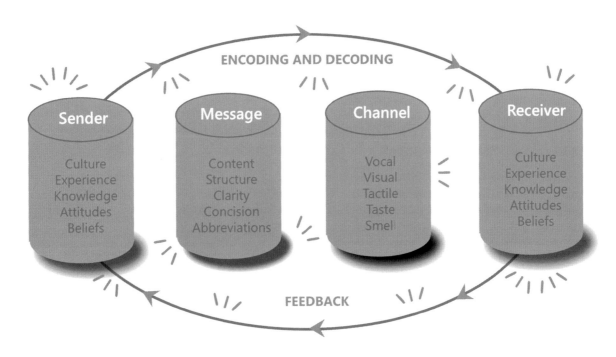

Figure 7.1 *The sender–message–channel–receiver (SMRC) and feedback communication model showing noise (interference) affecting all parts of the transmission process (Berlo, 1960 [10]).*

Sender (S)

The Sender is the speaker or writer of a message. According to Robert Bolton [13], a Sender can have three characteristics that enhance the effectiveness of their communication – whatever the message might be. These are *genuineness* (without false front or façade), *respect* (with patience, fairness, consistency, rationality, kindliness towards others), and *empathy* (understanding of another person's perspective). According to Thomas Gordon [14] there are twelve 'road-blocks' in three groups that make a Sender *less* effective – whatever the message might be – as shown in **Table 7.1**.

Table 7.1 *The charactesistics of Gordon's twlelve roadblocks to effective communication [14]*

Roadblock group	Roadblocks
Judging the other person rather than focusing on the issue	1 Criticising
	2 Giving abuse
	3 Diagnosing the sender's hidden agenda
	4 Evaulative praising
Sending solutions rather than agreeing them	5 Ordering
	6 Threatening
	7 Moralising
	8 Using leading questions
	9 Advising
Ignoring the receiver's concerns and input	10 Diverting
	11 Logical argument
	12 Reassuring

The second two of Gordon's groups amount to autocratic behaviour, which may often be misleadingly referred to as assertiveness. They are road blocks, but have a quick impact and in a crisis may be the only option. The best level of assertiveness is a balanced judgment. It can be escalated in stages, such as those outlined in the PACE (Probe–Alert–Challenge–Emergency) sequence described in *Module 3*.

Message (M)

For accurate *dispassionate* communication, messages should be clear, short and focused on the issue at hand – not on the sender or receiver. This approach frequently conflicts with emotional communication so it is not always appropriate. To tell a patient that '*You have cancer and with the best treatment available the prognosis of your condition is a median survival time of twelve months…*' is generally *not* good communication. Clarity and accuracy often have to be balanced against empathy.

Much of the subtlety we put into communication for emotional reasons does not translate well into other cultures or languages and is liable to lead to confusion. When speaking to someone with a limited grasp of English, softening a blow by saying '*I would rather not*' instead of '*I will not*' is liable to lead to a misunderstanding.

On average only five pieces of information can be kept in a person's short-term memory. The receiver can be overload by more than five pieces, or if too many messages are sent at the same time (e.g. e-mails!). If numerous points or messages are necessary, then the sender can help the receiver with a written copy of the message and by making the relative priority of the different points clear.

Messages come in two basic types – *mechanistic* and *transformational*. Of the two types, transformational messages are the more demanding to communicate accurately.

Mechanistic messages

These are like those of a machine. They are simple facts that can be passed from one person to another in a stream, like dates of birth, blood pressures and drug doses. There is no requirement for a person handling the message to understand its meaning. For example, the message 'Tell Dr Jones urgently that the serum potassium is 9.5 mM' can be given to a non-clinician who can deliver it accurately without understanding its significance (which is imminent cardiac arrest).

Transformational messages

These send understanding of systems or emotional feelings to the receiver. They are so called because they change, or transform, both the receiver's and sender's mental models.

STRUCTURED MESSAGES

Structured messages use a formula to present related pieces of information in a pre-agreed order. Their purpose is to avoid missing important information. In medicine we have a pre-agreed structure for communicating case histories (patient age, sex, presentation, history of presenting complaint, previous medical history, examination findings, investigation results and treatment plan). There are situations where a message structure is not agreed between the sender and receiver beforehand but it can still be used to help remember essential items. This is true in situations where we frequently communicate the same type of information. An anaesthetist who is specifying requirements to an assistant before induction frequently has the same list to communicate. Giving some thought to how best to structure this information (e.g. airway type, induction agent, muscle relaxant) and then using the same structure each time can aid clarity and reduce the likelihood of omissions. Structured communication is illustrated in **Figures 7.2a** and **7.2b**. They both refer to the equipment necessary for intubation. The structured version in **Figure 7.2** makes it much easier to spot what is missing. Structured communication is good for mechanistic messages but poor for transformational messages.

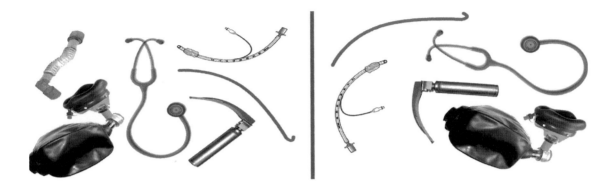

Figure 7.2a *Equipment needed for intubation. In the right-hand panel, one item is missing, but it takes time to spot which one; without knowing something was missing, it may go unnoticed.*

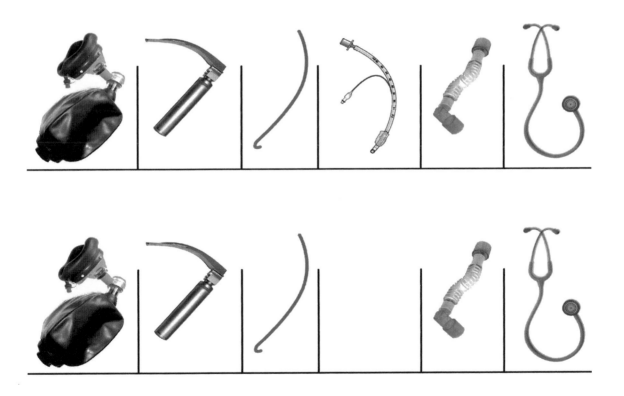

Figure 7.2b *The same equipment as in* **Figure 7.2a**, *but presented in a structured fashion. In the lower panel one item is missing, but now it is easy to spot it even without knowing that something is missing.*

NARRATIVE MESSAGES

In narrative or 'storytelling' messages, the items communicated all either state or support a common theme or premise. Purely structured communication ignores the associations between items and imposes a list-type structure to ensure that nothing is missed out. Of the two forms, narrative communication is much easier to understand and remember [15] and is the best method for transformational communication. The narrative approach starts with the most important facts to communicate and then fills in the background as supporting information. Good narrative takes careful forethought and this mental habit is worth forming. When you have a message to send that suits narrative, preview what you plan to say before saying it, and ask the following questions:

- What is the main point?
- Could it be shortened?
- Could it be clarified?
- Are there things that do not add to the message I could omit?
- Are there things that do add to the message that I could include?
- Have I got the main point first and supporting information second?
- Is the supporting information organised for maximum clarity?

STRUCTURED–NARRATIVE MESSAGES

There have been various attempts to combine narrative and structured messages. The best known method is SBAR (Situation–Background–Assessment–Recommendation). Its use in the intensive care unit has been reported [2] and it is the tool recommended by the *UK Resuscitation Council Guidelines 2010* [16]. Other structured forms of communication include *five-step advocacy*:

- Attention getting '*Excuse me, Dr Lamb.*'
- Stating a concern '*Mr Jones, oxygen saturations are dropping.*'
- Stating the problem as seen '*I think his pneumonia is progressing.*'
- Stating a solution '*Let's give oxygen and contact outreach.*'
- Obtaining agreement '*Does that sound reasonable, Dr Lamb?*'

This system specifies using names, a method by which the sender gets the attention of the receiver, and seeking feedback. Many teams have developed versions of these or other tools suited to their needs. What they do not do is aid good narrative. They are in essence structures, intended for use by junior staff. Such aids do not help with true narrative communication which is improved by knowledge, experience and intelligence, and are not under our control, at least not in the short term. What anyone can do, however, is think before sending.

NARRATIVE vs STRUCTURED MESSAGES

Structured communication is common in fields like aviation where the same essential components of information must be transmitted time and again. In medicine, the method has the disadvantage of being inflexible. While it prevents healthcare staff from missing out essential things to communicate, it gives little guidance on how to organise a message for the easiest comprehension unless it is highly stereotyped. Most medical communication is not highly stereotyped and therefore a narrative approach rather than a structured approach allows concepts to be communicated more clearly. For example, in **Vignette 7.1** the same essential facts are expressed in different ways, structured and narrative, for comparison between them. The structure used in the structured version of these communications may be appropriate for facts written down on a page where the reader can skip from place to place but the narrative version is far more suited to the serial nature of speech.

Vignette 7.1   Structured vs narrative versions

STRUCTURED VERSION

Surgical registrar calls anaesthetist:

'I am phoning about a 76-year-old man. **Complaining of** – pain in the back radiating into the right groin. **History of presenting complaint** – it came on fairly abruptly about three hours ago and has progressively worsened since. **Previous medical history** – exertional angina, stable, controlled on nitrates; he can climb one flight of stairs before stopping. **Social history** – lives with his wife who is fit; smokes twenty cigarettes per day; social drinker. **On examination** – cold sweat, pulse 100, BP 105/55, tender mass in abdomen. ?Pulsatile. Vital signs improving with resuscitation. **Investigations** – CT shows a ruptured abdominal aortic aneurysm below the renal arteries with aneurysmal dilation extending into the left common iliac artery. **Plan** – urgent transperitoneal repair.'

NARRATIVE VERSION

Surgical registrar calls anaesthetist:

'I have a man with a ruptured aortic aneurysm that needs urgent repair. Pulse is currently 100 with BP 105/55 improving with resuscitation. The diagnosis has been confirmed on CT. He is 76 with stable angina, can climb a flight of stairs without stopping and smokes twenty cigarettes per day.'

Surgical registrar rings consultant surgeon:

'We have admitted a 76-year-old man with a ruptured aortic aneurysm. CT shows it to be below the renal arteries but there is aneurysmal dilation of the left common iliac. He's a smoker with a history of stable angina but is otherwise reasonably well. He was in hypovolaemic shock on arrival but is responding to resuscitation. I've spoken to the anaesthetist Dr Y on phone number ...'

Consultant surgeon rings anaesthetist:

'Hi. It's Mr Z, the on-call vascular surgeon. I have just spoken to my registrar about Mr X. I will be coming in to do the operation. It will take me about twenty minutes to get there. Do you have a time estimate for starting yet?'

Good narrative communication differs from rigid-structure communication in two important respects.

First, before communication commences, the speaker organises the points he or she wishes to communicate into a hierarchy of importance. They then present the essential features first, with supporting information afterwards.

Second, when the speaker prioritises the information to present, he or she does so according to what the listener is likely to be interested in, rather than what they personally feel to be important. The speaker therefore changes the presented information depending on who is being spoken to. We can see this in **Vignette 7.1** where the Anaesthetist is particularly interested in the patient's exercise tolerance and smoking habit and less so in the detailed anatomy of the aneurysm. The Consultant Surgeon is interested in whether the patient is fit for anaesthesia and less so in his exercise tolerance, and shows more interest in the technical aspects of the aneurysm and its repair.

When the Consultant Surgeon rings the Anaesthetist the clinical details have already been communicated and the Anaesthetist's primary concerns are who is going to do the operation and what their availability is.

Narrative has the disadvantage compared with structured communication that it is easier to miss important items. It is clearly better than rigidly structured communication for most medical settings but it cannot entirely replace it.

Narrative communication works by association. In the current scenario, the issue is an aortic aneurysm. In order to form a narrative the sender must know the importance of an aneurysm and how it is relates to the clinical condition, the necessary treatment, and what the priorities are from the point of view of the various people they are speaking to. This knowledge of associations takes training and experience to acquire.

For these reasons, narrative communication is at its best when used by senior members of the team. Less experienced, more junior team members may not have the knowledge to use narrative communication effectively and are more likely to miss out important things. Junior members of the team depend more heavily on structured communication and senior members on narrative. At each point in a team member's professional development they have to strike a balance between structured and narrative communication, depending on their level of experience and knowledge. The best advice before speaking, therefore, is to consider both structured and narrative strategies, and to develop the best narrative possible while using structured tools to trigger the mention of issues (even if not fully appreciating their significance).

A further limitation of narrative communication is that it requires transformational communication on the part of the sender. The sender must have a mental model in order to form the narrative. If Person A explains a situation to Person B in narrative communication and Person B then goes and explains it to Person C, Person B cannot simply repeat the Person A's words. In order to communicate effectively, Person B must have understood what Person A said and then form his or her own narrative. If person B does not fully understand what Person A said, this narrative will be inaccurate or incomplete.

Structured communication can be passed on from person to person with much less reliance on each individual's understanding.

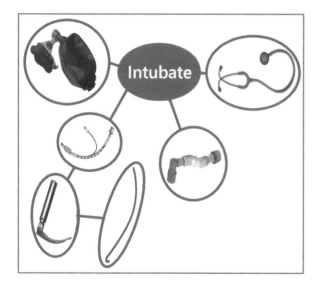 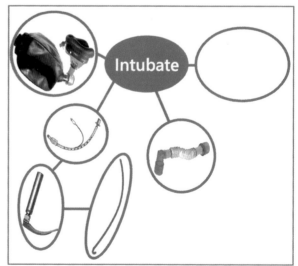

Figure 7.3 *Narrative version of* **Figure 7.2** *on the previous page. Again, there is a missing item. To anyone familiar with what is needed for intubatation, the images flow well and it is obvious that the stethoscope is missing. Someone who is not familiar with intubation will probably miss it.*

SOUND BITES

A sound bite is a simple, apparently logical or self-evident piece of information that is easily transmitted and remembered. It is more compelling if it is exciting, horrifying, or in some way vivid (the vividness effect) but this is debatable [17]. Sound bites pervade communication with multiple people. They are useful for getting a message across, but often lead to distortions (which is perhaps why they are so beloved in advertising and politics) because they reduce any issue to a simple memorable concept. When the reduction of the message is truly representative, it tends to be self-evident and we call it a statement of the obvious – rather than a sound bite.

Sound bites tend to bias complex issues towards one simple view or another, without (of course) any justification, so they should be chosen carefully. When a message contains a sound bite, it is likely that only the sound bite will be transmitted to most recipients; none of the supporting information will get through. Therefore, if there is a sound bite to be communicated, it must be the right one. Furthermore, if what is to be communicated is not really a sound bite, no sound bites should be used because they will obscure the message.

A common special case of the sound bite is the *blame bite*. Look at the example in **Vignette 7.2** where the heading is the sound bite and is a misleading distortion:

Vignette 7.2   Sound bite "MAN DIES AFTER DRUG ERROR!"

Here is the supporting information for this dramatic sound bite. A man with end-stage emphysema was admitted with a chest infection. Antibiotic treatment was started but the patient worsened and became semiconscious. After a lengthy discussion between the medical team and family, it was decided that there was no prospect of recovery and the object of treatment should be changed from treating the infection to relieving suffering. The antibiotics were stopped but the next day one dose was given in error. It made no difference to the situation and the man died peacefully, as expected, a few hours later.

Sound bites and blame bites have a particular role in teamwork – they form *the* communication link between the team and the world outside. Senior team members are likely to be more sensitive to the consequences of sound bites than more junior members, which can be divisive because it makes some members appear political, disingenuous and self-serving.

Another example is the very rare issue of surgically transmitted Creutzfeldt–Jakob disease (CJD). More attention and expenditure has been applied to this issue in the healthcare context than to the much more common and potentially more injurious problem of equipment maintenance. This looks like a political distortion of clinical priorities and can lead to acrimony unless the role of sound bites in communication between healthcare providers and their clientele is fully understood.

COMMUNICATING EMOTION

Rational thought occurs in language. Emotions are felt. This distinction comes across in communication also. The words we communicate with predominantly convey a rational message. Tone of voice and body language have a more significant contribution to the emotional component. This divide is surprisingly difficult to cross. It takes considerable skill for a communicator effectively to invoke emotion with pure language, and to express rational argument in feelings is extremely difficult, especially for those with a Thinking rather than Feeling personality subtype (see *Module 4*). In our minds, however, the link between emotion and rational thought is intimate. Our rational thought tends to follow where positive emotion leads and steer away from areas that lead to negative emotion. Knowledge of this link assists effective communication because it can be used for feedback control. We can read people's emotions from their body language and tone, and pursue areas of communication where they are responding favourably. When they are not, we can revise our strategy or content accordingly.

Channel (C)

Channel refers to the *modalities* by which information is exchanged. They include spoken words, tone of voice, facial expressions, gestures and body language, written text and graphic aids. Non-verbal cues can enhance understanding by:

- Confirming what is being said.
- Contradicting what is being said.
- Emotionally qualifying what is being said.
- Prioritising spoken points.
- Substituting for words.

The relative importance of these factors was investigated in a widely quoted (and misquoted!) series of experiments on conversational communication by Mehrabian *et al.* [18,19]. They studied words, tone of voice and non-verbal cues that did not agree with each other. They found that when non-verbal cues or tone did not match the words, then only 7% of the conveyed meaning came from the words, 38% from the tone of voice, and 55% from non-verbal cues. The contrived messages of Mehrabian *et al.*'s experiments may not be directly applicable to other situations, but the results do show that tone of voice and non-verbal body language add a lot to understanding. The importance of non-verbal cues in communicating emotional aspects of mental models is widely recognised, but they are equally important in rational models. **Vignette 7.3** is a student's account of learning a highly rational system.

Vignette 7.3   Channels of communication

Some years ago I was studying physics with the UK's Open University and took their course in quantum mechanics. The course ran for nine months in total. The teaching material was text books, with some audio and video programs. There were tutorial group meetings every two weeks but I was not able to attend many because of the shifts I was working at the time. I applied myself to the material, but three months into the course I was lost. I spent many hours poring over the course modules, and looking at other text books, television programmes and popular science books, but could not get my head round the basics of the quantum model. I managed to scrape through the assignments by adapting analogous worked examples – not by real understanding. I thought I was going to fail the exam.

Six months into the course there was a one-week summer school, which I attended. The first evening was encouraging in a way; the other students were just as baffled as I was! We met one of the seasoned tutors in the bar that evening and she made us all feel a lot better. Not only did most students arrive at summer school feeling like we did, but they left with solid understanding. She was absolutely right! A week later it all made sense, but looking back I cannot so easily identify what it was that made it click after so many hours of study had failed. We had good lectures, discussions with tutors, practical experiments, and discussions with other students. Something about this somehow got the quantum model into my brain.

The relevance of this is in understanding communication with restricted channels or *impoverished* communication. Face-to-face discussion, tutorials and class teaching have all channels available; they are the best means of communicating complex or analytical models. Telephone communication loses visual cues, and is poorer than face-to-face discussion, but it retains intonation and tone of voice as non-verbal cues. Written communication contains only the words; it is the most impoverished, and therefore the most difficult to understand and easiest to misunderstand. The right channel should be chosen for the message. If the message is complex or easily misunderstood, or if the consequences of misunderstanding are severe, then face-to-face communication is the best option.

WRITTEN COMMUNICATION

Written communication serves a different purpose to spoken communication. In most cases the two are not easily interchangeable. The strengths of written communication are that it can be referred to at any time after it has been written, it can be skimmed or dipped into (rather than read in sequence) as required by the reader, it can easily be sent over long distances, and it can be accessed by lots of people. To benefit from these advantages, the information must be easy to find! The NHS currently uses an information storage and retrieval system that dates from antiquity – handwritten notes. It may seem archaic, but it is the standard system, and it means there is only one place where written information relevant to a particular patient can be easily retrieved – the case notes – rather than private notes or handover sheets with numerous patient summaries.

There are weaknesses in written communication. Unlike the spoken word, there is a lack of non-verbal clues and of feedback (closed-loop communication), which can lead to deficiencies of communication that occur over and over again. For example, operating lists were produced in a department for several years using the patients' hospital numbers rather than their dates of birth. In theatre, however, patients were checked against the consent form and x-rays using their date of birth – so the list was not referred to. This was never corrected because the staff who wrote the lists never went to theatre and no one told them! This kind of recurrence does not occur with spoken communication because feedback is immediate.

The problem of lack of feedback goes further than this and good written communication requires a particular effort to focus on the reader rather than the writer. Common faults are alienating the reader with curt unjustified directives, stating things that are important to the writer but not the reader, and the use of excessively non-specific and politically correct language to avoid any blame, rather than enhancing clarity of communication.

These deficiencies of written communication do not affect all messages equally. Mechanistic communication, with simple unambiguous facts like dates and times and simple mental models, are little affected. Most affected are complex analytic models and emotional issues. Written communication is good for factual transfer, but bad for conveying understanding of complex issues, addressing concerns and conflict resolution. Telephone communication is somewhere in between, but for these issues face-to-face conversation should be used where possible.

COMPUTER-MEDIATED COMMUNICATION

By computer-mediated communication, we mean person-to-person communication channels, such as email, mobile phone text messaging and instant messenger services such as those provided by Yahoo, Microsoft and Research in Motion's Blackberry system. These are all convenient but potentially dangerous media.

It is very easy to send out a text message or email you later regret! Once a message is sent, you lose control over who reads it. It can be forwarded to any number of people or stored indefinitely, unknown and inaccessibly to you, and later found by powerful search software and taken out of context. Further, these systems are fast, with completely accurate message transmission, but we humans are not. For us, across communication – from breaking news stories to military operations to history to interpersonal messages – more speed means less accuracy. You cannot physically write and post an angry letter in seconds, but through these channels you can.

A familiar problem is the volume of texts and emails we all receive, much of it unsolicited. This makes going through an email inbox a tedious and low-priority task. Consequently, emails (particular those the recipient is not expecting) are liable to be ignored.

These media are bad at communicating emotion. Whatever the sender intended, the receiver is likely to interpret emotional content as more negative than intended, either seeing neutrality where positive emotion was intended, or negative emotion where neutral was intended [20]. As a consequence they lead to greater conflict escalation than other communication channels [21]. Experimental evidence shows that decisions made by groups communicating electronically are poorer than those of groups communicating face-to-face. Furthermore, the quality of decisions is worse with electronic media that are text only, compared to having an audio or video component, and are worse if they are non-synchronous, like emails, which do not invite an immediate response, than if they are synchronous like instant messaging. This makes email the worst computer-mediated communication medium of group decision-making [22].

HANDWRITING

Legibility is a dominant issue, but no matter how often it is addressed it never seems to make a difference. Issues like this should be shown – not told or preached. The reasons for illegibility, and specific areas when it matters most, should be emphasised, rather than making general statements and exhortations. One aspect of handwriting that must be commented on is the scope for medication errors, which was the subject of a US health department sentinel event alert [23]. Recurrent errors in drug administration are often due to unclear handwriting, particularly of numbers and unit symbols.

Problems commonly arise with certain abbreviations and digits.

> ■ The letter **U** used for 'unit', especially in units of insulin (UI) can look like **0** (zero)
>
> ■ The **µ** in **µg** used for **mcg** or microgram, can look like **m** for milli in **mg**
>
> ■ A decimal point with trailing zeros can be missed, e.g. **2.0** can look like **20**
>
> ■ A decimal point with no zero in front can be missed, e.g. **.2** can look like **2**

For side-specific interventions, especially surgical procedures, we should add one more point:

> ■ The *lower* case letters **l** and **r** (for left and right) can look like each other

As the NHS makes the change to electronic prescribing, another group of errors will no doubt emerge. Whether the overall rate of errors changes, and in which direction, remains to be seen. There is emerging evidence of reduced error rates [24] but in other safety critical areas such as aviation, over the longer term an over dependence on the infallibility of such systems has developed, especially in those with little experience of manual systems. *'To err is human but to really foul things up requires a computer'* (anonymous) as illustrated by the Stoke on Trent radiotherapy mistake.

Vignette 7.4   Radiation dosing

Between 1982 and 1991 the radiotherapy unit in Stoke-on-Trent in the UK suffered from an error that caused 1045 cancer patients to receive between 5% and 35% under-dosing of radiotherapy. As a consequence an estimated 492 patients suffered earlier tumour recurrence. The error arose because prior to 1982 staff applied a correction factor to doses to allow for the attenuation of radiation over the distance between the body surface and the tumour. In 1982 a computer system was introduced that applied this correction automatically but staff were not aware of this feature of the system, so continued to apply the correction themselves. This resulted in the correction factor being applied twice. The error only came to light when a new computer system was installed in 1991 and a discrepancy between its dosing and previous dosing was recognised [25].

Another area worthy of mention is the use of abbreviations. The role of these in adverse events has been extensively documented [26]. There is significant evidence that the use of abbreviations, such as 'TLAs' (for three-letter acronym).

TLAs are poorly standardised and poorly understood.
Use them with care and write in plain English unless all relevant
readers will unambiguously understand what they mean.

Receiver (R)

Have you ever been reading when your mind has wandered off onto other things? You reach the end of a page realising you have not registered anything that was on it? This common experience happens with both reading and listening. When listening, it is more likely to happen when the Receiver is preoccupied with other concerns, or the speaker rambles on and does not get to the point. A common cause of not listening is when the Receiver is thinking about what to say next, or is looking for a gap in the speaker's flow to interrupt them – so-called *gap searching*. These are particularly important issues in situations of conflict or disagreement, and *active listening* is a prominent part of conflict resolution strategies.

ACTIVE LISTENING

The term active listening was coined by Thomas Gordon [27]. In his original formulation, active listening involves the listener paraphrasing what has been heard in his or her own words, then asking the speaker if that understanding was correct – in other words, closed-loop transformational communication. We would now classify this into two steps – active listening and feedback. Active listening requires questioning, whereby the receiver asks themselves *'What is being said here?'*. If there is no clear answer, they close the loop and ask the speaker. Active listening refers to the receiver. As well as active listening, this involves the receiver's assessment of the speaker (or writer's) credibility, and how receptive they are to the message being conveyed. The factors of speaker credibility, active listening, and receptiveness to the message all go up and down together. A speaker who does not appear credible is less likely to be listened to actively, and even if they are, the message they give is less likely to be accepted. Seniority is an important determinant of credibility, and one that the speaker cannot change, but other factors are under the speaker's control:

- Credibility is *enhanced* by clarity of expression, precision, confidence, and a reputation for sensible commentary.

- Credibility is *reduced* by rambling, non-specific communication for an excessive amount of time, inconsistency in the way things are perceived and reacted to, and a reputation of unreliability.

During active listening, the receiver should make attempts to engage the sender with positive body language and gestures that demonstrate the sender is being listened to, regardless of their credibility. It may be necessary, if the sender has diverted from the message, for the receiver to acknowledge this and check that they intended to move away from the original message. It should be done in a respectful and non-confrontational way that demonstrates the receiver has been actively listening and values the contribution of the sender. If done appropriately, active listening may prevent conflict purely by the sender having the feeling he had been listened to and understood in a non-judgemental manner.

FEEDBACK (CLOSED-LOOP COMMUNICATION)

Feedback means the Sender gets confirmation back from the Receiver that a message has been correctly understood. It is used synonymously with the term 'closed-loop communication' because of the loop sender – channel – receiver – channel – sender. The intention of communication is to convey concepts, facts and ideas from one person's mind to another's. Errors in understanding that arise can be corrected by *closing* the communication loop. The practice is widespread. In critical communication situations, such as air traffic control, read-back systems are used to confirm correct transfer of critical data. In education, students are asked to consult literature and then express the concepts they read about in their own terms in essay form; the idea is to test not only their ability to write essays, but also that they have grasped the concepts they have read.

When someone calls the emergency services to report that a building is on fire, the telephonist uses structured communication to get the essential facts of where the fire is and how many people are in the building, and always asks for a contact telephone number for the caller. This structured communication is then passed on down the chain and given to the fire crews who attend the scene. The contact phone number is to close the communication loop. If the fire crew need clarification or do not understand something, the caller can be contacted. Closed-loop communication aids accuracy in situations involving complex and critical information and is important in the theatre environment [28]. In simulated theatre communication situations, lack of closed-loop communications has been found to be one of the factors leading to underperformance [29] and it now forms part of a national patient safety goal in the USA [30].

Specific communication situations

Serial communicating through multiple people

Serial communication through multiple people occurs when information is passed from one person to another and then on to another. It is an unreliable method, but often unavoidable [31]. It is tolerably reliable for structured communication, but for narrative communication it is highly unreliable. It is widely used in healthcare and is one of the most frequent causes of disasters and litigation. Systems should be designed to minimise this form of communication. **Vignette 7.5** illustrates the point.

Vignette 7.5 Discharged subarachnoid haemorrhage

A 35-year-old mother presented to Accident and Emergency with a sudden headache. She was seen by a registrar. Concerned about the possibility of a subarachnoid haemorrhage, a CT scan was organised. This was normal. The registrar discussed the matter with the consultant who also saw the patient. The consultant was accustomed to treating headaches and also considered the history highly suspicious of a subarachnoid haemorrhage. He suggested a lumbar puncture.

The result was ambiguous, with some blood staining that could have been the result of the lumbar puncture itself rather than a haemorrhage. The consultant felt a haemorrhage had not been adequately excluded and asked the registrar to phone the neurosurgeons. The registrar rang the neurosurgical registrar and communicated a headache with a normal CT and non-diagnostic lumbar puncture. Detailed analysis of the lumbar puncture was suggested and the result implied that the blood staining was not due to subarachnoid haemorrhage. The neurosurgical registrar then told the neurosurgical consultant that a patient had been referred with headache, a normal CT and 'traumatic tap' lumbar puncture. The neurosurgical consultant did not accept the patient and she was discharged from Accident and Emergency.

She re-presented ten days later with a severe subarachnoid haemorrhage from which she died. The episode led to a complaint and in the course of its investigation the two consultants met. It became clear that had the concerns of the Accident and Emergency consultant been conveyed properly to the neurosurgeon he would have accepted the patient without hesitation for investigation and her life would probability have been saved.

None of the steps in this serial communication were in themselves unreasonable. The tests relied upon are not 100% accurate – no tests are – and vital information did not get through: a senior doctor, highly experienced in the diagnosis of headaches, felt subarachnoid haemorrhage remained a possibility *despite* the results. This got missed out when the story was relayed.

Things can be done to minimise the problems associated with serial communication. The most obvious is to avoid it altogether, but that is not always possible. The person at one end of a chain of serial communication must be aware of its fallibility. If something does not seem right, they should pick up the phone and speak to the person at the other end of the chain. The Accident and Emergency consultant in the case above remained concerned about his patient, but took no further action because he accepted the opinion of the specialists. He was unaware that his message had been distorted by serial communication, so that the very reason for the referral had been lost. *Be careful of serial communication* – know when it is occurring and how unreliable it is. If in doubt, *bypass* it.

Avoiding serial communication can be difficult. The chain consists of a person who originates the information, a person who receives it and, in between, one or more people who pass it on. In most situations, those at either end of the chain are more senior, or have more relevant knowledge or experience than those in the middle of the chain. This leads to an important conclusion: if you are initiating a chain of serial communication, then you should *structure* the message rather than leaving it as purely narrative. A useful method is to enumerate the specific points to be communicated. One structure that might have helped in **Vignette 7.5** is shown below, relating to three specifiic points:

- The patient was a young woman who had a headache and who was fully conscious (i.e. there was a lot to lose if they got it wrong).
- The investigation for a subarachnoid haemorrhage that was carried out gave inconclusive results.
- The Emergency Consultant considered the clinical picture suspicious despite the test results.

Parallel communicating to multiple people

Parallel communicating means giving a message to several people at the same time. The method covers both public speaking and group discussion, but it is the latter that is principally relevant to team-working, so this is the focus of this discussion.

In the healthcare environment, the method is used for team briefing, debriefing, collaboration, departmental meetings, teaching and recruitment. Parallel communication differs from one-to-one communication in several significant ways.

> ### Differences between parallel and one-to-one communication
> - There is a greatly reduced opportunity for feedback
> - The level of attention of individual listeners is generally lower
> - Uninterrupted speaking tends to go on for longer
> - The proportion of what is remembered and retained by listeners is variable but generally lower
> - Listeners become bored more easily

Group discussion is a complex business with a large research literature. Countless words have been written on how to handle committees, groups and teams, invariably from the point of view of the speaker. As far as teamwork is concerned, simply holding group discussions, without any specific training or agenda, can be a big advantage, but there are certain techniques for making the most of group discussions.

Group discussion must be done well to get the best out of a team and make it highest achieving. The primary rule for team discussions is to communicate *both* ways with *all* members of the team. Obvious as it may sound, failure to act on this is common. When addressing the team, what the speaker says should be of interest to as many members as is possible – ideally everyone. If there is an issue that is only of interest to a small minority then, if possible, it should be dealt with it in a subgroup, without taking up the time of all the members. An extreme, but common, situation is where the speaker spends time addressing an issue which is of interest exclusively to themselves and no one else in the team!

Speakers who do this find it surprisingly difficult to spot. One good way of dealing with it is to alter the group lead. In briefing situations, rotating the person who leads the briefing (from the anaesthetist through nursing staff, operating department practitioners (ODPs), and surgeons) over time helps each member of the group appreciate what it is that the others need to know.

From the point of view of listening, get input from the quiet members. The different personality types are covered in *Module 4*. Some will speak out in group situations and some will remain quiet. These preferences can be quite extreme. Early research into group communication found that the most talkative member of a group makes 40–50% of comments, and the second most talkative makes 25–30%, irrespective of how large the group is [32]. A quiet group member may sit in silence listening to an issue discussed about which they alone know the appropriate solution, and never say anything. Obviously for the team as a whole this is a serious drawback. Getting quiet members to speak up is notoriously difficult, but a good start is not to make matters worse.

When working with people who are known to be quiet, the first step is not to try and elicit anything from them but to give them particular space and pay careful attention when they do speak. Asking a direct question in public can appear threatening and the person will usually give a bland and non-committal answer. A more effective alternative is to make a private request for an opinion later on.

The three-point rule

The three-point rule is widely used in public speaking and group briefing. The human brain is good at assimilating three related points. Make four points – and one or more are likely to be lost. Two have less impact. The same message is presented in two ways below:

- **Message One:** *'I'm giving you the task of developing a system to prevent errors in theatre. The system is to be reliable and once implemented it must remain in use in the longer term.'*
- **Message Two:** *'I'm giving you the task of developing a system to prevent errors in theatre. It must work, it must work reliably, and it must work long term.'*

The second version has more impact even though it has been expanded from a message with two qualifiers to a message with three qualifiers, one of which is redundant ('It must work'). The three-point rule works on several levels.

When applied to our own communication it helps to clarify thoughts on what needs to be said. Then it helps make what is said more memorable. Finally, it helps the listener to structure their response to the messages. They are immediately keyed in to a three-point structure which they can then use mentally to formulate a response.

Organisational issues

Weak management, failure to engage or consult with staff, and interpersonal conflicts are just some of the organisational impediments to communication.

Specific measures for enhancing communication

- Ensure clarity of the organisational structure so it is clear who should communicate to whom, and minimise use of serial communications
- Use efficient information technology (IT) systems
- Clearly define roles and responsibilities of each person
- Ensure each person receives appropriate supervision and training, so they are familiar with the organisation's lines of communication and IT services
- Minimise physical barriers and the effects of predictable environmental noise
- Design buildings so that staff are located together, rather than in different sites or parts of the site
- Reduce distractions from background noise, poor lighting, inappropriate temperatures, out-of-date equipment and inappropriate staffing levels, etc.
- Carry out dedicated communication sessions
- Dedicated communication sessions such as handover, briefing, debriefing, appraisals, departmental meetings, and non-operational talk time are all organisational responses to such concerns

Handover

Handovers between teams ensures that all members understand the common task and their role in it, and have the necessary information to perform their role efficiently. They also promote cohesion on an emotional level [33]. These two purposes are served by timetabled briefing and shift handover.

The British Medical Association has published a booklet [34] on handover, which recommends the following:

- It occurs at a fixed time and place.
- There is clear leadership.
- Any new staff are introduced.
- It is done with as few distractions as possible (such as bleeps and phones).
- It is done inside – not outside – of working shifts.
- There are structured prompts of issues and patients to discuss.

Situations requiring handover with special care [35]

- During plant maintenance
- When safety systems have been overridden
- When deviation from normal working practice is in progress or recommended
- When the handover is from experienced staff to inexperienced staff

Debriefing

Debriefing is discussed more fully in *Module 5*. An objective of team communication is to maintain or improve the team's performance over a period of time. This is done by the team regularly reviewing their own performance and identifying areas in which it could improve.

This is the role of *debriefing*. There have been several attempts to introduce formal debriefing into healthcare workplaces, alongside briefing, but these attempts have generally failed. Debriefing tends to attract a lower priority than briefing because of its less immediate relevance. In the case of operating theatres, the tasks of different team members do not all end simultaneously so there is no easy time to arrange a meeting when everyone is finished even if they are still in the building.

In the longer term, the teams that debrief will be the best performing ones, and it is suggested that the system of hot debriefing is used. With this method, any issues that could be improved, or things that have gone particularly well and could be repeated, are discussed as soon as practical after they arise.

Operational talk times

In aviation, the times of take-off and landing are busy and risky. To reduce background noise, communication in the cabin is limited to operational talk only below heights of 10,000 feet. In healthcare the same method can be used during high-risk periods. Outside these periods non-operational talk has a role in team dynamics and should not be prohibited. Potential operational talk times are during anaesthetic induction and intubation, preoperative checking, and times of critical decision-making.

Communication skills training

People spend much of their lives communicating and are highly practised at it. It is therefore difficult for a lecturer to stand up in front of a group of people and convince them that doing what he or she says will improve their communication skills – it smacks of teaching your grandmother to suck eggs.

The one thing most people do not have in their wide experience of communication is an external viewpoint on how they are doing. One of the most productive ways of teaching communication skills is simply to provide people with an external viewpoint on their communication. The three main tools for doing this are group discussion, audio recordings and camcorder recordings. It is fairly straightforward to use these modalities to focus on different communication skills, but the approach does have one major disadvantage in the classroom setting. That is, that many people become highly anxious when they are being recorded or communicating with large groups, sometimes to the extent that their behaviour is materially altered.

This problem is minimised by keeping down the size of groups. Ideally group size should be five or less to encourage the less talkative members of the class to participate freely.

References

1 Von Fragstein M, Silverman J, Cushing A, Quilligan S, Salisbury H, Wiskin C, *et al.* UK consensus statement on the content of communication curricula in undergraduate medical education. *Medical Education*, 2008; 42(**11**): 1100–107.

2 Brindley PG, Reynolds SF. Improving verbal communication in critical care medicine. *Journal of Critical Care*, 2011; 26(2): 155–59 (epub 2011/04/13).

3 Sutcliffe KM, Lewton E, Rosenthal MM. Communication failures: An insidious contributor to medical mishaps. *Academic Medicine*, 2004; 79(2): 186–94 (epub 2004/01/28).

4 Gray A. Adverse *Events and the National Health Service: An Economic Perspective.* Oxford: UK National Patient Safety Agency, 2003.

5 Joint Commision. *Improving Patient–Provider Communication* (Video series in four parts), 2012.

6 Gillespie BM, Chaboyer W, Murray P. Enhancing communication in surgery through team training interventions: A systematic literature review. *Association of PeriOperative Registered Nurses Journal*, 2010; 92(6): 642–57 (epub 2010/12/07).

7 Lingard L, Reznick R, Espin S, Regehr G, De Vito I. Team communications in the operating room: Talk patterns, sites of tension, and implications for novices. *Academic Medicine*, 2002; 77(3): 232–37 (epub 2002/03/14).

8 Elks KN, Riley RH. A survey of anaesthetists' perspectives of communication in the operating suite. *Anaesthesia and Intensive Care*, 2009; 37(1): 108–11 (epub 2009/01/23).

9 Shannon CE, Weaver W. *The Mathematical Theory of Communication.* Urbana, IL: University of Illinois Press, 1949.

10 Berlo D. *Process of Communication: An Introduction to Theory and Practice.* New York: Holt, Rinehart and Winston, 1960.

11 Schramm W, Roberts DF. *The Process and Effects of Mass Communication.* Urbana: University of Illinois Press, 1971.

12 Barnlund DC. A transactional model of communication. In: Sereno KK, Mortensen CD (eds) *Foundations of Communication Theory*. New York: Harper and Row, 1970; pp. 83–102.

13 Bolton R. People Skills: *How to Assert Yourself, Listen to Others and Resolve Conflicts*. New York: Touchstone, 1986.

14 Gordon T. *Parent Effectiveness Training: The Proven Program for Raising Responsible Children*. New York: Three Rivers Press, 2000.

15 Rigney A. The point of stories on narrative communication and its cognitive function. *Poetics Today*, 1992; 13(2): 263–83.

16 UK Resuscitation Council. *Resuscitation Guidelines 2010*. Available at: http://www.resus.org; .uk/pages/guide.ht (last accessed January 2013).

17 Kisielius J, Sternthal B. Detecting and explaining vividness effects in attitudinal judgments. *Journal of Marketing Research,* 1984; 21(1): 54–64

18 Mehrabian A, Ferris SR. Inference of attitudes from nonverbal communication in two channels. *Journal of Consulting and Clinical Psychology*, 1967; 31(3): 248–52 (epub 1967/06/01).

19 Mehrabian A, Wiener M. Decoding of inconsistent communications. *Journal of Personality and Social Psychology*, 1967; 6(1): 109–14 (epub 1967/05/01).

20 Byron K. Carrying too heavy a load? The communication and miscommunication of emotion by email. *Academy of Management Review,* 2008; 33(2): 309–27.

21 Friedman RA, Currall SC. Conflict escalation: Dispute exacerbating elements of e-mail communication. *Human Relations*, 2003; 56(11): 1325–47.

22 Baltes BB, Dickson MW, Sherman MP, Bauer CC, LaGanke JS. Computer-mediated communication and group decision-making: A meta-analysis. *Organizational Behaviour and Humam Decision Processes*, 2002; 87(1): 156–79.

23 Joint Commission. Medication errors related to potentially dangerous abbreviations. *Sentinel Event Alert*, 2001; 23: 1–4 (epub 2002/03/21).

24 Ammenwerth E, Schnell-Inderst P, Machan C, Siebert U. The effect of electronic prescribing on medication errors and adverse drug events: A systematic review. *Journal of the American Medical Informatics Association*, 2008; 15(5): 585–600.

25 Ash D, Bates T. Report on the clinical effects of inadvertent radiation underdosage in 1045 patients. *Clinical Oncology of Royal College of Radiology*, 1994; 6(4): 214–26 (epub 1994/01/01).

26 Walsh KE, Gurwitz JH. Medical abbreviations: Writing little and communicating less. *Archives of Disease in Childhood*, 2008; 93(10): 816–17.

27 Gordon T. Leader Effectiveness Training (LET): *The No-Lose Way to Release the Productive Potential of People*. Toronto: Bantam, 1977.

28 Salas E, Wilson KA, Murphy CE, King H, Salisbury M. Communicating, coordinating, and cooperating when lives depend on it: Tips for teamwork. *Joint Commission Journal on Quality and Patient Safety*, 2008; 34(6): 333–41 (epub 2008/07/04).

29 Miller K, Riley W, Davis S. Identifying key nursing and team behaviours to achieve high reliability. *Journal of Nursing Management*, 2009; 17(2): 247–55 (epub 2009/05/07).

30 Arora V, Johnson J. A model for building a standardized hand-off protocol. Joint Commission *Journal on Quality and Patient Safety*, 2006; 32(11): 646–55 (epub 2006/11/24).

31 Owen C, Hemmings L, Brown T. Lost in translation: Maximizing handover effectiveness between paramedics and receiving staff in the emergency department. *Emergency Medicine Australasia*, 2009; 21(2): 102–107 (epub 2009/05/09).

32 Bales RF. *Interaction Process Analysis*. Chicago: University of Chicago Press, 1950.

33 Chen G, Kanfer R, DeShon RP, Mathieu JE, Kozlowski SWJ. The motivating potential of teams: Test and extension of Chen and Kanfer's 2006 cross-level model of motivation in teams. *Organizational Behaviour and Human Decision Processes*, 2009; 110(1): 45–55.

34 British Medical Association. *Safe handover: Safe patients. Guidance on Clinical Handover for Clinicians and Managers*. London: BMA, 2004.

35 Lardner R. Effective shift handover. *Foresight and Precaution*, 2000; 1(2): 413–22.

Stress and Fatigue

8

Key points for reflection

❶ Stress is only indirectly a consequence of stressors. It is a direct consequence of stressors exceeding coping resources.

❷ Ample evidence shows that stress leads to poorer performance and health risks.

❸ We have little control over our own stressors but we can control:

(i) Our coping resources.

(ii) The stressors we cause to others.

In this module we look at work-related stress and how it affects the performance and health of healthcare staff and, by implication, the safety of the patients they care for and of themselves. The causes and effects of stress have been recognised since ancient times, but (as with much of psychology) our current understanding has been developed over the past century.

Early work focused on the extremes of stress and stress reactions associated with warfare. *Shell- shock* was the prime example of this. The term was coined during World War One but the condition appeared in the American Civil War as *soldier's heart* or *nostalgia*. Shell shock, now known as *combat stress reaction* consists of fatigue, slowed reactions, difficulty prioritising and making decisions, and a sense of disconnection from the immediate environment. Although variable in its manifestations, combat stress reaction is a normal short-term reaction to extreme stress. It was ill understood during the early wars and confused with blast injury to the nervous system, desertion and cowardice among other things.

Wars continued to dominate the study of extreme stress and its effects. The modern term combat stress reaction dates from World War Two and *post-traumatic stress disorder* was identified as a result of the Vietnam War. Outside the context of warfare such extremes are rare, and mainstream research has focused on the nature and effects of lower levels of stress which are more common but tend to be sustained over longer periods of time.

This change from short-term extreme stress to longer-term milder stress changed what we mean by the word. Most research outside of warfare involves asking people if they *feel* stressed and the word has therefore come to mean *self-reported* stress.

Stress originates from the demands placed upon us, which are called *stressors*, but the relationship between stressors and reported stress is indirect. The direct cause of reported stress is when the demands placed on us exceed our ability to cope with them. For example, having a mortgage commitment of two thousand pounds a month is a fixed stressor; the stress it would cause someone on an average income would be considerable, but to someone on a high income it would be trivial.

The ability to cope with stressors depends on the mental, social and material support available, collectively known as stress coping *resources*. Resources are generally more important factors than stressors. Most surveys show that the worst stress among workers is suffered by those who are low down in an organisation's hierarchy. Such people tend not to have highly demanding jobs but do have little control over their working lives and it is this that gives them stress.

Another feature of resources is that they are generally more easy to manage than stressors, so resource provision is central to stress management. Despite their importance, much research ignores resources because they are difficult to measure and there is no doubt that stressors alone are associated with stress and its consequences. Stress is divided into acute and chronic forms.

ACUTE STRESS

This is the 'fight or flight' reaction to unexpected alarming situations and sudden severe stressors. The effects include fear, anger and fixation on narrow issues. Acute stress is less common than chronic stress and is usually unpredictable. It is expected to be reduced by improving workplace and patient safety. These are general issues but there are specific situations that cause acute stress, and the consequences of acute stress, that can be managed.

CHRONIC STRESS

Chronic work-related stress is not the same as protracted or often repeated acute stress. Chronic stress is typically seen as a consequence of the cumulative demands of the workplace. These include commitments, tasks that must be completed, frequent unprogrammed or unpredictable interruptions, and unnecessary tasks required to work out what is needed despite poor communication.

Chronic stressors tend to be the main target for stress management.

Stress measurement in the workplace

The main tool used in stress research is self-reported stress levels. There are numerous studies that show that 20–40% of working people report working under stress, with stress-related health problems or stress-related sick leave. In the UK, stress is the second most commonly reported work-related health problem after musculoskeletal disorders [1].

The current cultural and political climate in the UK inclines towards being sympathetic of stress-related problems and compensating for them. These problems are wide-ranging; they depend on self-reporting, and are generally not amenable to objective testing, often being associated with substantial secondary gain such as prolonged paid absence from work. These features indicate that while there is currently an epidemic of self-reported stress-related illness, it may have as much to do with secondary gain as it does with primary loss. These problems of self-reporting apply to interventional as well as observational research, although in the former case, relative change can be used as a measure as well as absolute values.

When planning stress-reducing interventions what we really want to know is their likely effect on non-self-reported measures, such sick leave rates and staff turnover, but the amount of available research to inform this is minimal.

Attitudes to stress

Workplace stress and its associated ill-health is currently a major issue across industry, primarily because of the economic importance of sick leave and the potential for employees to seek compensation against their employers for workplace-related incapacity. All industries, including UK healthcare, take the issue seriously, but healthcare is perhaps more resistant to it than most. There are several reasons for this resistance. They include the attitudes of the medical profession and the career history of the current generation of senior consultants and general practitioners. Doctors are well versed in the effects of stress, but tend to be judgemental about it, and about stress-related illnesses, many of which are so-called *non-organic*. Such conditions are thought to be 'in the mind' and imply a 'lack of moral fibre', or they are not considered to be 'genuine' illnesses. Sufferers of these conditions are therefore seen as being somehow less deserving than sufferers of more conventional *organic* diseases such as stroke, heart attack or cancer.

Another significant contemporary factor that may change in the future is the career history of the current generation of senior medical professionals. In the UK, doctors who qualified between 1970 and the early 1990s had a very different early career experience from those who qualified later. This is due to changes in junior doctors' working practices. In the earlier period, newly qualified doctors would enter the workplace as house officers doing one night in two or three on-call rotas, often totalling more than a hundred hours per week, with periods of over eighty hours continuous duty over the weekends. The intensity of work done during the nights on shifts of this type varied widely from specialty to specialty, but typically doctors started in the busy subjects of medicine and surgery and would expect little or no sleep during an on-call period. Junior doctors often had extensive responsibility and were expected to acquire the necessary skills 'on the job'. This was a stressful working environment. Those doctors are now senior consultants and GPs. Perhaps understandably, they tend to be unimpressed by concerns about the workplace stresses of those around them now.

Another factor that makes organisations resistant to stress management is the wide variability in stress tolerance between individuals. The senior decision-makers in organisations tend to be hard-working, driven and capable. Such people often think that intolerance of stress is a sign of personal weakness or inadequacy. They are frequently tolerant of stress themselves or, if they are intolerant, refuse to admit the fact, and tend to believe (as did US President Harry S. Truman) that people who '*cannot stand the heat should get out of the kitchen*'. This means that while senior decision-makers may understand the relationship between workplace stress and issues such as sick leave, they find it difficult to identify with the problem themselves. Healthcare culture is characterised by the idea of personal invulnerability, led by the medical profession. Consultants in general (and surgeons in particular) are more inclined to deny that their performance is degraded by stress and fatigue than professionals in other fields [2]. Such views are based on personal experience but published research tells a different story. There exists a body of evidence that healthcare workers are particularly prone to stress [3], that this can be managed [4] and that it affects patient safety [5]. Furthermore, stress-related illness is common among healthcare staff and is associated with significant impairment of patient care [6].

Stressors

Stressors are the demands placed upon people. Their effect on depends on the demand itself and the individual's ability to respond adaptively and cope with it. Deadlines are stressors; help with the task and time are resources that reduce the effect of the deadline on us. **Table 8.1** (overpage) lists some common stressors and their associated resources. Most research looks only at stressors because resources are less practical and more expensive to measure. The stressors shown are manageable; they are chronic low-level stressors that can be identified and moderated, or coping resources can be provided. They are also difficult to quantify, which has led to another approach to the measurement of stress: counting life event stressors.

Table 8.1 *Chronic stressors and associated resources*

Chronic stressors	Comments	Resources
Time pressure	■ Too much pressure gives stress; too little, causes boredom ■ Staff who control their own workload find their balance; those who do not are prone to stress or boredom ■ Time pressure reduces surgical dexterity under experimental conditions [7–9]	■ Time ■ Control over workload ■ Flexibility of commitments ■ Help with tasks from others
Noise	■ Includes background noise ■ Non-operational talk during critical tasks ■ Construction and maintenance work noise	■ Freedom to avoid it ■ Ear protection ■ Operational talk times
Change	■ Affects different personalities differently ■ Stresses judging temperaments more than perceiving ones	■ Consultation about and explanation of change ■ Flexibility about change and its implementation
Distractions	■ Affects judging temperaments more than perceiving. Distracting tasks reduce surgical dexterity under experimental conditions [7,9]	■ Co-workers who can deal with distractions such as phone calls while critical tasks are in progress
Not knowing what is expected of you	■ Common and easily manageable	■ Communication and briefing from co-workers
Supervisors and managers	■ Particularly autocratic or toxic leadership behaviour	■ Participation in decision making
Divided loyalties	■ Between home and work ■ Particularly relates to time pressure	■ Control over working hours ■ Control over shift patterns
Lack of control	■ Greatest workplace stressor ■ Lack of job control is associated with cardiovascular disease [8]	■ Democratic leadership style

Life events are not chronic and cannot general be modified though in some cases coping resources can be provided. They are things like sitting exams, bereavement, changing jobs and getting married. Their advantage is that data can accurately and reliably be collected from subjects on their life event history and the method is widely used to investigate the effects of stress on health and performance.

The best known list of life event stressors is that of Holmes and Rahe, the 1967 version of which is reproduced in **Table 8.2** [10]. This *social readjustment rating scale* ranks a number of life events with respect to their associated relative effects on stress and health. The rating scale gives each of them a numeric value that that has been worked out relative to the stress of 'getting married' (this event scores as 50).

The scale allows cumulative stress over time to be calculated.

Table 8.2 *Social readjustment rating scale of relative effect of life events on stress and health [10]*

Life event	Life-change units
Death of a spouse	100
Divorce	73
Marital separation	65
Death of a close family member	63
Imprisonment	63
Personal injury or illness	53
GETTING MARRIED	**50**
Dismissal from work	47
Retirement	45
Marital reconciliation	45
Change in health of family member	44
Pregnancy	40
Business readjustment	39
Sexual difficulties	39
Gain of a new family member	39
Change in financial state	38
Death of a close friend	37
Change to a different line of work	36
Change in frequency of arguments	35
Major mortgage	32
Foreclosure of mortgage or loan	30
Change in responsibilities at work	29
Trouble with in-laws	29
Leaving of child from home	29
Outstanding personal achievement	28
Spouse starts or stops work	26
Begin or end school	26
Change in living conditions	25
Revision of personal habits	24
Trouble with boss	23
Change in working hours or conditions	20
Change in schools	20
Change in residence	20
Change in recreation	19
Change in church activities	19
Change in social activities	18
Minor mortgage or loan	17
Change in sleeping habits	16
Change in eating habits	15
Change in number of family reunions	15
Vacation	13
Christmas	12
Minor violation of the law	11

Adverse effects of stress

Behavioural effects

Behavioural patterns such as irritability, hostility and apathy are often caused by stress, but the key clue that someone is over-stressed is the change in their behaviour rather than behaviour per se. New patterns of hostility, alcohol or tobacco use, apathy, absenteeism or carelessness and so on in someone who normally does not show these behaviours is an indicator of serious chronic stress.

Emotional patterns

As with behavioural patterns, it is the change in emotional patterns that is most suggestive of a stress reaction. Most stress-induced emotions are part of our stress-coping resource and are positive (such as determination, concentration, pride in success) but when stress exceeds resource, negative emotions including cynicism, depression, anxiety and irritability will appear.

Systemic diseases

Holmes and Rahe's social readjustment rating scale (**Table 9.2**) [10] was used in the 1960s to study the patterns of stress that preceded the onset of symptoms in patient groups and controls. The patients were affected by heart disease, tuberculosis, skin disease or pregnancy. All four groups showed clustering of stressors in the two years preceding the onset of symptoms [11] and these differed significantly from controls. In a prospective study, they used the scale to measure stress in the crew of US navy ships and found that crew members with over 300 points in a six-month period reported a third more illness to medical staff than those scoring under 100. Most of these illnesses were minor and there was no proportional difference in illness severity between the more and less stressed crew members [12].

The social readjustment rating scale (**Tab;le 8.2**) and disease correlations have been revised numerous times since the 1960s, but always with broadly similar finding: that cumulative stress is associated with the onset of disease.

Although stress has numerous associations with disease incidence and severity, some caution in interpretation is necessary. Ill health is a major stressor and associations between stress and disease may be because a disease causes stress rather than the other way round.

Another problem is that the sections of society most prone to ill health also tend to be those who are prone to stress. Low socioeconomic status, for example, is associated with both. Mindful of these reservations, acute stress appears to enhance resistance to acute infections [13], but other effects and the effects of chronic stress are negative.

Chronic stress seems to cause a non-specific depression of defence mechanisms. It is associated with an increased risk of cardiovascular disease, but its most pronounced associations are with exacerbation of existing disease. Stress causes cancer to behave more aggressively [14,15]. Whether it has an influence on the incidence of cancer is less clear but there is some evidence that it increases it [16].

Numerous other diseases show this effect too. Stress is associated with worsening control of inflammatory bowel disease [17]. It has a significant effect on the time it takes for wounds to heal, which is extended by around 25% by stress [18], and there is some evidence that stress delays postoperative recovery in general [19]. Few surgeons will perform non-urgent surgery on patients who are highly distressed or frightened. Tuberculosis has also long been known to be related to state of mind, with a positive, optimistic and cheerful outlook being associated with faster recovery times [20].

The longstanding concepts of 'fighting off' a disease and 'dying of a broken heart' date from the time when mortal diseases characterised by a chronic balance between body defence and disease progress were common. Among these diseases, tuberculosis and leprosy are currently seen as chronic diseases in which progress is sensitive to stress. Other conditions, such as syphilis, are now easily treatable so recent data on the behaviour of the chronic condition does not exist, but it probably is stress sensitive. The closest and best described disease associations of stress are with mental illness. Both neuroses (anxiety states) and disorders of affect (depression) can be provoked or exacerbated by stress, as has been repeatedly observed.

These relationships between organic conditions and stress only account for a minority of stress-related ill health and lost work days in most studies. The commonest manifestations of stress are symptoms that resist diagnosis on objective testing (such as tension headaches, chronic fatigue, irritable bowel syndrome and atypical chest pain), and conditions that are virtually pandemic but whose clinical manifestations are highly variable and subject to psychosomatic exacerbation or dissembling (such as arthritis and spondylitis).

Cognitive function effects

The effects of stress on cognitive functioning are complex and not without controversy, as discussed in the following section on the Yerkes–Dodson relationship below. Experimentally, high levels of stress have been found to impair short-term memory, decision-making, forward planning and prioritisation. This last one – prioritisation – is significant because it reflects the situation we all recognise of stress impairing our ability to see things in proportion. Stressors often cause people to concentrate on things obsessively, so they fail to see the true importance of the stressors themselves in the fuller context and running of their lives [21].

Yerkes–Dodson experiments

In 1908, Yerkes and Dodson [22] published the results of a series of experiments on mice. In these experiments, mice were placed in a chamber with two exits — one dark tunnel and one light tunnel. Both tunnels had bare wires in the floor through which electric shocks could be delivered. The light tunnel led back to their nesting chamber and the dark tunnel led to a dead end, and the position of the tunnels was interchanged at random.

The experiments were designed to study how long it took the mice to learn to go through the light tunnel. Motivation was added by giving the mice an electric shock through the wires if they went into the dark tunnel. Two things were varied: the size of the shock and the difference in grey tone (light level) between the dark and light tunnels [22]. The results are shown in **Figure 8.1** overpage.

The results seemed to show that when the difference between light and dark was *strong* (black *vs* white), the learning was faster with larger shocks. This is shown by the bottom line, Curve II on the graph. When the difference between light and dark was *intermediate* (shown by the middle line, Curve I) or *slight* (top line, Curve III), the task was more difficult and the learning took longer, but it was faster for intermediate shocks than for either small or large ones.

The finding that for difficult tasks, intermediate levels of stress, arousal or motivation are better than either slight or marked levels, led to the controversial and *often misquoted* Yerkes–Dodson law – that performance increases to a peak with increasing stress, then declines with further increases in stress. This proposed relationship between stress level and performance is an example of hormesis (see Box overpage).

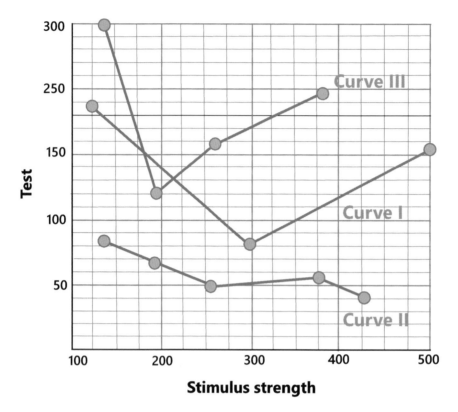

A graphic representation of strength of electrical stimulus to condition of visual discrimination and rapidity of learning. Ordinates represent value of electrical stimulus in units of stimulation; abscisae represent the number of tests given. Curve I represents ther esults of the experiments of Set I. Wach dot indicates a value of stimulus which was used in the experiments. For example, the first dot to the left in Curve I signifies that the stimulus whose value was 125 units gave a perfect habit, in the case of the four individuals trained, with 187 tests; the second dot, that for the stimulus value of 300 units, 80 tests were necessary; and the third that for the stimulus value of 500, 155 tests. Curves II and III similarly represent the results of the experiments of Sets II and III, respectively.

Figure 8.1 *Relation between strength of electrical stimulus and visual discrimination and learning in mice. Curves I, II, and III plot the results of three sets of experiments (from Yerkes and Dodson 1908; with original caption for explanation).*

What is hormesis?

The Yerkes–Dodson curve is an example of hormesis. This effect is commonly encountered in pharmacology, toxicology and environmental health. It refers to an agent that has an effect that rises with dose up to a maximum, then falls with further increases in dose, passing again through zero to become negative. The effect of alcohol intake on the incidence of heart disease is one example. The effect has been extensively investigated in relation to ageing, with radiation, oxidative stress and food restriction all showing hormesis in experimental conditions.

There are several criticisms of the original experiments and attempts to repeat the findings in mice and other animals have had mixed results [23].

The difficulty is in separating the effects of motivation, arousal and distraction because most experiments use stimuli that can potentially give all three of these. It has repeatedly been shown that task performance increases with increasing motivation and declines with increasing distraction.

What is not so clear is whether low levels of distraction can increase performance or whether high levels of motivation can reduce it. Some results suggest that this is true and, even if it is not, the Yerkes–Dodson law may have practical value because many real-life situations have elements of both motivation and distraction.

It has been suggested that situations of low arousal can be made safer by adding stressors. Long, straight sections of road can be made safer by adding gentle bends [24] because they require a higher level of attention to navigate. However, this is an easy rather than hard version of the driving task and the Yerkes–Dodson law refers to complex tasks.

The Yerkes–Dodson law has also been criticised for treating stress as unitary and primarily influenced by physiological responses, taking inadequate account of the interaction between physiological and psychological factors in stress [25]. The alternative *catastrophe* model proposes that physiological arousal displays a mild inverted-U relationship with performance when cognitive anxiety is low, but that catastrophic declines in performance can occur if both physiological arousal and cognitive anxiety are high [26].

Yerkes–Dodson effects have been claimed for memory [27], visual perception [28], and eye-witness recall [29]. They have also been claimed for simulator-assessed laparoscopic surgical dexterity. Whether these effects are *true* hormetic responses to individual stimulants is not at all clear.

The stylised graph shown in **Figure 8.2** appears often in the literature. It is useful for teaching purposes, but the fact that its message remains unproven must be emphasised. It also suggests markedly different outcomes compared to alternative theories, suggesting a gradual rather than a catastrophic decline in performance as stress increases.

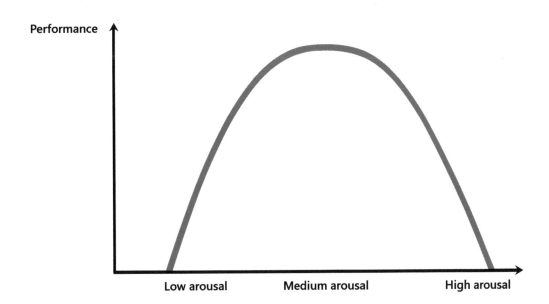

Figure 8.2 *A stylised version of the Yerkes–Dodson relationship as found in the popular psychology press. Treat this with caution!*

Health and Safety Executive (HSA) stress management system

There is no doubt that high levels of stress are implicated in a large amount of lost productivity and ill-health across the UK. The matter is taken seriously by the Health and Safety Executive (HSE) who have funded much of the research into the area through the Nottingham University Institute of Work, Health and Organisations.

The default way of managing stress is reactive. That is, if an individual complains of being overstressed, the matter is investigated and appropriate measures are taken. Options include adjustments to tasks, information systems, or paid sick leave. The HSE now recommends a more proactive approach which it refers to as risk management. This involves the stages of identifying a reducible stress problem, diagnosing the cause, and then intervening to reduce the risk of stress. To this end, the HSE has developed an indicator tool, a questionnaire of thirty-five items relating to the stressors mentioned above. This is available free of charge from the HSE website [30].

Organisations have a legal obligation to manage the work-related stress their employees are exposed to. They are expected to do this with primary prevention or risk management, rather than purely treatment of affected employees. They should assess any stressors and, where reasonable, reduce them. The HSE has also outlined a means of doing this in the three phases summarised below.

Phase One: Risk assessment

The basic tool of the risk assessment is to ask workers about their jobs and their experience of work-related stress. Specifics about the particular work environment are asked, as well as general indicators of stress that are fairly non-job-specific, such as whether they feel worn out or tense, are often absent, intend to leave, and are satisfied with their job. What the HSE means by risk assessment is a significant, and costly, investigation akin to management consultancy.

Professional observers first enter a department and familiarise themselves with its working before mounting a formal interview program in which staff are asked to identify stressors. They may go on to conduct wider surveys. All data are analysed and stressors identified, and an inevitably lengthy report is written. This process takes several professionals six to eight weeks to complete [31].

Phase Two: Translation

This involves designing interventions to reduce stress. If anything needs to be done at all, priorities will be ranked, options will be identified, costed and planned. Deciding whether something should be done at all is a significant issue. In the experiments and developmental work funded by the HSE, all five hospitals involved in stress-factor risk assessment and action decided something needed to be done! It is fair to assume that any risk assessment exercise will identify things that 'need' to be changed [31].

Phase Three: Intervention

Intervention design starts with the list of stressors from the translation phase. This process necessarily involves more contributors that the earlier phases and only becomes feasible using a 'common script negotiation' (see box). Six steps are suggested, of which the first three are *ideas*-based, and the second three are *action*-based.

1. IDENTIFYING STRESSORS

The assessment phase produces a long list of issues as perceived by different members of staff. The first step in managing this list is to look for common factors that may be behind groups of issues. Dysfunctional individuals, lack of communication and lack of dedicated clerical time are commonly among these underlying factors. The resulting reduced list of factors is then prioritised.

2. ASSESSING FEASIBILITY

The factors identified in *Step 1* are examined to determine the feasibility and cost of improving them.

3. CHOOSING THE INTERVENTION TYPE

Factors regarded as feasible to improve from *Step 2* are then considered. The type of intervention is selected – where type is either primary prevention (in which stress is limited or eliminated at source) or secondary prevention (in which staff are provided with resources to help deal with the stressor), or rehabilitation (in which staff are treated for the effects of stress). Interventions are also classified from an organisational point of view between geographical re-arrangements, communication-based changes, and staff re-deployment, recruitment or dismissal.

4. IDENTIFY WHO MAKES THE CHANGES AND WHO BENEFITS

In this stage, the people who are to make the stress-reducing changes are identified and referred to as the agency, and staff whose stress interventions are intended to reduce are referred to as the targets.

5. PLANNING ACTION

Once the agents and targets have been identified, they get together to plan the details of how the implementation is to be done, in terms of who is to be recruited or instructed to create timetables, and so on.

6. AGREEING THE TIMEFRAME

In this final step feasible timelines and appropriate milestones or deadlines are set for completion of the intervention.

A further phase of repeated stress assessment is carried out in order to gauge the effectiveness of interventions, analogous to 'closing the audit loop'.

Common script negotiation

When complex issues are being considered by groups of people such as committees or collaborations, it is necessary for all participants to work around an existing text or 'common script'.

Individual members then suggest changes, deletions or additions and these proposals are decided on by the group. Working from 'nothing' leads to the inconsequential discussions that are a familiar aspect of many meetings.

The HSE approach to stress management was used in a well-funded HSE stress intervention research programme in several NHS hospitals. It showed benefits in self-reported stress rather than the more objective measures of patient outcomes, staff turnover and absenteeism. The approach is subject to several limitations.

Firstly, there is a close relationship between avoiding stress and serving the ubiquitous, but less worthy, motives of idleness and greed. Many changes aimed at reducing stress also serve these motives. This overlap probably explains why whenever staff stress is looked for, it is found. There is significant evidence of confirmation biases in the completion of psychometric assessments and, for example, the self-reported rates of post-traumatic stress disorder are much higher than those based on expert clinical assessment. If stress is found, there is pressure to do something about it. And pressure is likely to result in action, but there is no guarantee that those actions will have any benefit other than the obvious, such as providing resources for tasks clearly under-provided for. This means that wherever stress management is implemented, costs can be expected, but the benefits are uncertain.

Secondly, the effectiveness of assessment and change programs like this are dependent on finding issues that cause stress and are correctable. The pilot research process identified certain manageable difficulties, but these were simple things such as staff shortages, which were widely known about, or lack of administrative time, which is also easy to diagnose. In a reasonably competently managed organisation, most of these will be spotted and corrected automatically. Consequently, as with many management interventions, stress management is most effective when the organisation is most dysfunctional. Such interventions are therefore best as a response to failure.

Thirdly, there is the difficulty of identifying triggers for such risk assessment. Triggers such as an unusually high staff turnover or absenteeism are reasonable, but the intervention has not been demonstrated to improve these things. On the other hand triggers such as self-reported stress levels or their equivalent would lead to widespread application with considerable attendant costs.

Cultural stress management

The limitations of the HSE approach to stress management make it uneconomic in most situations. Instead we suggest a cultural model of stress management in which stress is not looked at in isolation but is incorporated into human factors training generally. The issues of teamwork, leadership and communication all have direct bearings on levels of stress, and understanding of the importance of stress adds motivation to improve performance in those same areas.

Specific issues that the study of stress brings to those topics are that frequently there is little we can do to control the stressors we personally experience but we can control what resources are available to deal with it. Another important point is that while we may have little control over the stresses we personally experience, we frequently have greater control over the stresses of those around us.

With appropriate teamwork, leadership and communication skills we can work with those around us to reduce the stress we all experience far more effectively than anything we can achieve as lone individuals.

Conflict resolution

Conflict resolution is a major issue in healthcare where staff must deal with violence and aggression from the public. In 1999, the NHS began a campaign of 'zero tolerance' against violence and aggression and has extensive training material for this. Our present purpose is not to duplicate this, but to deal with the issue of conflict between team members. Team conflicts are traditionally classified into three types:, namely *task*, *relationship*, and *process*.

TASK CONFLICTS

Task conflicts involve differences of opinion about what should be done and how it should be done. Unlike the other two forms of conflict, this can be positive and beneficial, as it includes discussions about planning and policy, and is part of the process of choosing between alternative options.

RELATIONSHIP CONFLICTS

These types of conflict arise out of interpersonal animosity and are usually expressed in terms of complaints about lack of communication, unfair distribution of resources, or victimisation, but these are secondary to interpersonal dislike. Partly because of this tendency to use surrogates for the main issue of conflict, relationship conflicts are the most difficult to resolve.

PROCESS CONFLICTS

Process conflicts are disagreements about delegation and who should do what. Unlike task conflicts, they are personalised by linkage with individual team members' skills and time usage.

Conflicts are ubiquitous in teams. Research on this subject has focused on *conflict resolution* rather than conflict avoidance. As is the case with many human factors models, conflict models are largely descriptive and are not much help in guiding what to do.

Conflict resolution strategies are not specific to task, relationship or process conflicts but all apply to each type. In a major study on the performance of fifty-seven teams of postgraduate business-school students involved in tasks that were of relevance to their academic success in the course, researchers were able to map the teams into four groups using two dichotomies: well performing or improving *vs* poor performing or deteriorating, and high *vs* low team-member satisfaction [32]. **Figure 8.3** (overpage) summarises the results of this study.

Conflict resolution strategies (*see Figure 8.3*)

Pluralistic strategies: Apply to all members of the group

Particularist strategies: Apply to satisfy or contain individual members

Reactive strategies: Apply in response to an existing problem

Preemptive strategies: Apply in order to preempt the effect of any conflict

---

From this study emerged *three* aspects of conflict management that were consistently associated with high team-member satisfaction and good or improving performance of the team as a whole. These were:

- **Focusing on the issues** rather than the way they are presented by team members.

- **Explicitly discussing the reasons behind decisions** made in allocating tasks to team members and their acceptance of them.

- **Allocating tasks to members who have the relevant expertise** rather than by other methods such as volunteering, default, convenience or willingness.

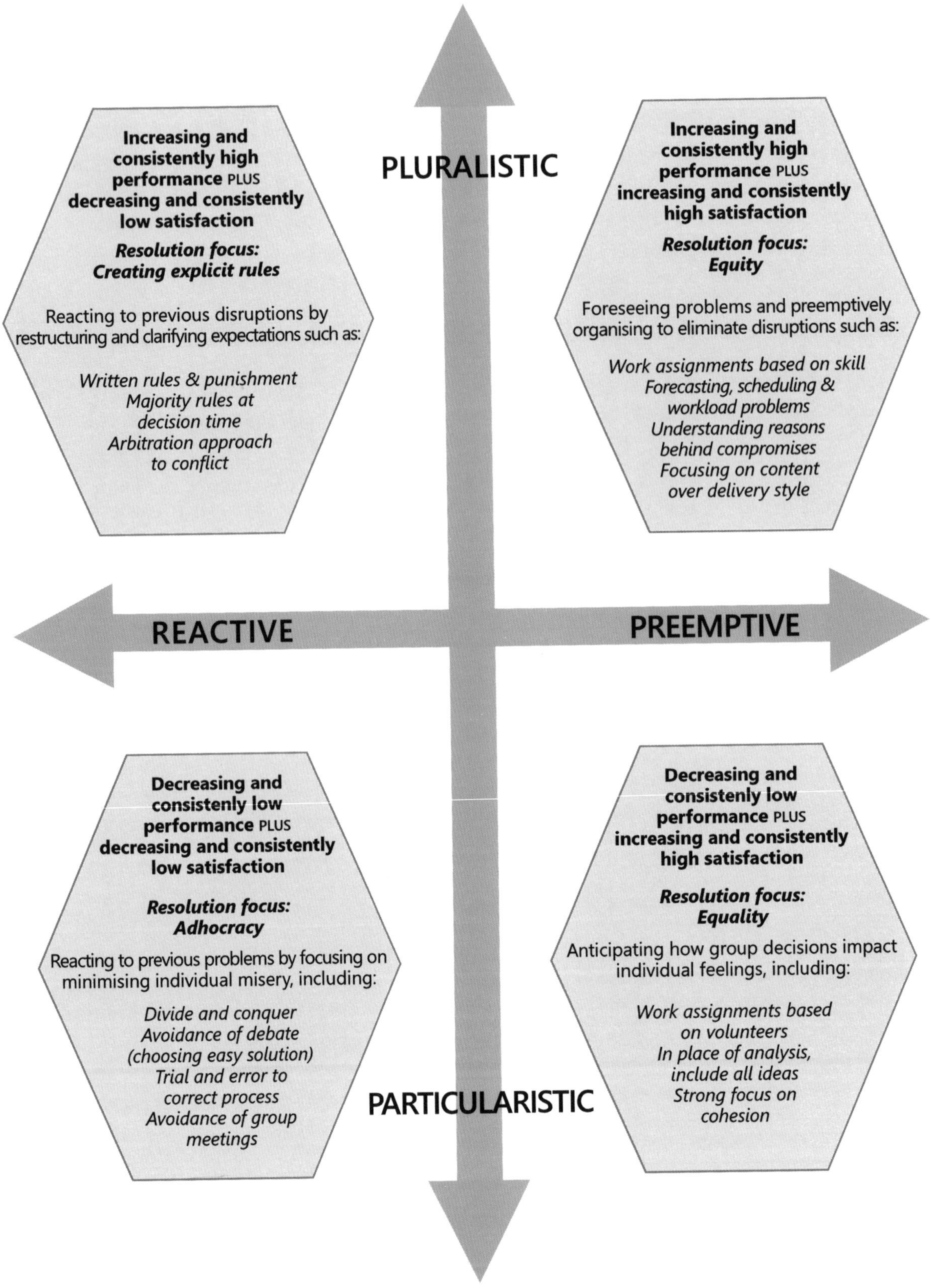

PLURALISTIC

REACTIVE

PREEMPTIVE

PARTICULARISTIC

Increasing and consistently high performance PLUS decreasing and consistently low satisfaction

Resolution focus: Creating explicit rules

Reacting to previous disruptions by restructuring and clarifying expectations such as:

*Written rules & punishment
Majority rules at decision time
Arbitration approach to conflict*

Increasing and consistently high performance PLUS increasing and consistently high satisfaction

Resolution focus: Equity

Foreseeing problems and preemptively organising to eliminate disruptions such as:

*Work assignments based on skill
Forecasting, scheduling & workload problems
Understanding reasons behind compromises
Focusing on content over delivery style*

Decreasing and consistenly low performance PLUS decreasing and consistently low satisfaction

Resolution focus: Adhocracy

Reacting to previous problems by focusing on minimising individual misery, including:

*Divide and conquer
Avoidance of debate
(choosing easy solution)
Trial and error to correct process
Avoidance of group meetings*

Decreasing and consistenly low performance PLUS increasing and consistently high satisfaction

Resolution focus: Equality

Anticipating how group decisions impact individual feelings, including:

*Work assignments based on volunteers
In place of analysis, include all ideas
Strong focus on cohesion*

Figure 8.3 *Matrix of different conflict resolution strategies (pluralistic, particularistic, reactive and preemptive) on performance and satisfaction in teams (adapted from [32]). For more details on the strategies, see previous page.*

Anger management

Whereas conflict resolution is largely concerned with managing disagreement with others, anger management is about managing ourselves. Anger is a normal human behaviour pattern, but one with particularly destructive consequences. Angry outbursts, temper tantrums and attacks of rage are common in childhood, but as we grow older most of us learn to control them. People vary in their susceptibility to anger from placid docile individuals to irritable and quick-tempered ones. At the angry end of the spectrum this behaviour pattern can be detrimental to an individual, and the group in which they work, and for this reason anger management programs are commonplace.

Formal estimates of the prevalence of problematic anger are not available, but informal estimates suggest around 5% of the population are affected [33]. Research into the effectiveness of anger management treatment is complicated by the number of outcome variables used. These include self-reported frequency of angry thoughts, behaviour patterns, measures of physiological arousal, self-esteem and response to experimental provocations. The field is also complicated by the range of treatments tested, which number over ninety. In meta-analysis, a range of well-delivered anger management interventions may be moderately effective at improving these outcome measures, but it is not possible to demonstrate consistent superiority of one treatment strategy over another [33].

Treatments for anger are psychotherapeutic in nature and involve a range of theoretical models including cognitive behavioural and psychodynamic approaches.

COGNITIVE BEHAVIOURAL THERAPY (CBT)

CBT is a school of psychotherapy that treats problems by focusing on their directly observed triggers, progression and consequences in the here and now, rather than probing for and influencing hidden causative factors from the past as does psychodynamic therapy. CBT for destructive anger explores provoking factors and how to respond to them, the self-sustaining effect of thoughts and behavioural reinforcement in anger escalation, and the consequences of a person's anger on themselves and those around them. It is often administered as group therapy which creates an environment in which individuals can openly discuss their problems with others who have personal knowledge of them and without judgement from those unaffected by destructive anger.

PSYCHODYNAMIC THERAPY

This form of therapy is from the Freudian school of psychoanalysis that explores putative underlying primal motivations and influences originating from repressed memories. The theory is that by bringing these to conscious recognition their baleful effects can be mitigated.

Programs involve either an intensive course over a few days, or repeated sessions over weeks or months, with detection and treatment of relapse if disruptive behaviour should return. In the USA, several programs are available specifically for medical staff. In 2008, The UK Department of Health opened a Practitioner Health Programme for medical staff in the London area that does address anger, but it is mainly concerned with substance abuse. The Cardiff Deanery has for several years been running a programme for doctors with behavioural problems, mainly anger and aggression related.

Outside of these areas, the usual approach is to demand that the disruptive individual stops the behaviour on pain of discipline [34]. This is suboptimal, firstly because people respond better to inducements than to threats, and secondly because it has not been shown to be effective, whereas as other approaches have [35].

A common fallacy in anger management is the hydraulic theory, largely attributable to early psychodynamic theorists, that angry emotions are like a fluid under pressure that must be let out or will lead to ill health because they are 'bottled up'. Experimental results show this to be false. Expressing anger, 'taking it out' on inanimate objects by doing acts of violence to them, or consciously seeking 'outlets' for anger, all appear to promote higher levels of anger and aggression, impair self-control and delay resolution in anger-provoking situations [36].

Post-traumatic stress disorder

Post-traumatic stress disorder (PTSD) arises after highly stressful psychological events [37]. By definition, these involve a person witnessing an event that poses a risk to life or injury to themselves or other people. A single event is enough to trigger the disorder, but the risk rises with repeated exposure [38] and if actual injury is sustained [39].

It is estimated that 50% of the people in Western countries will experience an event sufficient to trigger PTSD in their lifetime [40] and of these, 10–20% develop the condition. The overall prevalence is 7–9% [41]. The condition can be incapacitating and often delays or prevents a return to work. Some groups witness such events in their working lives and they are more prone to PTSD. This aspect of stress should be addressed when dealing with at-risk groups, including anyone on front-line service where such events are encountered such as ambulance crew, police officers, accident and emergency staff and theatre staff.

Unlike other disorders, PTSD is not abnormal in nature but in duration. People's response to severe stressors include:

- **Reminders of the events**—flashbacks, intrusive thoughts, nightmares.
- **Excitation**—insomnia, agitation, irritability, anger.
- **Inactivation**—avoidance, withdrawal, confusion, depression.

These reactions to psychological trauma resolve within one month in the normal population. In people with PTSD, they persist beyond one month for acute PTSD and beyond three months for chronic PTSD, or they reappear after an interval of normal recovery in delayed-onset PTSD. This is shown in **Figure 8.4** overpage.

Previously, debriefing was advised as a preventative measure after severe psychological trauma. This was found to increase – not reduce – the rate of PTSD. Normal recovery occurs in most people after such stresses and involves a progressive decline in the memory of and attention given to the stressful event. This is impeded by re-visiting the event in debriefing. The relevance to healthcare professionals who are at risk of the condition is in secondary prevention strategies used after a traumatic event to minimise the risk of PTSD. Both treatment and secondary prevention are aimed at social support and avoidance of memory triggers. There are three so-called *Ps to Avoid*, as shown below [42].

The Three Ps to Avoid

☒ **P**athologise (symptoms within a month of the events are a normal response)

☒ **P**sychologise (work through the issues by debriefing or group therapy)

☒ **P**harmacologise (i.e. treat with anxiolytic drugs)

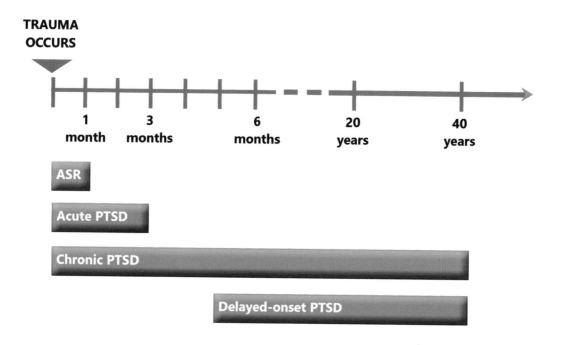

Figure 8.4 *Typical reactions to trauma at different times after the occurrence of the initial trauma (based on Zohar, 2011 [32]). ASR = (normal) acute stress reaction; PTSD = post-traumatic stress disorder.*

Fatigue

The word 'fatigue' is used to refer to two distinct conditions – lack of sleep and cumulative stress. Sleep deprivation is variously referred to as tiredness, fatigue or sleepiness. Sleepiness is a major cause of accidents in transportation, surpassing the effects of drug and alcohol use [43]. Medical duty-hours across the Western world have been reduced over the last twenty years, but surveys conducted in the 1990s reported substantial rates of tiredness-related mistakes made by doctors, many of which were fatal [44].

Research on fatigue is hampered because there is no easy way of measuring it. Simply asking people if they feel sleepy is unreliable, and more formalised measures such as the multiple sleep latency test are difficult to administer. This test measures how long it takes a fall asleep in a sleep-inducing environment, where sleep onset is detected by electroencephalography. With this test, people normally fall asleep in within ten to twenty minutes; five to ten minutes suggests mild-to-moderate sleepiness, and less than five minutes suggests severe sleepiness. In one study using this test [45], anaesthetists had an average latency during a normal working day of six or seven minutes and after a twenty-four-hour on-call period it went down to just under five minutes [45].

The pupillographic sleepiness test (PST) was developed in the 1990s. With sleepiness or full dark adaptation, there are fluctuations in the diameter of the pupil of several millimetres over periods of one or two seconds. It is these fluctuations that are measured in the PST. The method has been used to assess physician sleepiness during the day and after nightshifts, with similar results to sleep latency [46].

The basic cause of sleepiness is sleep deprivation. The amount of sleep deprivation someone can tolerate without becoming significantly sleepier at work is also dependent on other tiring factors, such as extremes of temperature, stress, noise, vibration, and how boring the task is (with an increasing problem of sleepiness the more boring it becomes). Experiments on drivers show they are more likely to crash due to fatigue on straight, featureless sections of road than they are on winding roads.

Fatigue has a number of detrimental effects on a range of performances:

● **Motor skills.** Loss of two hours sleep in one night has been reported to produce an impairment in motor performance equivalent to drinking two or three pints of beer [47].

● **Communication.** Studies observing the performance of teams engaged in prolonged tasks find that the clarity and frequency of communication declines with fatigue [48].

● **Social.** Fatigue leads to an increase in childish behaviour, characterised by impatience, irritability, and lack of courtesy [49].

● **Decision-making.** Impaired decision-making with increasing fatigue has been reported for people who drive, play sports, and in healthcare and in aviation [50].

Sleep deprivation has a cumulative effect on performance, but restoration to normality is not sensitive to the amount of sleep – it only takes one night sleep to fully recover, however much sleep deprivation there has been.

Circadian rhythms

Circadian rhythms are the daily physiological rhythms of blood pressure, temperature and wakefulness. These rhythms run in time with the light–dark cycle of day and night and when that changes (e.g. due to jet lag), circadian rhythms are 'entrained' to the new hours, adjusting themselves at a rate of about one hour per day. With the widespread availability of artificial lighting, we rarely appreciate the extremes of light and dark occurring during a twenty-four-hour day. This is because the conscious part of vision has a very wide dynamic range of adaptability to light levels. The circadian rhythm is governed not by the conscious visual pathways involving rods and cones, but by light-sensitive retinal ganglion cells. These respond slowly to changing light levels, and are mainly sensitive to blue light; they are involved in non-image forming functions such as entrainment of circadian rhythm. They do not show the same adaption qualities as rods and cones, and most artificial evening and night-time lighting is not intense enough to fool this non-image forming system into entraining the circadian rhythm. This is why full-time nightshift workers do not usually adapt their circadian rhythm successfully.

The endogenous circadian rhythm that occurs when subjects are denied any clues of the time of day is exactly twenty-four hours long [51]. Misinformation dating from early studies is still quoted, suggesting that endogenous circadian rhythms are highly variable in length, with an average of around twenty-five hours. The problem with these studies was that they allowed subjects to turn on and off artificial lighting at will. They were denied access to any time clues and when they felt tired they went to bed and turned the light off. When rested, they woke up and turned the light on. When the results were interpreted it was assumed that the timing of sleep was determined by endogenous circadian rhythms.

Actually there are many other determinants of feeling tired, such as what we have been doing, how much sleep we have, and whether we have been napping. These subjects' circadian rhythms were being entrained by their chosen light exposure.

Shifts and jet-lag

The false finding that endogenous circadian rhythm was longer than twenty-four hours was thought to explain why jetlag and shift changes are better tolerated if they go ahead of the body's biological clock, rather than behind it. The reason is actually simpler than that. Shift changes are most disruptive of sleep if they result in sleep deprivation.

Changing from an early to a late shift results in tiredness during the shift and sleep when it is over. Changing from late to early results in lack of tiredness at the end of a shift, and sleep does not follow, so there is sleep deprivation for the start of the next shift. For this reason, shifts tend to go 'early late night early' rather than 'early night late early'. Jetlag, for the same amount of time, has less effect on tiredness if a person travels east rather than if they travel west. Advancing age increases the tiring effects of jetlag and shift working.

> Adjusting circadian rhythms to jetlag or shift changes takes time. A rough approximation is that it takes twenty-four hours to adjust to every hour's difference in sleep pattern.

Shift work is inevitable in healthcare and there is no ideal arrangement. Current evidence suggests that the most effective option is for people to be on particular shifts for prolonged periods, rather than change shifts often. Irrespective of the type of shift system or the speed at which workers move from one shift to another, only a minority of workers show significant circadian adjustment [52]. This has a bearing on the safety and efficiency of night-time work.

Night-time working

In healthcare it has long been known that nocturnal surgery has worse results than comparable operations done during the day time. Out-of-hours operations are done because rapidly progressing disease dictates urgency. Much of the increased morbidity and mortality of out-of-hours operating is no doubt explained by this case-selection effect, and it is not possible to convincingly separate the effects of staff tiredness from this. In other industries, such as engineering, aviation and transport, these selection effects do not occur but a nocturnal safety difference is still apparent [53].

No reasonable analysis of the evidence can deny that as well as case-selection factors, team performance contributes to the poorer results of critical interventions done at night and this fact should be considered when deciding what should be done. To balance this disadvantage, interventions should only be undertaken at night if the expected disease trajectory over the hours until morning suggests that the harm done by delay would be even greater.

Furthermore, inexperienced staff members tend to underestimate available time and have less reserves of skill to compensate for lowered performance at night. The message to draw from this is that the often contentious issue of what operating theatre teams should do at night is best decided with direct involvement of senior staff.

Sleep hygiene

Minimising fatigue involves making the most of opportunities to sleep in the form of sleep hygiene, rest breaks and napping. Shift workers who are required to sleep during the day require extra protection from sleep disturbance due to noise and light. Special opaque and closely-fitting window blinds should be used, and other occupants of the building should be informed to minimise any disturbance. Rest breaks and napping during nightshifts is a controversial matter. Night-workers who are required to be vigilant, such as those on lookout or monitoring safety equipment, clearly should not sleep on the job. In healthcare, in particular, there are large numbers of nightshift workers who do not have this role, but rather are on standby to do often complicated tasks as they become necessary. Evidence suggests that allowing napping in such individuals improves performance [54,55].

Fatigue from chronic stress

The second form of fatigue is related to cumulative chronic stress. The theory is that over time the stresses of the workplace cause a form of fatigue that leads to demotivation, 'burnout', apathy about performance, and disillusionment. This form of fatigue, if it exists – which is not certain – differs from tiredness in that it is not relieved by sleep.

The theory is that it is relieved by a vacation or change of scene, as in 'a change is as good as a rest'. In contrast to tiredness and sleep deprivation, the research base behind this theory is minimal. There is some evidence that a vacation produces a modest and relatively short-lived improvement in self- reported health and well-being [56] but there are insufficient data available to comment more specifically on the truth or otherwise of the above theory.

Conclusions

Workplace stress is an often elusive but ubiquitous and important health-related issue. Some stress is inevitable but much of it, particularly as it affects staff working lower down in command hierarchies, is avoidable - as is the ill-health, loss of work, and staff turnover that go with it. Some specific approaches to stress management are not without controversy but the general awareness and application of human performance and limitations has the beneficial side effect of stress reduction.

References

1 Health and Safety Executive. *Work-related stress: Together we can tackle it.* Available at: http://www. hse.gov.uk/stress/ (last accessed January 2013).

2 Sexton JB, Thomas EJ, Helmreich RL. Error, stress and teamwork in medicine and aviation: Cross sectional surveys. *British Medical Journal,* 2000; 320(7237): 745–49.

3 Rees D, Cooper CL. Occupational stress in health-service workers in the UK. *Stress Medicine* 1992; 8(2) 79–90.

4 Marine A, Ruotsalainen J, Serra C, Verbeek J. Preventing occupational stress in healthcare workers. *Cochrane Database System Review,* 2006 (4).

5 Lundstrom T, Pugliese G, Bartley J, Cox J, Guither C. Organizational and environmental factors that affect worker health and safety and patient outcomes. *American Journal of Infection Control,* 2002; 30(2): 93–106.

6 Wallace JE, Lemaire JB, Ghali WA. Physician wellness: A missing quality indicator. *Lancet,* 2009; 374(9702): 1714–21.

7 Arora S, Sevdalis N, Nestel D, Woloshynowych M, Darzi A, Kneebone R. The impact of stress on surgical performance: A systematic review of the literature. *Surgery,* 2010; 147(3): 318–30 (epub 2009/12/17).

8 Belkic KL, Landsbergis PA, Schnall PL, Baker D. Is job strain a major source of cardiovascular disease risk? Scandinavian *Journal of Work, Environment and Health,* 2004; 30(2): 85–128.

9 Moorthy K, Munz Y, Dosis A, Bann S, Darzi A. The effect of stress-inducing conditions on the performance of a laparoscopic task. *Surgical Endoscopy,* 2003; 17(9): 1481–84 (epub 2003/06/24).

10 Holmes TH, Rahe RH. The social readjustment rating scale. *Journal of Psychosomatic Research,* 1967; 11(2): 213–18 (epub 1967/08/01).

11 Rahe RH, Meyer M, Smith M, Kjaer G, Holmes TH. Social stress and illness onset. *Journal of Psychosomatic Research*, 1964; 54: 35–44 (epub 1964/07/01).

12 Rahe RH, Mahan JL, Arthur RJ. Prediction of near-future health change from subjects preceding life changes. *Journal of Psychosomatic Research*, 1970; 14(4): 401.

13 Dragos D, Tanasescu MD. The effect of stress on the defense systems. *Journal of Medicine and Life*, 2010; 3(1): 10–18 (epub 2010/03/23).

14 Moreno-Smith M, Lutgendorf SK, Sood AK. Impact of stress on cancer metastasis. *Future Oncology*, 2010; 6(**12**): 1863–81 (epub 2010/12/15).

15 Thaker PH, Lutgendorf SK, Sood AK. The neuroendocrine impact of chronic stress on cancer. *Cell Cycle*, 2007; 6(4): 430–33 (epub 2007/02/22).

16 Chida Y, Hamer M, Wardle J, Steptoe A. Do stress-related psychosocial factors contribute to cancer incidence and survival? *Nature Clinical Practice Oncology*, 2008; 5(8): 466–75.

17 Mawdsley JE, Rampton DS. Psychological stress in IBD: New insights into pathogenic and therapeutic implications. Gut, *2005*; 54(**10**): 1481–91 (epub 2005/09/16).

18 Christian LM, Graham JE, Padgett DA, Glaser R, Kiecolt-Glaser JK. Stress and wound healing. *Neuroimmunomodulation*, 2006; 13(5/6): 337–46 (epub 2007/08/22).

19 Mavros MN, Athanasiou S, Gkegkes ID, Polyzos KA, Peppas G, Falagas ME. Do psychological variables affect early surgical recovery? *Plos One*, 2011; 6(5).

20 Calden G, Dupertuis CW, Hokanson JE, Lewis WC. Psychosomatic factors in the rate of recovery from tuberculosis. *Psychosomatic Medicine*, 1960; 22: 345–55 (epub 1960/09/01).

21 Flin RH, O'connor P, Crichton M. *Safety at the Sharp End*. Aldershot: Ashgate, 2008.

22 Yerkes RM, Dodosn JD. The relation of strength of stimulus to rapidity of habit-formation. *Journal of Comparative Neurology and Psychology*, 1908; 18(5): 459–82.

23 Brown WP. The Yerkes-Dodson law repealed. *Psychological Reports*, 1965; 17(2): 663–66 (epub 1965/10/01).

24 Robertson IH, O'Connell R. Vigilant attention. In: Nobre K, Coull JT (eds) *Attention and Time*. New York: Oxford University Press, 2010.

25 Hardy L, Parfitt G. A catastrophe model of anxiety and performance. *British Journal of Psychology*, 1991; 82: 163–78.

26 Wilson M, Malhotra N, Poolton J, Masters R. Clarifying assumptions about intraoperative stress during surgical performance: More than a stab in the dark: Reply. *World Journal of Surgery*, 2012; 36(2): 481–82.

27 Mair RG, Onos KD, Hembrook JR. Cognitive activation by central thalamic stimulation: The Yerkes-Dodson law revisited. *Dose-Response : A Publication of International Hormesis Society*, 2011; 9(3): 313–31 (epub 2011/10/21).

28 Woods AJ. *The Consequences of Hyper-Arousal for Human Visual Perception*. Washington, DC: The George Washington University, 2010.

29 Deffenbacher KA. Eyewitness recall, the Yerkes-Dodson law, and optimal-level theory. *Medical Law Review*, 1985; 4(4): 361–72 (epub 1985/01/01).

30 Health and Safety Executive. *HSE Management Standards Indicator Tool, 2007* . Available at: htpp://www.hse.gov.uk/stress/standards/pdfs/indicatortool.pdf (last accessed January 2013).

31 Cox T, Randall R, Griffiths A. *Interventions To Control Stress At Work In Hospital Staff. Norwich*. UK

Health and Safety Executive, 2002 . Available at: http://www.hse.gov.uk/research/crr_pdf/2002/crr02435. pdf (last accessed January 2013).

32 Behfar KJ, Peterson RS, Mannix EA, Trochim WMK. The critical role of conflict resolution in teams: A close look at the links between conflict type, conflict management strategies, and team outcomes. *Journal of Applied Psychology*, 2008; 93(2): 462.

33 Di Giuseppe R, Tafrate RC. Anger treatment for adults: A meta-analytic review. *Clinical Psychology: Science and Practice*, 2003; 10(1): 70–84.

34 Margerison N. Problem psychiatrists? *Advances in Psychiatric Treatment*, 2008; 14: 187–97.

35 Adshead G. *Intervention Programmes for Disruptive Physicians*. London: Winston Churchill Memorial Trust, 2008 . Available at: http://www.wcmt.org; .uk/reports/384_1.pdf).

36 Zillmann D. Cognition and excitation interdependencies in the alation of anger and angry behaviour. In: Potegal M, Knutson JF (eds) *The Dynamics of Aggression: Biological and Social Processes in Dyads and Groups*. Hillsdale, New Jersey: Lawrence Erlbaum Associates, 1994.

37 American Psychiatric Association. *Diagnostic and Statistical Manual of Mental Disorders*, 4th edn. Washington, DC: AMA, 1994.

38 Zatzick D, Jurkovich G, Russo J, Roy-Byrne P, Katon W, Wagner A, *et al.* Post-traumatic distress, alcohol disorders, and recurrent trauma across level 1 trauma centers. *Journal of Trauma*, 2004; 57(2): 360–66 (epub 2004/09/04).

39 Sherin JE, Nemeroff CB. Post-traumatic stress disorder: The neurobiological impact of psychological trauma. *Dialogues in Clinical Neuroscience*, 2011; 13(3): 263–78 (epub 2011/10/29).

40 Kessler RC, Berglund P, Demler O, Jin R, Merikangas KR, Walters EE. Lifetime prevalence and age-of-onset distributions of DSM-IV disorders in the National Comorbidity Survey Replication. *Archives of General Psychiatry*, 2005; 62(6): 593–602 (epub 2005/06/09).

41 Zohar J, Juven-Wetzler A, Sonnino R, Cwikel-Hamzany S, Balaban E, Cohen H. New insights into secondary prevention in post-traumatic stress disorder. *Dialogues in Clinical Neuroscience*, 2011; 13(3): 301–09 (epub 2011/10/29).

42 Zohar J, Sonnino R, Juven-Wetzler A, Cohen H. Can post-traumatic stress disorder be prevented? *CNS Spectrums*, 2009; 14(Suppl. 1): 44–51 (epub 2009/02/10).

43 Akerstedt T. Consensus statement: Fatigue and accidents in transport operations. *Journal of Sleep Research*, 2000; 9(4): 395 (epub 2000/12/21).

44 Wu AW, Folkman S, McPhee SJ, Lo B. Do house officers learn from their mistakes? *Quality and Safety in Health Care*, 2003; 12(3): 221–27.

45 Howard SK, Gaba DM, Rosekind MR, Zarcone VP. The risks and implications of excessive daytime sleepiness in resident physicians. *Academic Medicine*, 2002; 77(**10**): 1019–25.

46 Wilhelm BJ, Widmann A, Durst W, Heine C, Otto G. Objective and quantitative analysis of daytime sleepiness in physicians after night duties. *International Journal of Psychophysiology*, 2009; 72(3): 307–13.

47 Dawson D, Reid K. Fatigue, alcohol and performance impairment. *Nature*, 1997; 388(6639): 235.

48 Whitmore J, Fisher S. Speech during sustained operations. *Speech Communication*, 1996; 20(1/2): 55–70.

49 Horne JA. Human sleep, sleep loss and behavior: Implications for the prefrontal cortex and psychiatric-disorder. *British Journal of Psychiatry*, 1993; 162: 413–19.

50 Friedl KE, Mallis MM, Ahlers ST, Popkin SM, Larkin W. Research requirements for operational decision-making using models of fatigue and performance. *Aviation Space Environmental Medicine* 2004;75(3):A192-A9.

51 Duffy JE, Wright KP. Entrainment of the human circadian system by light. *Journal of Biological Rhythms*, 2005; 20(4): 326–38.

52 Spencer MB, Robertson KA, Folkard S. *The Development of a Fatigue/Risk Index for Shiftworkers.* London: Health and Safety Executive UK, 2006.

53 Smith L, Folkard S, Poole CJ. Increased injuries on night shift. *Lancet*, 1994; 344(8930): 1137–39 (epub 1994/10/22).

54 Howard ME, Radford L, Jackson ML, Swann P, Kennedy GA. The effects of a 30-minute napping opportunity during an actual night shift on performance and sleepiness in shift workers. *Biological Rhythm Research*, 2010; 41(2): 137–48.

55 Tremaine R, Dorrian J, Lack L, Lovato N, Ferguson S, Zhou XA, *et al.* The relationship between subjective and objective sleepiness and performance during a simulated night-shift with a nap countermeasure. *Applied Ergonomics*, 2010; 42(1): 52–61.

56 De Bloom J, Kompier M, Geurts S, De Weerth C, Taris T, Sonnentag S. Do we recover from vacation? Meta-analysis of vacation effects on health and well-being. *Journal of Occupational Health*, 2009; 51(1): 13–25 (epub 2008/12/20).

Index

A

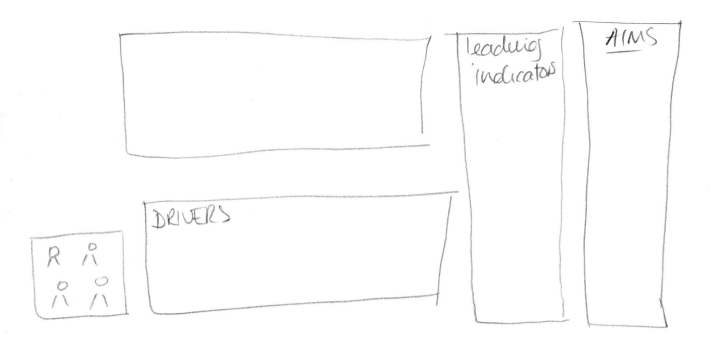

leadings indicators

AIMS

DRIVERS

R

Tale of 2 wards